Research and Kno
at Work

How can we make sense of the complexities of research in the workplace?

What is 'working knowledge' and how is it being shaped and managed?

Rejecting the idea that there are ready-made solutions to the challenges of constructing and managing knowledge in organisations, this book addresses the changing nature of knowledge construction and what can be achieved through innovative research practices. Key issues and debates include:

- working knowledge into the 21st century;
- the highly contextualised nature of research at work;
- critical and postmodern perspectives on knowledge construction;
- innovative research practices and performance implications;
- the impact of globalisation;
- the influences of new technology, language, power and culture upon the 'construction' of knowledge.

Leading experts from North America, Japan, Britain and Australia illustrate both practice and theory issues, making this a valuable resource for researchers, teachers and students in the field of human resource management, policy-makers and all those concerned with continuing professional development.

Dr John Garrick is a senior researcher and policy analyst at the Research Centre for Vocational Education and Training at the University of Technology, Sydney. **Dr Carl Rhodes** is a consultant and manager in organisation development, change management and human resource development, and is an Associate of the Faculty of Education at the University of Technology, Sydney.

Research and Knowledge at Work

Perspectives, case-studies and innovative strategies

**Edited by John Garrick
and Carl Rhodes**

London and New York

First published 2000 by Routledge
11 New Fetter Lane, London EC4P 4EE

Simultaneously published in the USA and Canada
by Routledge
29 West 35th Street, New York, NY 10001

Routledge is an imprint of the Taylor & Francis Group

Typeset in Baskerville by Taylor & Francis Books Ltd
Printed and bound in Great Britain by
TJ International Ltd, Padstow, Cornwall

British Library Cataloguing in Publication Data
A catalogue record for this book is available
from the British Library

Library of Congress Cataloging in Publication Data
Research and knowledge at work/edited
by John Garrick and Carl Rhodes.
Includes bibliographical references and index.
1. Employees–Effect of technological innovations on. 2. Technological
innovations–Economic aspects. 3. Organizational learning. I. Garrick,
John. II. Rhodes, Carl.

HD6331.R44 2000
331.25–dc21   99-087147

ISBN 0–415–21337–1 (hbk)
ISBN 0–415–21338–x (pbk)

Contents

Contributors

Ronald Barnett is Professor of Higher Education and Dean of Professional Development, Institute of Education, University of London. He has written some of the most influential texts of the past decade on developments in higher education, knowledge formation and work. His most recent book, entitled *Realizing the University in an Age of Supercomplexity*, offers a fundamental reworking of the way in which we understand new knowledge and the future of higher education.

Marie Brennan is Professor of Education at the University of Canberra. Since coming to academia from the Ministry of Education in Victoria, Australia, she has continued her interest in research on educational injustice and school reform, as well as on pedagogical matters including the uses of post-structural theories in professional practices.

Dennis Calvert is Professor of Medicine and Public Health at the University of Wollongong in Australia. He has a background as both a physician and a research scientist specialising in public health medicine, and currently teaches in public health and in the areas of his research, which centres on nutrition and exercise, buttressed in some cases with pharmacological treatment.

Stewart Clegg is Professor of Management in the Faculty of Business, University of Technology, Sydney. He has produced award-winning books such as the *Handbook of Organization Studies* (1996, in conjunction with Cynthia Hardy and Walter Nord), as well as other books that have been influential, including *Frameworks of Power* (1989) and the recent *Changing Paradigms: The Transformation of Management Knowledge for the 21st Century* (1998).

Richard Edwards is Reader in Education at the Open University, UK. His research and writing interests span developments in higher education, flexible learning and the application of postmodern ideas to contemporary work practices, lifelong learning and the legitimations of knowledge. With Robin Usher, he has written *Postmodernism and Education*, and is the author of several other significant texts on the learning of adults.

Christine Ewan is Pro Vice-Chancellor (Academic) at the University of Wollongong in Australia. Her academic interests span public health, higher education and research policy. She is currently Chair of the Environmental Health Council of Australia and of the Management Committee of the National Breast Cancer Centre, and a member of the Committee for University Teaching and Staff Development. She was formerly a Council Member and Chair of a Principal Committee of the National Health and Medical Research Council and a member of the Wills Committee Review of Health and Medical Research Strategy for Australia.

John Garrick is currently attached to the Dean's Unit in the Faculty of Business, University of Technology, Sydney, as Academic Consultant for Work-Based Learning. He is a Senior Research Fellow with the Research Centre for Vocational Education and Training, the author of *Informal Learning in the Workplace: Unmasking Human Resource Development* (1998) and co-author of several recent Routledge books on learning and work.

Kenneth Gergen is Professor of Psychology at Swarthmore College, USA. He is the author of numerous internationally acclaimed books on work, self and knowledge development in postmodern times, including the influential *The Saturated Self: Dilemmas of Identity in Contemporary Life*.

Bill Green is Professor of Curriculum Studies at the University of New England, Australia. His research and teaching interests encompass the cultural politics of knowledge formation, curriculum and literacy studies, and also postgraduate research pedagogy and doctoral education.

Alison Lee is Associate Professor in the Faculty of Education at the University of Technology, Sydney. Her current research interests are in the area of postgraduate research education and the new forms of knowledge production.

Carla Lipsig-Mummé is Professor and Director of the Centre for Research on Work and Society at York University in Canada. Her research focuses primarily on trade unions and the emerging work order.

John McIntyre is the Director of the Research Centre into Vocational Education and Training (RCVET), University of Technology, Sydney. John has an extensive research background related to learning at work, which includes the successful tendering for government and private industry grants, negotiating research contracts, implementing diverse research methodologies and managing key aspects of the university/government/industry interface.

Keiko Morita is the Japan major co-ordinator at the Institute for International Studies, University of Technology, Sydney. She has research interests in Japanese management practices including *kigyo shudan* (enterprise conglomerates) and their effects on employees. Originally from Kobe Jyogakuin University, Keiko completed her doctoral studies at the University of Hull, and currently consults on a regular basis with Japanese companies and universities.

Carl Rhodes is a consultant and manager in organisation development, change management and human resource development. He is also an Associate of the Faculty of Education at the University of Technology, Sydney, with research interests in the applications of narrative and literary theory to understanding organisations.

Jill Sanguinetti has particular interests in participatory action research. She is currently the Victorian Co-ordinator of the Adult Literacy and Numeracy Australian Research Consortium (ALNARC) and is based at Victoria University, Australia.

Hermine Scheeres is Senior Lecturer and Program Director in the Faculty of Education at the University of Technology, Sydney. Her work brings together expertise in discourse analysis with an analysis of the changing workplace. Hermine's current research focuses on the construction of identities in restructuring workplaces.

Nicky Solomon is a Senior Lecturer in the Faculty of Education and Program Manager for Work-Based Learning at the University of Technology, Sydney. Her current research focus is on the new kinds of knowledge produced through the relationships between universities and workplaces.

Robin Usher is Professor of Education and Senior Policy Advisor (Postgraduate Education) in the Office of the Pro Vice Chancellor (Research and Development) at RMIT University, Melbourne, Australia. He has written numerous influential texts on the practices of adult education, postmodern theory and 'knowledge practices' within and around work.

Rosie Wickert is the Director of Organizational Development in the Faculty of Education at the University of Technology, Sydney. She is particularly known for her ground-breaking research concerning the links between adult literacy, learning and policy development and uses of post-positivist conceptual and methodological approaches to policy analysis.

Foreword

Kenneth Gergen

For the better part of the twentieth century the twin concepts of knowledge and research have enjoyed broad and positive consensus. Empirical science not only provided the models of rigorous research, but indeed served as the ideal for adequate thinking in all walks of life. Simultaneously, the bodies of accumulated knowledge served as compelling witnesses to the power of science to produce endless benefits to humankind – in health, economic prosperity, education, defence and more. The workplace was similarly enchanted by the concepts of knowledge and research. Organisations increasingly entrusted their futures to scientifically trained consultants, and incorporated visions of scientific management into their modes of operation. More visibly, many major industries of the century – automobiles, aircraft, electrical appliances, weapons and the like – owed their existence to the fruits of systematic empirical research. A strong commitment to basic research meant good business.

Within recent decades, however, the chorus of hosannas to knowledge and science has begun to thin; the voices are far less rapturous. At the outset, too many organisations seemed to employ scientific knowledge solely for purposes of self-gain. Issues of the greater good were removed from consideration. Further, the technologies resulting from research often bit back: pesticides unsettled fragile food chains; cities became polluted; highway planning destroyed communities; and so on. Most dramatically, the by-products of research often seemed used for immoral ends – subjugating peoples, colonising cultures and controlling lives. For many the image of Dowe Chemical napalm setting fire to human bodies in Vietnam was emblematic. Partly owing to these shifts in attitude, storms of intellectual protest were gathering. Placed in question by a growing band of philosophers, sociologists, historians and the like were the epistemic authority of the sciences . Increasingly the sciences were accused of ideological and moral naiveté (if not malignancy), and seemed bent on totalitarian (single truth) ends. What is often termed 'post-empiricist' or 'post-foundational' critique is now a major fixture in the academy, and so clamorous is the critique that we now confront 'the science wars'.

It is within this context that the present volume acquires a special significance. Rather than the mutual rancour and resulting scepticism of recent decades, the present offerings take on the daunting challenge of digging out what constructs worthwhile working knowledge. They set in motion dialogues essential for seeing the issues in broader historical context, considering advantages and disadvantages inhering in both foundational and post-foundational orientations to knowledge, and inviting new alternatives in both conceptualisation and workplace practice. The collection of chapters is richly textured and polyvocal, and there is no one way of reading, no master narrative or bottom line. In a global condition of pluralist realities and moralities, such an orientation is right on target. I can but share, then, several significant ways in which I found myself illuminated. First, in my view the work is fascinating in its revelation of the multiple ways in which the very concept of knowledge is being transformed in the workplace. As the traditional view of knowledge as justified true belief settles into history, we find a precious clearing for emerging conceptions of what it is to know. With the traditional concept of truth linked to outmoded assumptions about the correspondence between words and world, organisational practices now invite us to consider new forms of justification. The present volume illustrates the potentially deadening effect on organisations of the traditional conception of knowledge particularly when linked to hierarchical structure. At the same time, however, we are introduced to pragmatic or instrumental conceptions of knowledge, for instance as linked to profit-making and commercial agendas. And the working knowledge of this book also indicates the shortcomings of such conceptions. Attention is directed, then, to blurring old boundaries (for example, between pure and applied knowledge, knowledge and work, research and practice, and knowledge and information) and to ways of multiplying conceptions of knowledge and its legitimation.

I also found myself significantly informed in this work by treatments of emerging new complexions of collaboration, and the implications of these admixtures for conceptions and practices of knowledge at work. As the capacity of any single voice to command full authority wanes, and as realities of global interdependency become more apparent, so does collaboration seem imperative for what Stewart Clegg in Chapter 5 terms the 'intelligent organisation'. We thus see in this work the significance of educational practices that link in new ways the academic researcher with inhabitants of the workplace; we explore the advantages of conjoining academic researchers with both government policy-makers and trade unions. As understandings are shared, conceptions and values mixed, we find that new and more broadly beneficial conceptions and practices of research can result.

Finally, I took delight in the ways various contributions treated emerging alternatives to traditional empiricist methodology. It is one thing to criticise the empiricist tradition and yet another to generate alternatives that not only realise the ideals implied within the critiques but also prove useful to organisations. Yet myriad efforts are in the making, and the present work furnishes useful insights into their successes as well as failures. Narrative, interpretive, participatory and dialogic methodologies, for example, have rapidly expanded in popularity and sophistication in recent years. As the present volume demonstrates, they have also enriched the workplace in many ways. At the same time, however, we are alerted here to various limitations inhering in these methodologies. With the strong emphasis placed on collaborating across domains, such an outcome may be anticipated. No longer can we anticipate a single best solution; unceasing openness to dialogue may be essential.

In an important sense the great dramas of recent decades effectively unmasking scientific authority and unleashing the marginalised voices have passed their zenith. The major critiques have been richly and compellingly elaborated, and the doors opened wide to a pluriverse of voices. Yet we are left now with the hard task of sorting, synthesising and creating viable theories and practice, all within the rush of rapid technological and global change. It is to this task that I see the present work devoted. Herein lies a treasure trove of resources for those dialogues that may shape the future of the workplace, one that may hopefully be more inclusive, humane and life sustaining.

1 Legitimising knowledge at work

John Garrick and Carl Rhodes

That workplaces are now viewed as sites of 'valid' knowledge is now virtually a given. Contested, but powerfully present, knowledge is placed in the
context of an era of 'knowledge workers' and workplace reforms. This is a
context where organisations exist in an information age in which many
aspects of working life are subject to highly automated and informated
systems and networks. In this postmodern context the legitimising of new
knowledge is occurring through a variety of work-based research practices
and the ramifications of this are dramatic, complex and contested. In these
sites of contestation changes to knowledge are being played out. Such
contestations exist at a time when the assumptions of modern management, and the notion of organisations as institutions where managerial
power is employed for organisational health, are being eroded. This
erosion has been ushered in as societies face periods of 'social decay,
resource scarcity, and social conflict because of declining reserves of
natural resources, resistance to environmental pollution, changing work
expectations, and declining confidence in established institutions' (Gephart
Jr 1996: 31). These changes, and the theories that emerge related to them,
have implications on the very nature of what we might call knowledge.
Questions such as 'when and how is it produced?', 'who gets to say what,
and why?', 'what counts and what doesn't?', 'what is really useful?' and
'how are notions of usefulness constructed?' are all at play in this contemporary meltdown of what constitutes 'legitimate' knowledge.

As a response to these changes, this book aims to conceptualise new
ways that knowledge is being 'legitimised' through various formal and
informal workplace-based research practices. We have sought to examine
the new legitimations critically, and to analyse possible directions for future
developments in work-based research and 'knowledge' formation. The
book will provide a state of the art research-based and theoretically aware
picture of developments in this area. This is not to suggest that the book
pretends it can capture or impute a totality to what is happening to

research or knowledge. More importantly, the book intends to chronicle some different perspectives on the changes that are occurring and to examine how these changes have been effected and understood in different contexts. The resulting opportunity that the book provides is a discussion of ways in which workplace 'knowledge' is being conceptualised and an exploration of the various institutional processes of contemporary society that strive to legitimise such knowledge. In doing this, the chapters variously address the connections between contemporary work research methodologies and practices and the shifting social and institutional processes of work/knowledge construction. The scope covers the relationships between work and knowledge, formal and informal education, work sociology, power, discourses of difference, identity, and more particularly how contemporary research practices in organisations affect/construct knowledge.

This book is targeted at an audience from a range of disciplines and professions. 'Work' itself is a practice that spans many disciplinary boundaries, as knowledge from any discipline might be used in work contexts. For this reason, the book is intended to have a wide readership and should be appropriate to any work context in which research is conducted or used. Outside this wide applicability, the primary readership is intended to be students and academics in business and management schools who have an interest in areas such as human resource management, human resource development, industrial relations, training and development, management learning and organisational development. It will be of particular value to those undertaking work-based research as either research practitioners, academics or postgraduate students, as well as to managers involved in research activities. In order to cater to such a diverse audience, as few assumptions as possible have been made about the levels of awareness readers have of the issues being discussed or of any theoretical perspectives.

The work in research and the research in work

The idea of 'research at work', which is a central theme of the book, can be viewed in two interrelated ways. First, 'research at work' can be conceived in terms of the methodologies and practices that researchers use in doing inquiry into different aspects of work. From this perspective, the interest is in what researchers do, how they do it, to (or with) whom they do it, for whom they do it, and the consequences of doing it. In examining research in this way, the focus is both on formal/academically legitimised research and on more informal practices that people use to develop knowledge at work. This also raises the question of 'who is the researcher?' in terms of how professional identities of researchers are constructed and legitimised through institutionally defined research practices. Second, 'research at work' can be thought of as related to the way that research-based knowledge is employed in workplace situations. Here, the focus is on how research is used for non-research practices as well as on how the difference is produced between practices called research and those cate-gorised as other than research. This book will be concerned with each of these perspectives and the relation between them.

The *uses of research* and the *doing of research* are not easily separated in the sense that both can be seen as research practices. But it is precisely these practices, in their many forms, that this book will be examining. As such, a key objective of the book is to present and develop innovative research practices through a critical analysis and questioning of work-based know-ledge. Such a questioning of knowledge and the modes of its production are entwined with the legitimacy of research in both formal and informal settings. In particular, the notions of what counts as research, who counts as a researcher and, particularly, the assumptions of scientism are also under scrutiny. Contemporary times have seen a questioning of the 'still overwhelming belief that science constitutes, by far, the most valuable part of human learning and accomplishment' (Chia 1997: 73). Such a questioning asserts that 'scientific knowledge does not represent the totality of knowledge; it has always existed in addition to, and in competition and conflict with [other kinds] of knowledge' (Lyotard 1984: 7). This conflict has been manifested in recent times in university degrees and research programmes that are increasingly accompanied by a gen-eral de-differentiation of disciplinary-based knowledge, new forms of institutional hybridity and a vocationalisation of curricula involving partner-ships between public and private sectors, universities and industries, faculties and business organisations. These developments accompany rapid changes in work cultures and contexts, as increasingly a knowledge- and information-based re-ordering of capacities is required both of organisa-tions and of the individuals who work in them.

What then do we know about the effects of this re-ordering of institu-tional capacities in relation to how knowledge is being produced and legitimised? Furthermore, how are such processes shaping (and being shaped by) key research stakeholders? There are crucial tensions here – between the professional discourses of research and the larger economic, social and organisational 'logics' that both contextualise and constrain the legitimising practices of research at work. For instance, at the same time as new research capacities are being fostered and enacted in workplaces, new professional identities and subjectivities are emerging. The new knowledge workers carry with them the possibility (and promise) of more enriched and productive work lives. From the perspective of many employers, the ultimate value to the organisation of an employee is their ability to *apply* their knowledge. Productivity in firms depends not only on the aggregate capabilities of individuals taken separately, but on the development of effective interaction patterns and teamwork (Bowman 1995: 69). But the new interaction patterns can also contain and represent some disturbing and highly pragmatic interests. At the epistemological level, such interests are frequently framed by discourses of human capital theory where people are regarded as economic subjects, as sellers of labour and as resources that can be bought and sold in the employment market. It is precisely the more glaring effects of such theories on the legitimising claims of 'research at work' that this book seeks to explore.

'Knowledge' and research in work contexts

As this book focuses on contemporary trends in the legitimisation of particular types of 'knowledge' it is fitting that we further clarify our own ways of working with the key terms, particularly 'knowledge' and 'research'. With the de-differentiation of disciplinary-based knowledge has come an emphasis on instrumental knowledge. This instrumentalisation of knowledge is connected to the questions of whether knowledge is considered to be 'useful', whether it can be applied to work contexts, and whether it can generate a competitive edge or profits. 'Knowledge' in this sense is not about the pursuit of *a priori* valid truth-claims. In short, the Enlightenment notions of truth, reason, critique and ideology have been 'downsized' to comply with the contemporary 'order of things'. Rorty puts a pragmatic spin on this: 'truth is what currently counts as good in the way of belief' (in Norris 1993: 54).

Leading up to the beginning of the new millennium, there has been a distinct turn against the discourse of Enlightenment values and beliefs and an accompanying turn in favour of the practical application of knowledge and skills in work contexts. To help us examine such turns and to interrogate some of the new applications of research at work, we have tried to position this volume in a sceptical stance with regard to contemporary knowledge construction and the productions of 'what counts as good in the way of belief'. To an extent this approach draws from the ideas of Michel Foucault who, in 'What is Enlightenment?', rejects universalist premises and argues that 'knowledge' is historically de-limited. In his terms (1997: 316):

> What remains of that delusory Enlightenment project is not so much a theory, a doctrine, or ... a permanent body of knowledge that is

accumulating … but an ethos, a philosophical life in which the critique of what we are is at one and the same time the historical analysis of the limits that are imposed on us and an experiment with the possibility of going beyond them.

What we have here is the beginnings of a carefully worded expression of doubt about the Enlightenment, and a rejection of 'belief' in its 'project'. This doubt is of value in critically examining contemporary knowledge practices, and the Foucauldian questions 'how are we constituted as subjects of our own knowledge?', 'how are we constituted as subjects who exercise or submit to power relations?', 'how are we constituted as subjects of our own actions?' and 'how can the growth of capabilities be disconnected from the intensification of power relations?' remain pertinent to this study. It is also our intention, however, by positioning the book in relation to these questions, to de-mystify the ideas of the postmodernising philosophers. For instance, we ask about the relevance to contemporary work of the collapsing of the whole range of ontological distinctions between fact and fiction, philosophy and literature, history and poetry, truth and appearance, life and art. Such blurred distinctions can be read as both conceptually exciting and problematic. But what does it all mean for employees and managers seeking to meet present-day requirements of workplace knowledge and skills? We argue that there are important connections to be made here, and see advantages in using postmodern ideas to interrogate trends in research at work, such as how work-based research practices are immersed in power/knowledge formations. For the moment, however, we turn our attention to the question 'why is it that at this historical moment the boundaries between work and research are increasingly blurred?'

The merging of research and work: why now?

Today's workers need to be multi-skilled; either that or, for many, contemplate (and enter) retrenchment or unemployability. To be multi-skilled implies several things. First, one needs to have the ability to perform a number of traditionally distinct occupational roles and be able to move across different work areas. This means acquiring and applying knowledge and skills across a range of jobs (cross-skilling). To do this effectively in our post-industrial work environments, employees are expected to develop pertinent and complex knowledge and skills such as in the use of electronic databases, the internet and other industrial communication and negotiation processes. Second, employees are required to develop understandings of work tasks (domain knowledge). This entails the capacity to engage in higher-order thinking skills related to problem-solving, critical thinking and research (up-skilling). The evolution of the 'multi-skilling' of workers has led to the notion of 'knowledge workers', whereby the components of cross-skilling, up-skilling and higher-order thinking skills (including research) are merged. It is, to an extent, the highly competitive nature of our contemporary industries, coupled with globalised markets, changing production and management technologies, that have both discursively and materially compelled employers – in most developed economies – to multi-skill their workforces.

In this book we are not going to examine whether such industrial trends are really necessary, but rather our interests are in the effects of these phenomena on the legitimisation of knowledge and the new productions of workplace meanings and belief systems. For instance, as workers at a variety of levels are increasingly required to become problem-solvers, this implies developing the capabilities to gather information, analyse data, identify trends, map dominant discourses, and so on: they are essentially doing forms of research work. At present there are very few texts that reveal much about the effects of this 'research at work' – either on new knowledge production or on knowledge-workers' selves. This book is interested in both, and the following section addresses some of the questions raised in relation to the effects of 'research at work' on professional identities.

The work that research does

People not only work at research but research also does work. And it is the striking absence of critical literature about the effects of research in the context of contemporary organisations that we are concerned about. We are ourselves in a process of legitimising certain ways of viewing knowledge production. We are piecing together particular stories that contribute to the shaping of understandings of the topic: stories that critically addresses the ways in which research is often conducted in workplaces, how it has been conceptualised, the processes of contemporary society that are enabling workplaces to produce and make valid knowledge claims. We have thus sought contributions that address the connections between the social and institutional processes of research, how one might actually conduct research in organisations and the ensuing impacts on subjectivities at work.

There are, of course, substantial literatures on each of the research topics explored within this book. For instance, volumes have been written on scientific research, action research, ethnography and interpretive research more generally. There is a growing body of works on the uses of post-structural ideas in research in organisations, and much has been written about research using information and communication technologies. Each has its own interests and concerns, and it is outside the scope of this book to address them all. We do, however, recognise that the term 'research' is ontologically, epistemologically and ethically charged. The key decision we have made is to foreground *the legitimising* of new knowledge that comes from work-based research practices in organisational contexts. We are viewing 'organisations', and the many dimensions that come with organisations, as important *contextual* features that shape what research is and what it does. Having made this key decision, the chapters that follow come from practising researchers who have practical experience in using the approaches they write about. Each draws on ideas about research at work that is extending and challenging what is already known about the topic.

Overview of the book

Our aim has been to put together an exciting and challenging collection of new and original writings, each of which takes its place in a critical examination of 'research at work' and its implications for the legitimising of new knowledge. Our intention is that this will generate discussion and dialogue and provide an access point to cutting-edge ideas about research in work contexts. To achieve this we are presenting chapters from leading researchers and practitioners who have directly engaged with the various approaches that are highlighted. The book shows that there are many ways of viewing 'valid' research and gives practical illustrations of what can be done in a range of workplaces and through a range of theoretical perspectives.

As a result of our focus on the social aspects of research and knowledge, we are emphasising the influences of context, culture, power and language, which has meant less space is allocated to more conventional technical (how to do it) considerations. The book is not about the technical aspects of research, although some chapters do address such issues; research perspectives that focus on theory/practice relationships and statistical methods are well represented in standard texts and we do not wish to replicate such topics here. Instead, the emphasis of this book is more on the implications of research *in the context of work* and what these implications mean for those who have responsibilities for 'knowledge management' – developing organisations' capacities to produce new knowledge.

The book is organised into three sections. The first, 'Knowledge, learning and the practice of work', focuses on an examination of the meanings of research and knowledge in and around contemporary workplaces. In Chapter 2, 'Working knowledge', Ronald Barnett traces the way that working knowledge has been shaped by contemporary changes in culture and society. Barnett suggests that technological change and the economic rationality of the workplace have given rise to work as a site for knowledge, as a source of knowledge and as a way of validating knowledge. Barnett argues that working knowledge is of value in that it adds a pragmatic edge that is concerned with its actions and effects on the world. At the same time, he offers a scepticism that if knowledge is legitimised only 'because it works', then we run the risk of closing off debate by judging knowledge solely on the basis of instrumentally oriented technological and market rationalities. Chapter 3, 'Research on work, research at work: postmodern perspectives' by Richard Edwards and Robin Usher, describes a conceptual framework that postmodernism can provide for understanding workplace research practices. In doing so, they bring to the fore the power of language, discourse and text in research at work. To illustrate this postmodern framework, Edwards and Usher examine human resources development in organisations, as they see such practices as embodying the relationship between knowledge and power. The outcome of this is a focus on the discursive nature of workplace practices where knowledge might be legitimated in a multiplicity of ways beyond a narrow definition of systemic enhancement. In the last chapter of Part I, 'The crisis of scientific research', Christine Ewan and Dennis Calvert assert that scientific research is in a state of crisis. To explore this crisis, they use illustrative examples from medical and health research to describe how the balance between research as the pursuit of knowledge and research as the pursuit of economic return has been radically altered. They argue that this has changed the definitions of what research is, where it is done and by whom it is done. Rather than lamenting this change or invoking a nostalgic past, Ewan and Calvert argue that future researchers need to participate creatively in defining and constructing a research environment for the next century in the face of the economic, social and technical conditions that research now faces.

Part II of the book, 'Whose knowledge? Collaboration and research in and around work', explores the way that knowledge is being used and is changing in various institutional contexts. Chapter 5, 'Globalising the intelligent organisation' by Stewart Clegg, uses a series of case studies to explore issues of power, knowledge and learning in organisations. The chapter examines how 'intelligently' these organisations have tried to achieve learning capacities. The contrast made is between exploratory learning – which focuses on improvisation, innovation, risk-taking and flexibility – and exploitative learning – which seeks to specify and employ particular organisational practices. In drawing these comparisons, Clegg concludes that organisational learning must go beyond 'cleverness' and strive for the insight, imagination and understanding that might lead to 'intelligent' organisations. In Chapter 6, 'Knowledge and control in the Japanese workplace', Keiko Morita draws on the work of Max Weber to examine how knowledge and control have been employed in contemporary Japanese workplaces to create an 'iron cage' of regulation and oppression. Morita discusses the development of this 'iron cage' through a review of the hierarchical structure of Japanese industry and the labour relation practices of leading Japanese companies. Examples of this are presented, first, through a discussion of how Japanese quality management practices have enabled increasing amounts of control over workers' lives, and, second, through a discussion of how *karoshi* (death from overwork) has spread as a problem affecting nearly all job types and industries in Japan. The chapter concludes with a question as to whether the future will see the Japanese industrial relations system free itself of the 'iron cage' or replace it with some new 'super-alloy cage'. In Chapter 7, 'Organisational knowledge, professional practice and the professional doctorate at work', Alison Lee, Bill Green and Marie Brennan examine the changing relationship between research, knowledge and work as constituted in the emergence of the professional doctorate in Britain and Australia in the 1990s. They argue that the professional doctorate marks a redefinition of research, work, knowledge and professional practice – one that proposes a reconfiguration of the role of the university in the production of knowledge between academic disciplines and workplace practices. In this reconfiguration, they foresee that new kinds of knowledge and new ways of producing knowledge will be developed, involving new relationships among participants and new kinds of research writing. Chapter 8, 'Research and engagement with trade unions: bridging the solitudes' by Carla Lipsig-Mummé, looks at how economic and social conditions in the 1980s and 1990s have led to new forms of collaboration between trade unions and academic researchers. Lipsig-Mummé argues that the growth of the 'knowledge economy', the macro social move *right* and the weakening social authority of unionism have led to a profound self-questioning within trade unions. The chapter shows how, in this globalised environment, new uses for research are being created that are linked to member education and public policy through new collaborations between unions, researchers and educators. The chapter concludes by suggesting that research needs to connect with training, education and implementation so as to sow the seeds for the future of social and political change. John McIntyre and Rosie Wickert in Chapter 9, 'The negotiated management of meanings: research for policy', introduce the idea of 'policy knowledges' to explore the relationship between research and policy. Drawing on a discussion of two examples of commissioned research, McIntyre and Wickert argue that 'research for policy' exemplifies a role for the academy in contemporary 'modes' of knowledge formation. They suggest that research can contribute to a co-production of policy knowledge through collaboration and reciprocal understanding between academics and policy-makers. Chapter 10, 'Research partnerships at work: new identities for new times' by Hermine Scheeres and Nicky Solomon, critically examines the position of the academic researcher in contemporary collaborative research practices that are emerging between universities, governments and workplaces. Drawing on their experiences in two research projects, Scheeres and Solomon review the relationship between work, education and economy. In so doing, they argue that collaborative research produces new kinds of academics who are drawn into the economics of the global workplace and whose positions are neither compliant nor resistant to economic relationships, but instead might constitute the academic as an active subject in the collaborative production of research knowledge.

Part III, 'Changing practices of research at work', turns its attention to an examination of a sample of emerging methodologies and theorisations of research at work. In Chapter 11, 'The construction of working knowl-edge and (mis)interpretive research', John Garrick addresses some of the common uses (and misuses) of interpretive research methods in contempo-rary workplaces. This examines how such research practices frame the subjectivity of people at work in a relationship that privileges the researcher and can, at times, marginalise the researched. This relationship is enacted in research texts in which researchers can colonise the research subjects by re-telling their stories without necessarily acknowledging the power of the re-interpretation that inevitably occurs in this re-telling. In conclusion, Garrick suggests that interpretive research needs to be ques-tioned in terms of the discourses surrounding its practice and to account more critically for the researcher in the production of working knowledge. Chapter 12, ' "Doing" knowledge at work' by Carl Rhodes, approaches research at work in terms of the study of organisational learning. In partic-ular, Rhodes questions theorisations of 'dialogue' that exist in mainstream organisational learning literature. In doing so, he suggests that researching communication and dialogue at work has backgrounded the social and discursive differences that operate unreconciled in organisations. Drawing mainly on the work of Mikhail Bakhtin, Rhodes argues that research at work can be theorised in a way that accounts for diversity, difference and power imbalance without trying to resolve them with idealistic yet power-laden and managerially oriented notions of consensus and 'shared meaning'. In Chapter 13, 'An adventure in "postmodern" action research: performativity, professionalism and power', Jill Sanguinetti discusses the application of postmodern and post-structuralist ideas to the practice of action research. By telling the story of an action research project in which she was involved, Sanguinetti demonstrates the research practice she calls 'discourse mapping'; a practice where contending discourses are analysed and fed back to research participants. It is argued that this approach to research can explore discursive positions, subjectivity and power so as to facilitate a greater reflexivity on the part of researchers and participants. In Chapter 14, 'Virtual research in performative times', Robin Usher and Richard Edwards review the impact of new technologies and globalisation on the forms of contemporary knowledge and on the changing modes of knowledge production. They suggest that these changes relate to a blurring of the distinction between information and knowledge that has broken down traditional notions of what knowledge 'is'. The 'virtual' research they refer to relates to the way that knowledge is now mediated 'virtually' through information technology as well as the way that research practice itself is now broader in its possible meanings than traditional university-based ideas about research. In reviewing these trends, Usher and Edwards suggest that the impact of the new technologies has been an increased dissensus as to what constitutes knowledge and greater questioning of what practices might be considered to be 'research'. In the final chapter, 'Inside the knowledge works: reviewing the terrain', we briefly review the main themes and critical issues that that have emerged from the contributions to the book.

In summary, the chapters in the book are intended to explore research practices from different points of view and in different contexts. In so doing, each chapter problematises aspects of work-based research and working knowledge in order to contribute to the development of a critical understanding of these phenomena. Taken together, the different chapters represent a multi-faceted set of theorisations and descriptions of research at work. This is intended to go beyond the confines of just being a book on research methodology and move towards an examination of the meaning of knowledge at work, as new knowledge is embodied in the nexus between academically and theoretically legitimated approaches and the practice of work.

References

Bowman, M. (1995) 'On-the-job training' in M. Carnoy (ed.) *International Encyclopedia of Economics of Education*, Oxford: Pergamon (pp. 69–74).

Chia, R. (1997) 'Process philosophy and management learning: Cultivating "foresight" in management' in J. Burgoyne and M. Reynolds (eds) *Management Learning: Integrating Perspectives in Theory and Practice*, London: Sage (pp. 71–88).

Foucault, M. (1997) *Ethics, Subjectivity and Truth*, vol. 1, edited by P. Rabinow, New York: New Press.

Gephart Jr, R.P. (1996) 'Management, social issues, and the postmodern era' in D.M. Boje, R.P. Gephart, and T.J. Thatchenkery (eds) *Postmodern Management and Organizational Theory*, Thousand Oaks: Sage (pp. 21–44).

Lyotard, J.F. (1984) *The Postmodern Condition: A Report on Knowledge*, translated by G. Dennington and B. Massumi, Manchester: Manchester University Press.

Norris, C. (1993) *The Truth about Postmodernism*, Oxford: Blackwell.

Part I

Knowledge, learning and the practice of work

2   Working knowledge

Ronald Barnett

The forms knowledge can take

Knowledge changes. That is a commonplace. Less understood and less remarked upon is the point that what counts as knowledge also changes. The underlying tacitly held assumptions in society as to what, in general terms, knowledge looks like gradually – or not so gradually – give way to new ideas as to the form that knowledge might take.

In the Athenian senate, not only theoretical knowledge (theoria) but also practical wisdom (phronesis) was understood to be a legitimate route to gaining understanding of the world. Senators, after all, had to think on their feet and to have their wits about them: they never knew from which direction might come a stab in the back. Later, in medieval times, with the formation of a priestly stratum, knowledge was essentially the knowledge of texts. He who commanded the key texts (chained in the monastery libraries) was likely to be venerated, but, in an era before the printing press, the spoken word also carried with it a force of its own (Gellner 1991). Rhetoric, accordingly, was a key element in the curriculum of the medieval universities.

Over the last one hundred years, knowledge has come to be defined largely as the product of organised and often large-scale 'research', often disseminated to schools and universities through textbooks and stored in libraries. Over the decade of the 1990s, new technology in the form of computers and associated information systems has come to form a kind of *sine qua non* of the production of knowledge. For many fields of knowledge the use of the computer in some form has come to be taken as a likely, if not a necessary, condition of valid knowledge. Not only in the academic world, the process is also evident in the world of work. In the latter, computerised management information and the transition by companies to 'informated networks' have added authority to knowledge claims. For example, demographic data may be used to legitimise the development of a particular product, marketing campaign or company strategy.

The ways we frame knowledge in constructing the world, our 'epistemologies', are – as Ernest Gellner persistently reminded us – social in character (Gellner 1992). What we take valid knowledge to be in general is shaped by culture and society: our rules of knowledge are not just or even primarily matters for philosophers, but are matters of general interest and, social determination. What counts as valid knowledge, in one age, slips away, sometimes easily and sometimes not without a fight, to be replaced by another way of engaging with the world that comes to be seen as natural and indisputable, at least for a time.

As we move into the twenty-first century, we are arguably facing yet another fundamental epistemological transition. Crudely put, it is a shift from knowledge understood as a matter of what one knows, to knowledge understood as a matter of what one can do. There are several strands in this transition. But the key direction is clear: from knowledge as contemplation to knowledge as action.

As Gibbons and his associates have insisted (Gibbons *et al.* 1994), this transition is not a matter of academic knowledge being applied to domains of action: it is rather the recognition that knowledge is generated *in action*. Characteristically, the knowledge-in-action that is most highly prized in the modern world is that which is produced in situ in the domain of work; that is, in settings that are systematic, collective, often large-scale and oriented towards production, profit and growth. Accordingly, *working knowledge* – as we might term it – is knowledge that is generated by and in the work situation; it works for its producers, securing economic or other gains, and it works as a form of intellectual labour, taking the place of human manual labour, and claiming attention in its own right.

Unravelling this working knowledge and assessing its legitimacy are two tasks in front of us here. Accordingly, the first half of the chapter takes the form of a mapping exercise, in which key features of working knowledge are identified, while the second half changes tack, moving to assessing the legitimacy of working knowledge as a bona fide form of knowledge. The chapter ends by offering some suggestions as to how working knowledge might be strengthened.

What's in a name?

How can we give sense to this idea of working knowledge? In the Western tradition, as we have noted, knowledge has come to stand for ordered conceptual frameworks, providing systematic holds on the world, expressed in written and spoken language. We talk of bodies of knowledge, and we associate them with systematic strategies to add to those bodies of knowledge through 'research', which is increasingly undertaken in teams and then reported in an academic literature (which is increasingly being pursued in electronic forms). Knowledge only becomes 'knowledge' when it is public, captured in the form of propositions or theories which, depending on the knowledge field, have their own tests of truth and which, in turn, can be publicly examined and evaluated, preferably in writing (Hirst 1974). This, indeed, is one of the functions of academic journals: to make available a public forum for the examination of knowledge claims. In this way, Knowledge – with a capital K as it were – emerges into a world 'independently' – either of the external world or of the world of minds and their thoughts (Popper 1975). We may picture knowledge, accordingly, as an edifice, having a durable character, that has stood the test of time, the result of much hard labour but with a public face. Karl Popper, indeed, invoked the image of the erection of a building in capturing the evolution of 'objective knowledge'.

However, alongside this idea of knowledge as publicly constructed through shared understandings in language, other ideas of knowledge have developed over the past fifty years that are much more grounded in action. Experiential learning, action learning, knowing-how and problem-solving are indicative terms: they point us to ways of interacting with the world that are perceived to yield worthwhile knowledge. Michael Polanyi's ideas of 'personal knowledge' (1958) and 'tacit knowledge' (1968) are, forty years later, rediscovered as apparently helpful concepts in making sense of 'knowing in firms' (von Krogh *et al.* 1998). This knowledge is gained in situ, through interactions not with propositions, theories or formally expressed facts about the world, but in direct engagements with the world in particular settings as they arise, especially in the domain of work. And so an idea of 'working knowledge' begins to emerge.

Working knowledge has a number of aspects to it. It is not a coherent idea but stands for a range of claims, for example, that:

1   Knowledge is only authentic if it can be put to work (*work as the site of knowledge*).
2   Work is a site in which knowledge can be generated (*work as a source of knowledge*).
3   Work can offer a means of testing claims to knowledge (*work as a form of validating knowledge*).

Some equivocations run through these claims. First, they slide between working knowledge as *the* path to knowledge or as just *a* path to knowledge.

There are hawks and doves on this issue. Some, for example those advocating the idea of 'competence' as the key concept for education and training, might want to argue the strong thesis, that work holds the golden palm: it alone offers the way to 'true understanding'. Others would be happier with the milder thesis that knowledge in work is just one legitimate way of understanding the nature of knowledge.

Second, there is a key distinction to be made between the generation of knowledge (or, to put it more technically, its *production*) and its assessment (or its *validation*). Again, there would be hawks and doves on this issue. The hawks will claim that it is the world of work, or at least the domain of action, that not only produces knowledge but ensures its validation. They are wholehearted pragmatists. The doves take a more nuanced line. They would contend that the world of work is entirely legitimate as a domain in which knowledge can be produced, but would allow that the kind of knowledge produced in work settings could still, and perhaps should, be tested in a more independent setting according to conventional tests for truth.

Lastly, there is embedded in our three propositions a radical thesis but one which again is susceptible to stronger or weaker formulations. It is the thesis that knowledge in action constitutes quite a new way of gaining a hold on the world. It constitutes, in the language of Gibbons and his associates (1994), a World 2 as distinct from the World 1 of more theoretical forms of knowing (Edwards and Usher expand on this matter in Chapter 3). Here, the hawks would argue that working knowledge, as embedded in solving real-time problems in the glue of actual situations as they present in the world, is replacing knowledge in a theoretical context and, indeed, *should* be seen in this way. Putting it more formally, our epistemologies are changing – from knowing-in-theory to knowing-in-action – and not before time. From knowing as description to knowing as prescription.

The idea of working knowledge, then, heralds large changes in the ways in which we engage with the world and in which we come to form what are taken to be valid or worthwhile claims about the world. What is emerging is nothing less than a potential revolution in what we take knowledge to be.

Capital, capital

Recently, the notion of 'intellectual capital' has gained currency. It points to the fact that, in the 'knowledge society' (Stehr 1994), organisations will prosper so long as they draw significantly upon intellectual resources of their own. To maintain its currency, this intellectual resource has to be maintained, renewed and developed; otherwise, the value of this capital will dwindle. 'Many organisations are now appointing chief knowledge officers' (Nonaka *et al.* 1998), presumably to take command of their organisations' intellectual capital. How does this notion of intellectual capital relate to the idea – being developed here – of working knowledge?

The idea of intellectual capital has virtue in that it reminds us that the mind can constitute a potent resource in the modern world, alongside machinery, material technology and mere physical labour. It has the drawback, however, in that the notion of intellect is both unduly cerebral and is characteristically held to be an attribute of individuals. The form of its knowledge products is held to be propositional in character, propositions that are susceptible to manipulation by the mind: the intellect shows itself in the formal knowledge that an individual holds of the world. The idea of working knowledge, on the other hand, still implies that knowledge is being put to work (and so fits with the notion of knowledge as capital) but goes beyond the cerebral and the individual dimensions. Working knowledge emphasises that knowledge is inherent in human processes, actions and all interactions: it is thus not purely cerebral. Working knowledge indicates that knowledge may be apparent at the level of groups, systems and organisations, just as much as it is at the level of individuals.

We therefore emerge with the following initial classification of working knowledge:

	Individual	*Group*	*Organisation*
Proposition-based knowledge			
Process-based knowledge			

Such a framework produces immediate challenges. Propositions may be held by individuals, but to what extent are they held by groups and organisations? Groups increasingly are making collective statements, amounting to knowledge claims. Even organisations are doing so. We do not have to confine ourselves to so-called mission statements: increasingly, companies are making public pronouncements – for example, on environmental issues, on issues connected with drugs (in the pharmaceutical industry), on matters to do with information and data accessibility (in the computer industry) – which are tantamount to knowledge claims. They are, in effect, saying: this is how the world is. They are making claims that can be tested.

The idea of proposition-based knowledge, defined at the group or organisational levels, is therefore relatively straightforward. More problematic is the idea of process-based knowledge in such collective form. There is an increasing readiness to recognise the existence of process knowledge as a key aspect of the capabilities of individuals in professional life, indeed, their very professionalism (Eraut 1994). But to include processes within the ambit of 'organisational knowledge' is to present immediate difficulties.

First, knowledge-constructing processes within organisations are themselves diverse and embrace both technical and bureaucratic systems and forms of communication and interaction. The communicative dimension of organisational knowledge would, in turn, raise issues of 'voice' and ethos: what are the characteristic forms of engagement across an organisation? To what extent do staff see each other as colleagues, able to express and to develop a point of view? To ask these questions reminds us that organisational knowledge is not a fixed entity but is dynamic, and might and should be expanding in continuing processes of knowledge creation (Nonaka *et al.* 1998), and that those processes can be buttressed – or, indeed, severely limited – by opportunities and encouragements given to human interaction.

Second, and just as challenging, is the very idea of organisational knowledge (see Magalhues 1998). Even if we allow for both systems and communicative processes, to what extent are we entitled to employ the term 'knowledge'? We might talk of the knowledge capacities of an organisation, but in what way might we talk of organisational knowledge? This seems to imply that organisations *as such* possess knowledge yet it also implies that knowledge may be organisational in character.

On the one hand an organisation may be said to be a repository of knowledge in the sense not just of the contents of the minds of its individual employees but more significantly in the sense of its capacities to draw on, to wield and to deploy knowledge. Here, we can entertain the ideas of the *knowledge position* and a *knowledge audit* of the organisation. In the knowledge society, in a world awash with knowledge, the issue arises as to where an organisation is positioned in terms of knowledge. With which knowledge networks is it connected (Castells 1997)? For instance, we are seeing the rise of corporate universities – such as that in the UK spawned by British Aerospace (Kenney Wallset, 2000) – but they are not noted for their sponsorship among their employees of a receptivity to Greek philosophy or the nineteenth-century novel. A knowledge audit would reveal that they focus on technical and managerial knowledge; and, even there, will want to develop among their employees certain usable knowledges – and their associated skills – with likely productive value for the organisation.

This possession of organisational knowledge locates an organisation epistemologically, as we might say. It points to the dominant *knowledge inter-*

ests of the organisation (compare the knowledge interests of a local community health centre with those of a multi-national drugs company). But it also points to what might be termed the *epistemological voice* of the organisation. On what topics can it speak with authority? With which departments of state and of which ministers might it have or would it wish to have their ear (the Department of Trade and Industry? The Department of Health? The Defence Department?).

On the other hand, alongside organisational knowledge as the knowledge positioning of an organisation, lies the organisational dimension of knowledge. This dimension affirms that knowledge can be organised systematically by an organisation. It also tells us that the sum is more than the parts: knowledge produced and garnered within an organisational setting and supported by the resources of that organisation can be given added value; or, at least, is given particular kinds of value. By taking knowledge seriously, by investing organisational effort in its knowledges, an organisation imparts extra dimensions to its knowledge resources. Here again we are pointed back to knowledge processes.

Activities and interactions within an organisation may be forms of knowing-in-action, albeit of a collective kind. Problem-identification and problem-solving in teams becomes a kind of action research. Knowing becomes embedded in organisational practices. In turn, sophisticated and collective frames of understanding may emerge, often captured in visual form (in graphs, diagrams, tables, three-dimensional and dynamic computer models, and so forth).

These knowledge processes will have their own tacit structures, characteristic of the organisation concerned and imparting an organisational 'culture'. Forms of communication (the extent to which they are open, hierarchical and frequent), the favoured modes of communication (whether oral, written, computer-based, visual) and the extent to which communication is cross-disciplinary will all shape the character of the organisation's knowledge processes.

The concept emerges, therefore, of an organisation's *knowledge capital*. An organisation's knowledge capital is its ability to marshal and deploy its knowledge. That ability is a function of the range of knowledges at its disposal and the processes which they work. Knowledge capital, accordingly, takes on something of the following elements:

Disciplines: Range; interchange across the disciplines
Modes of communication: Hierarchical/dialogical, individual/team-based
Forms of communication: Visual, oral, written, computer-based
Processes: Systems/procedures, tacit/codified

Performance indicators: Team-building, new tangible product, new purpose/new 'mission'

These elements are not in themselves necessarily aspects or components of knowledge capital. They come into play as knowledge capital – become *working knowledge* – insofar as there is a collective, epistemological value added. The organisation not only does things; it does things in an informed way. Knowledge resources are orchestrated through both human and non-human means. Effort is put into securing a deeper collective understanding of the challenges faced and of working out shared strategies and new collective self-understandings. Investments are made in developing the knowledge and understandings of employees, perhaps even setting up the company's own corporate 'university'. Knowledge capital is thus put to work, adding further value to existing knowledge capital.

Working it through

Working knowledge, epistemological voice, knowledge position, process and knowledge capital: collectively, these concepts amount to nothing short of a revolution in our general conception of knowledge and knowing. From individuals to organisations; from states of mind to interactive processes; from propositions to processes; from public-but-explicit (in the written word) to public-but-tacit (in ineffable powers and processes): working knowledge challenges our traditional understandings of knowledge.

Questions at once arise. Are those traditional conceptions of knowledge sidelined? Is our global age (Albrow 1996), with an effervescent dynamism that calls for a collective response-in-action, in effect also asking us to repudiate familiar notions of knowing, which are buried deep in Western culture? If there is to be a place for individuals, for propositional knowledge and for explicitness, what is to be its relationship to working knowledge? And then, having sorted out those relationships, how might we place working knowledge itself? Is it 'real knowledge'? By what criteria might it be justified, if at all, *as* knowledge?

There are no clear answers to these questions. Nevertheless, a first move might be to say that, in keeping with the spirit of our 'postmodern' times, there are no universal principles by which we can legislate on the matter. There are no indisputable principles we can wield that can sort out bona fide knowledges from more doubtful or even masquerading knowledges. There are both philosophical and sociological issues at stake here. At the philosophical level, any set of arbitrating principles would be suspect: their own grounds would be contentious. For example, on what grounds might numerical descriptions of the world be favoured, or falsifiable propositions be considered especially worthy? There are no 'first principles' available to us that do not provoke further questions in turn (Rorty 1989). Philosophically, then, it would seem that we are obliged to be generous in our sense as to what is to count as a serious candidate for the title of 'knowledge'. If 'working knowledge' is felt by enough people to be knowledge, then knowledge it is.

Sociologically too, legislation seems to be off-limits. The global world would appear to be calling for multiple knowledges. Our knowledges expand so as to be more responsive to the demands of a fast-moving age, characterised by the compression of time and space (Giddens 1991). If we are to make sense of our world and prosper in it, new forms of knowledge – at once process-oriented, collective and pragmatic in character – may well have to be embraced. And, in any event, new knowledges are now with us.

In the age – now passigng – in which formal propositional and scientific knowledge counted as knowledge, it was generally accepted who the authorities were; or, at least, one could readily find out. Now the epistemological authorities are less clear, if indeed they exist at all. Indeed, in being a property of organisational potential (and of organisational process), knowledge seems to be distributed between all involved in those manifold knowledge processes. On this view, to be seen to be invoking an idea of knowledge as such – of knowledge with determinable rules and standards (Knowledge with a capital K, as it were) – would seem to be behind the game. The world has moved on. No epistemological rules here, seems to be the only sensible reading.

But the arguments for epistemological clarity should not be allowed to be won too easily. Yes, we live in a world that calls for multiple knowledges, especially knowledges that work, that are in the work, and that are seen to be in work. Those knowledges are fundamentally different from the formal systematic knowledges celebrated in universities. But they still wish to be known as knowledges, claiming to offer legitimate constructions of the world: they seek validation and approval *as* knowledge. They cannot both repudiate the idea of knowledge and, simultaneously, stake a claim as knowledge. Notwithstanding the difficulties that attach to legislating, then two tasks remain. First, there is that of making sense of the idea of working knowledge as 'knowledge' – how do we locate it philosophically? What forms of knowledge does it open up? Second, what judgements are available to us about working knowledge, even against the background of the difficulties of epistemological judgement?

Making it count

Working knowledge is both hard and soft. That working knowledge works gives it a hardness. This knowledge takes no prisoners. Either it has outcomes, preferably in the bottom line, that count in favour of the organisation, or it does not. On the other hand, its lack of explicitness provides it with a softness. This is not a knowledge that can be tested publicly in the academic journals. It is not 'there' in any secure sense. Its forms and its means of evaluation are manifold, fuzzy and indeterminate. Further, whereas formal knowledge is susceptible of tests that are arguably universal, working knowledge is often company-specific: its tests are whether it works for this company.[1] Working knowledge, accordingly, has an ineffable quality.

This dual character – hard and soft at the same time – makes working knowledge a slippery customer. It can claim to be robust; its test of worth is its success in the world; its outcomes are there for all to see. Does it provide a more economic product? Does it lead to more efficient working practices? Does it allow more control over an open environment? Does it provide for greater projection of the company? These tests are not academic tests, but they are public for all that; and they provide an apparent robustness for this working knowledge. But its softness, the way in which the legitimising tests will slip and slide from one day to another, make it elusive. One day, managers may feel secure in their judgements and practices because the company's shares rise in value; on another day, they affirm the robustness of the company's knowledge capital because they have more product lines than their competitors; on yet another day, they will be plagued by ambiguity as knowledge-in-work declares itself in the inventiveness that is, embedded in their products and in the rapidity with which new product developments are made; and on yet another day, this knowledge-in-work may show itself in the numbers of graduate entrants to the ranks of that company's employees, drawn especially from degree courses in the technologies and in the computational fields.

One response, in reflecting on this dual character of working knowledge, is that we are hardly in the domain of knowledge at all. At best, it might be said, the term 'knowledge' is being used in an honorific way. Its slipperiness, its elusiveness and its fuzziness – in being associated with indeterminate processes and capacities – are characteristics that rule out the presence of 'knowledge' as such. It may be that formal knowledge from one or more of the 'academic' knowledge fields comes into play (and in many technological fields, necessarily so) but their transposition into knowledge-in-work brings a transition from knowledge as contemplation to knowledge as action. So the phrase 'knowledge-as-action' still leaves us with a conundrum: in what sense, if at all, are we in the presence of knowledge?

'Knowledge', in the Western tradition at least, has had conceptual connections with truth and understanding. Does truth come into play where working knowledge is present? The fundamental difficulty is that the formula beckons: truth is what works. But, quite apart from its question-begging character ('works' against what criteria?), we run into a near-double tautology, in which both working knowledge and truth are both defined in terms of work. What we need is an independent formulation of truth that doesn't depend on work; *and* we need a definition of 'work' that doesn't refer to work. Both of these hopes seem forlorn.

This seemingly pedantic discussion about truth criteria has profound implications. The idea of working knowledge both claims that we are in the presence of knowledge yet also wants to distance itself from conventional propositional knowledge. So where do we locate 'working knowledge' and how might we evaluate this form of knowledge? On the first count, 'working knowledge' indicates a pragmatic turn in our orientation towards what counts as knowledge, Garrick and Rhodes point out in Chapter 1. Working knowledge is not only in work; it is what works. On the second count, our evaluations have to be guarded as what works, is a matter of judgement made by those in power. For Lyotard (1984), truth takes on a performative aspect, being no longer a matter of the better argument but outcomes shaped by criteria such as economic growth, organisational projection and consumer satisfaction. The academic world *has been* too precious over its truth criteria and its truth assessment processes – they should be challenged and widened. But working knowledge can too easily become a vehicle for pushing through prior value systems and projects unconcerned with truth and knowledge as such. Without independent sorts of validity, working knowledge is likely to be a set of ideological carriers.

A mixed blessing

One comment on the argument so far is that it has distinguished too sharply between conventional propositional knowledge on the one hand and working knowledge on the other. Even while it has been acknowledged that working knowledge itself comes in many forms, and that it is not a unitary phenomenon, still it has portrayed working knowledge in terms of processes, capabilities and outcomes; in other words, in terms of the instrumental dimension. Propositional knowledge has often been put to one side as if that could not be said to be part of working knowledge.

Such a characterisation of working knowledge, holding it apart from propositional knowledge, is misguided, so it could be alleged. Indeed, in support of such a counter-attack, it might be pointed out that 'professional knowledge' is a concept that brings together both propositional and process knowledge. We look to professionals both for their mastery of a particular domain of propositional knowledge *and* – in virtue of the value of that domain of knowledge to a sphere of practical life (health, the law, building construction, and so forth) – we also look to professionals to be adept in handling that knowledge in the processes of engaging with particular circumstances that we, as clients, present to them. Propositional knowledge and process knowledge: both come together in professional knowledge (Eraut 1994).

Further, in support of there being a fuzzy boundary between propositional and working knowledge, it might be pointed out that not only are many domains of work dependent on particular bodies of propositional knowledge but they are themselves intimately involved in developing those bodies of knowledge. The chemical industry, medicine and the pharmaceutical industry are among the major players in this respect. Professions and sectors of industry such as these are not just built around 'evidence-based' practice: they are themselves engaged in building up the body of 'evidence' on which their practices are based.

'Research and development', we can pertinently notice, is a term that has its locus within the domain of work. An increasing proportion of research is conducted in work settings. We should distinguish (1) research conducted in specialised, often state-funded, institutes (for example, on road safety or on cancer): here, specialised research institutes orient their activities towards the 'solution' of problems in the world; (2) so-called 'think tanks', whether aligned to particular political causes (such as the environment) or political parties or more independent, that both conduct research and commission research focused on particular social issues; (3) sectors of industry (such as the chemical industry or the information technology industry) that conduct research in order to produce economically viable products; (4) professions (such as medicine and engineering) that seek to extend the knowledge base of their profession so as to offer more effective services to their clients.

The relationships between research and work are strong in some cases – (3) and (4) – and weaker in others – (1) and (2). At one end of the axis, so to speak, there is an intention of informing policies; a mid-position on the axis is that of intending actually to shape policies; and at the other end lies the situation in which knowledge is bound up in a product or activity itself. Despite these variations, a central issue in relation to each setting is the extent to which the knowledge process is itself coloured by the general character of the hoped-for action. This is not, we should note,

a matter of ideology configuring the knowledge activity in any straightforward sense, nor of the knowledge claims being pre-figured by a
premonition of the likely outcomes, although both of these influences
may be present. It is, to put it sharply, the matter of the domain of truth
being dominated by pragmatic concerns. Nothing so crude as 'truth is
what works' need be invoked as a spectre. It is rather, as stated, the possibility that considerations of truth are influenced by considerations of
effectiveness in the practical domain. To the extent that that happens, we
are removed from the domain of the better argument and, in that event,
we start to close off options for constructive debate, for consideration and
for examination.

Working knowledge, then, emerges as a mixed blessing. On the one
hand, it brings knowledge up against the external world. It looks for a pay-
off of some kind. It asks: 'What is the use value of your knowledge claim?'
It encourages a concern with action and effects in the world. It can even
propel a momentum in addressing problems in the world of manifest
human concern. In themselves, these features of working knowledge are
laudable. For too long, academic knowledge was dominated by an interest
in knowledge-in-itself. Purity, intellectual rigour (the criteria of which took
their contours from the separate disciplines) and the support of one's
academic peers: these *were* the hallmarks of knowledge production in the
academic domain. The more removed from the world of action, practice
and (especially) work, the better. That such unduly narrow definitions of
knowledge should now be challenged is surely proper; and not only on
epistemological grounds, for those definitions of knowledge represented an
academic ideology and ruled off-side other potentially worthwhile definitions.

Working knowledge, while heralding a welcome alternative definition of
knowledge, is faced with its own problematic: it is deficient precisely where
the academics' propositional knowledge was strong. What are the tests for
truth, independently of the aphorism that it is 'what works'? Ultimately, is
this not a situation in which money talks? Propositional knowledge is
public, open to debate and subject to scrutiny in open argument: working
knowledge is, at best, tacit and at worst deliberately managed to achieve
particular ends that are hardly up for debate in an organisational context
(for instance, the company's mission is not on the table). Indeed, the knowledge products themselves will often be patented so as to prevent
replication. So far as propositional knowledge comes into play, it will often
be kept literally secret: the company's researchers will be limited in the
extent that they can write up their findings for fear of reducing their
company's competitive advantage.

To speak, then, of working knowledge or even of 'the new production of knowledge' (Gibbons *et al.* 1994), is to concede too much. Indeed, in the Western tradition, 'knowledge' has stood for improvement of our understanding of our world, an improvement of understanding acquired through open consensual debate. In this new knowledge, saturated by pragmatic interests, improvement is simply what the market or the shareholders will bear, or which will assist in projecting the company's profile. It is a domain in which, far from there being an open debate in which a wide range of people can join (as with propositional knowledge), the forces of commerce and politics can wield undue power and control. Ultimately, we are in the process of rival rationalities (MacIntyre, 1990). On the one hand, an argumentative rationality in which matters can be brought out into the open and argued through by the contesting parties; on the other hand, a performative rationality in which effects in the world count, effects that are the outcome of unequal forces and interests, especially those of the transnational companies.

Conclusion: working knowledge – it would be a good thing

To return to our starting point, the Athenians had a place for working knowledge or, as Aristotle termed it, practical wisdom. More recently, we have come to recognise the existence of professional knowledge as a valid form of knowledge. Both of these claims to knowledge point to understanding-in-action and can justifiably claim the term 'knowledge' since, in both instances, there are consensual courts of scrutiny and debate that can be brought to bear on the actions in question: the 'Athenian forum' in the one case, the professional journals that set out and attempt to develop in open debate the profession's knowledge and ethical base and professional bodies that can try alleged professional misdemeanours.

Working knowledge, however, lacks these superstructural elements. For working knowledge, work is both site and instrument of evaluation: knowledge is in work and it is what works. Despite the calls from the corporate sector that, as putative learning organisations, companies should encourage new ideas and even critical ideas (Senge 1990), thoroughgoing critique is largely discouraged. The concept of 'whistle-blower', after all, gains its purchase from the limits placed on open evaluation of working practices and assumptions. Working knowledge is often devoid of open scrutiny.

This critique of working knowledge is not, it should be noted, a critique of knowledge-in-work as such. Donald Schön (1983) decisively and subversively demonstrated, in his examination of *The Reflective Practitioner*, how knowledge of an action-oriented character is embedded in professional activity. But that professional knowledge is not only open, as Schön pointed out, to real-time critical reflection by the professional practitioner and to public demonstration and examination in teaching situations; it is also open to more public representation, scrutiny and evaluation (which Schön perhaps failed fully to recognise). In that sense, professional knowledge is potentially open-ended, even in its action elements. And just this happens in practice: witness the critical attention being given to 'keyhole' surgery to determine its efficacy.

It follows that if 'working knowledge' is to be a coherent construction and not just a dressing up of particular elements of work in a technological age, or a cloak for technical and financial interests, superstructural components that allow for such reflexivity need to be built into its construction. Transparency, openness, unrestricted use of peer-assessed journals, scrutiny by expert panels, the development of professional associations and increasing contact with the academic world (in which these values and practices are hopefully surviving), and structural links between companies and universities: these would be among the possible constituents of such an epistemological infrastructure for openness and debate. There are signs that much of this may be taking shape, albeit embryonically. At the same time, within companies, appraisal processes, distributed responsibilities, flatter hierarchies, greater opportunities for interaction spawned by modern information and communications technologies and the call from shareholders for greater accountability: developments such as these are sponsoring a climate of openness and mutual evaluation within the business world. In a global world, saturated by information available through the internet, openness may turn out itself to be a pragmatic option that 'works'.[2]

Without such a structural reflexivity accompanying working knowledge, we cannot seriously maintain that we are in the presence of 'knowledge'. Much more is at stake than mere terminology. What is at stake is both the character of what we take knowledge to be and, even more seriously, the extent to which we are moving towards, or away from, a more open society and a more open world. Ultimately without the necessary superstructural attention, 'working knowledge' – to the extent that it became an acceptable term – would signify a closing of our options and a closing of our world.

Notes

1   The idea of 'autopoiesis', recently developed and much vaunted in the literature on knowing in firms, specifically underlines the view that organisational knowledge has to be seen as a matter of a self-productive set of systems *within* an individual company, through which a company develops its own character. In other words, it allows without question that company-specific processes can count as knowledge, whereas the idea of knowledge in the Western tradition has contained elements of universality. 'Autopoiesis' also elides organisational self-productive capacities with organisational learning. See Magalhues (1998) for such a doubly unquestioning stance.

2   Admittedly, however, such industry–universities interactions may represent a Trojan horse for giving academic science itself an ideological character (Dickson 1988; Feenberg and Hannay 1995).

References

Albrow, M. (1996) *The Global Age*, Cambridge: Polity.

Castells, M. (1997) *The Rise of the Network Society*, Oxford: Blackwell.

Dickson, D. (1988) *The New Politics of Science*, Chicago: University of Chicago Press.

Eraut, M. (1994) *Developing Professional Knowledge and Competence*, London: Falmer Press.

Feenberg, A. and Hannay, A. (eds) (1995) *The Politics of Knowledge*, Bloomington: University of Indiana Press.

Gellner, E. (1991) *Plough, Sword and Book*, London: Paladin.

Gellner, E. (1992) *Reason and Culture*, Oxford: Blackwell.

Gibbons, M., Limoges, C., Nowotny, H., Schwartzmann, S., Scott, P. and Trow, M. (1994) *The New Production of Knowledge*, London: Sage.

Giddens, A. (1991) *The Consequences of Modernity*, Cambridge: Polity Press.

Hirst, P. (1974) *Knowledge and the Curriculum*, London: Routledge and Kegan Paul.

Kenney-Wallset, G. (2000) 'Plato.com: The role and impact of corporate universities in the third millennium', in P. Scott (ed.) *Higher Education Re-formed*, London: Falmer.

Lyotard, J.-F. (1984) *A Report on Knowledge*, Manchester: Manchester University Press.

MacIntyre, A. (1990) *Three Rival Versions of Moral Enquiry*, London: Duckworth.

Magalhues, R. (1998) 'Organisational knowledge and learning' in G. von Krogh, J. Roos and D. Kleine (eds) *Knowing in Firms: Understanding, Managing and Measuring Knowledge*, London: Sage.

Nonaka, I., Umemoto, K. and Sasaki, K. (1998) 'Three tales of knowledge-creating companies' in G. von Krogh, J. Roos and D. Kleine (eds) *Knowing in Firms: Understanding, Managing and Measuring Knowledge*, London: Sage.

Polanyi, M. (1958, republished 1978) *Personal Knowledge: Towards a Post-Critical Philosophy*, London: Routledge and Kegan Paul.

Polanyi, M. (1968) *The Tacit Dimension*, New York: Doubleday.

Popper, K. (1975) *Objective Knowledge*, Oxford: Clarendon Press.

Rorty, R. (1989) *Contingency, Irony and Solidarity*, Cambridge: Cambridge University Press.

Schön, D. (1983) *The Reflective Practitioner*, New York: Basic Books.

Senge, P. (1990) *The Fifth Discipline: The Art and Practice of the Learning Organisation*, London: Century Business.

Stehr, N. (1994) *Knowledge Societies*, London: Sage.

von Krogh, G., Roos, J. and Kleine, D. (eds) (1998) *Knowing in Firms: Understanding, Managing and Measuring Knowledge*, London: Sage.

3 Research on work, research at work

Postmodern perspectives

Richard Edwards and Robin Usher

This chapter is deliberately subtitled 'postmodern *perspectives*' since we take the view that there is no single or simple definition of the 'postmodern'. It is itself a contested area and as such its contribution to researching the workplace cannot be said to be uncontentious, either in what it might tell us about workplace practices or in terms of what it implies and suggests about research in general and researching the workplace in particular. It is possible to characterise a situation in which, for some, postmodern perspectives might be thought of as researching postmodernity, where the latter is thought of as the 'reality' of emerging workplace practices. These practices are associated with flexible specialisation, flatter structures, human resource development (HRD) – in short, what is usually subsumed under the term 'post-Fordism'. For others, however, postmodern research involves locating social practices, including those of the workplace, within theoretical frameworks that produce different and multiple understandings of those practices. Insofar as workplaces explicitly adopt 'multiple under-standings', we might then be able to talk of a postmodern workplace as a 'reality'. However, that 'reality' itself might take many forms, as the post-modern perspectives in circulation can be quite different.

This chapter does not attempt to neatly tie down the issues already raised, nor to come up with simple and generalisable conclusions. Neither is it concerned with describing and analysing specific examples of research on the workplace. Instead, its main theme relates to the multiple significa-tions that the title itself suggests. In adopting this title – an act both deliberate and playful – we sought to welcome, in an exemplary post-modern way, the 'play' that is thereby opened up. What is suggested is a range of possibilities for researching postmodern workplaces. The need for carrying out research in a postmodern way is suggested, which includes issues of language, discourse, text, power, subjectivity and reflexivity being highlighted rather than ignored or suppressed. This is one important sense of 'research *on* work'. But 'research at work' can have more than one signification – not only can it refer to researching the workplace in a straightforward sense, but less obviously it can also refer to research generated in the workplace. We term this 'research *in* work', and this encompasses the work that research does: research *at* work, where research is 'world constructing' rather than simply 'world explaining'. This is a postmodern notion that brings to the fore the power of language, discourse and text in the practice of research.

This thematic will be worked through in a chapter of four parts. First, we will outline some of the different notions of the postmodern in play. Second, we will focus on what is held to be a central aspect in postmodern perspectives, the linguistic turn, the increased role and importance assigned to language and discourse in understanding social practices. Here we will touch on the work of some of those writers whose work is commonly associated with these perspectives, in particular the work of Foucault. The third section will examine some of the main texts that can be said to provide a postmodern perspective on the workplace. In particular, we will highlight studies that focus on the practices of human resource development, practices that embody the interrelationship of knowledge and power. Finally, we will point to the multiple senses in which the notion of 'research at work' can be understood and the reflexivity in research practices that this highlights. To reiterate once again, this chapter does not touch upon research methodology or how to go about researching the workplace, but rather its focus is the conceptual framework that the 'postmodern' provides for developing different understandings of workplace practices.

Postmodern perspectives/perspectives on postmodernity

The meaning and significance of postmodernity is subject to an enormous amount of contemporary debate encompassing areas traditionally covered by separate academic disciplines and work practices: for example, literature, architecture, the media, advertising, cinema and music. The notion of 'postmodernity' has been deployed in a variety of ways:

> As an historical period, an aesthetic style, and a change in the condition of knowledge; to conceptualise difference – a distinctive form beyond the modern – as well as similarity – a variant of the modern, or its limit form; and to describe affirmative or reactionary and critical or progressive discourses and movements.
>
> (Smart 1992: 164)

Often it is associated with ways of characterising the present, which can result in the suggestion of a historical trajectory from the traditional to modernity, and from there to postmodernity. Postmodernity, therefore, has been constructed as a new historical era, a position in our view that is highly problematic in that it denies complex configurations of change, rupture and continuity. In this chapter, we do not wish to suggest that post-modernity is such a new historical period; however, the development of postmodern perspectives is nonetheless associated with attempts to under-stand contemporary practices from a position that prior orthodoxies – conservative and radical – are no longer as telling as they once were, and where this position is itself open to critique.

In economic terms, the current conjuncture has often been charac-terised as a period of revitalised capital accumulation based on globalisation that has helped bring about, and has resulted from, new forms of production, distribution and consumption. Globalisation involves the integration of the economies of nation-states through market mecha-nisms, accompanied by increased transnational flexibility of capital and labour markets and the introduction of new forms of information tech-nology. With globalisation comes increased economic competitiveness and a requirement for flexibility. This has resulted in a shift towards neo- and post-Fordist forms of work organisation in a fragmented and volatile market for goods and services, where smaller scales of production and customised design for market niches have tended to displace pre-existing forms of mass production for the homogenised consumers of the mass market. Marketisation and a culture of consumption become central to the economy as a whole. Changes in products, services and working practices reconstruct the workplace, the organisation of work, and the social defini-tion of skills.

Alongside, and as part of, changes in the economy are changes in cultural forms. First, these changes are in the realms of culture narrowly defined – film, music, entertainment, fashion, architecture and art. Modernist 'seriousness', which includes the search for deep, often hidden meaning, is contested by postmodern 'playfulness', pastiche and self-referentiality, as the possibility of providing secure and deep meanings is overwhelmed by the proliferation of signs and images. Here, the playful does not signify the trivial, but an alternative strategy that can transgress and dislocate dominant conceptions of meaning and power. Second, there are changes in the significance of culture generally to the economy and the society, where the hitherto tight boundary between the realm of culture and the realm of the socio-economic, and the dominance of the latter over the former, breaks down. Cultural goods become commodities to be consumed. Such consumer goods are 'infected with aesthetic considerations, becoming signs of style and taste, and losing their functional qualities' (Gabriel and Lang 1995: 107). Here, the cultural and the aesthetic displace, or come to be valued more highly, than the functional, with style and design playing an increasingly significant role in ensuring consumption of products and services, and with image and lifestyle playing an increasing role in the decisions of many consumers. The domain of the aesthetic, hitherto the preserve of high culture and the elite associated with that culture, now pervades everyday life and, equally, everyday life now invades high culture – the emphasis on culture in its broadest sense is, as we shall see in a moment, particularly significant in the contemporary workplace.

It is the attempt to characterise and understand certain processes of contemporary change that is the concern of those working with postmodern perspectives. We noted earlier the somewhat problematic notion of postmodernity as a historical era. It has also and perhaps more usefully been termed a condition of 'hypercommodification' (Crook *et al.* 1992), a condition where the commodity becomes the culturally dominant and where the dominant commodity form is the image. The communication/media revolution means that people are engulfed by images to the extent where the distinction between reality and image breaks down in a condition of virtuality or 'hyper-reality' (Baudrillard 1988). The hyper-real, as characterised by Baudrillard, is a world of constantly proliferating images, of simulacra, copies without originals, which become a desirable reality to be consumed and where experience becomes contingent and less well defined rather than coherent and determinate. In this process, new forms of experience proliferate, experiences that are not rooted in a stable and unified 'self', a concept itself conceived by postmodernism as a modern patriarchal construct. Hyper-reality is characterised by a continual shaping and re-shaping of subjectivity and identity. Postmodern sensibilities are attuned to the pleasure of new experiences, part of a constant making and re-making of a lifestyle and biography and where, therefore, there is an emphasis on the subjective.

For many writers, the postmodern signifies a different regime of capital accumulation associated with globalisation and flexibility:

> In the current and coming waves of automation this [industrial] *system of standardised full employment* is beginning to soften and fray at the margins into flexibilisations of its three supporting pillars: labour law, work site and working hours … Flexible, pluralised forms of underemployment are spreading.
>
> (Beck 1992: 142)

Destandardisation produces and is a product of greater flexibility, where 'flexibility' has become a central policy goal for governments around the globe in their bid to increase national economic competitiveness (Edwards 1997). For Harvey (1991: 147), contemporary times are an era of flexible accumulation which rests on:

> flexibility with respect to labour processes, labour markets, products and patterns of consumption ... These enhanced powers of flexibility and mobility have allowed employers to exert stronger pressures of labour control on a workforce in any case weakened by two savage bouts of deflation, that saw unemployment rise to unprecedented post-war levels in advanced capitalist countries.

Destandardisation, risk and individualisation are all aspects of moves to increase the flexibility of the workplace and the workforce. With this comes an increased requirement for reflexivity on the part of organisations and individuals, and the necessity to learn in order to keep up with or be ahead of the bewildering pace of change. Organisations become reflexive and attempt to cast themselves as 'learning organisations'. The capacity for organisations to reflect on and learn from their practices in order to be more flexible, efficient and/or profitable and/or effective has become a central feature of organisational and management theory. This is one of the reasons for the emphasis on workplace culture. To enable organisations to change, the workforce has to have networks of communication within which to channel information and views, the opportunities to learn associated with facilitating flexibility and change, and ways of participating in decisions about these processes. Workers need to 'think' change – to have a positive attitude towards and be prepared to accept change. 'Culture' assumes the significance it has because it is seen as structuring the way people think, act and understand their experience, and in forging a sense of identity. Changing workplace culture is therefore seen as a way of effectively shaping subjectivity in a non-coercive and self-managed way.

Flexibility, therefore, has come to be equated with change and the acceptance of change. In one sense, this mirrors and reinforces the sense of instability, insecurity and uncertainty that Lyotard (1984) argued characterised a postmodern condition of knowledge. For Lyotard, modernity is characterised by an emphasis on progress and faith in rationality and science as the means of its realisation. He pointed to the role of the 'grand narratives' of modernity, of social progress and emancipation through knowing the world better; that narratives have legitimised certain forms of knowledge and knowledge production, but are now greeted increasingly with 'incredulity'. Progress in modernist terms is judged by such things as mastery of the physical and social worlds, the growth of scientific knowledge, the spread of a particular kind of rationality and the development of rational, enlightened and autonomous people. Stemming from the Enlightenment, Lyotard argued that the grand narratives provided a teleological rationale for the development of the role of the modern nation-state and of the educational project which supported that development.

Lyotard argued that the grand narratives of modernity now no longer have the ability to compel consensus. Emancipation through the application of scientific rationality has been shown to be, at best, ambiguous and, in certain situations, far worse. The trajectory of scientific rationality leads to Hiroshima and the Holocaust, nuclear tests in the Pacific and China, environmental degradation and risks to humanity. The very progress science has brought about stimulates doubt about the continued sustainability of the project of modernity. Increasingly, the grand narratives are seen as masterful narratives and narratives of mastery, functioning to legitimise the Western, male mission of sovereignty. Their declining influence and power in the contemporary period has also thrown into doubt the subaltern narratives they have helped to shape. Master signifiers are no longer quite as masterful. Universal messages are now seen as historically located, cultural constructs whose universality and consequences are open to question. Teleological certainty has been replaced by open-ended ambivalence. In recent years, therefore, the extent and level of doubt over progress has resulted in doubt over the capacity of science to represent the truth of the world, and, therefore, the claim of scientific research to be the only legitimate mode of knowledge production. Here, one way of understanding the 'postmodern' is as a condition where people have to make their way without fixed referents and traditional anchoring points in a world characterised by rapid and unpredictable change, uncertainty and ambivalence. Here, knowledge is not only constantly changing, but as we argue in Chapter 14, the impact of information/communications technology is becoming more rapidly, indeed overwhelmingly, available. At the same time, what constitutes knowledge is itself increasingly contested. The postmodern rationale for knowledge is that knowledge is legitimated by its performativity, its capacity to enhance the efficiency and effectiveness of the economic and social system. 'Performative usefulness' rather than 'truthfulness' of knowledge is emphasised – a manifestation of the decentring of knowledge that is, we would argue, a feature of the postmodern condition.

Postmodern perspectives, then, are at one and the same time both aspects of the contemporary world and ways of understanding it. Reflexively there is the attempt to provide a discourse for the world they seek to explain, a discourse that highlights notions of decentring, ambivalence and contingency which interlink with the thrust of postmodernity in a socio-cultural and economic sense. However, a reflexive caution is necessary since 'the "postmodern" discourse generates its own concept of "modernity", made of the presence of all those things for the lack of which the concept of "postmodernity" stands' (Bauman 1992: 95). In other words, postmodern perspectives, being themselves discursive, construct modernity in particular ways, some more inclined towards distinguishing absolute breaks than others.

For those for whom a postmodern discourse is interpretatively powerful, it is only through identifying such changes in this way that critical practices and possibilities can be established. This does not mean establishing firm boundaries between the modern and postmodern. Indeed Lyotard (1992) argued that the postmodern is the constantly reworked interface between the past and future, with the implication that the modern and postmodern are moments found together in dynamic tension and interaction. Further, Foucault (1986) suggests that it is wrong to think of history in terms of discrete periods and of complete changes in these. Rather, modernity and postmodernity are perhaps more usefully seen as different and conflicting attitudes and discourses that are present in the contemporary moment. Burbules (1996) argues that the postmodern attitude, if it can be summed up at all, is one of doubt based on an inability to believe, marked by narrative tropes of irony, tragedy and parody. This attitude is indicative of the terrain of ambivalence and uncertainty (of which it is partly a product), enhancing and opposing aspects of modernity. Similarly, Kellner (1995: 47) has argued that:

> the discourse of the postmodern is a cultural and theoretical construct, not a thing or state of affairs ... the discourses of the postmodern produce their objects, whether a historical epoch of postmodernity, or postmodernism in the arts ... the family of concepts of the postmodern are merely conceptual constructs meant to perform certain interpretive or explanatory tasks and are not transparent terms that merely reflect established state of affairs.

This points to two aspects of postmodern perspectives which are central to the position we are seeking to develop here. The first is the constructed nature of the postmodern: in other words, that the postmodern constructs a way of seeing rather than simply modelling reality. The second is that the postmodern attempts to engender understanding and explanation without falling into a totalising mode of speaking. Pivotal to both is a focus within the postmodern on language, discourse and text, its own as well as those of the social practices it seeks to explain.

Telling tales – researching discourse

The notion of 'discourse' has become increasingly important in academic and public debates in recent years. Primarily, this can be seen as a response to the perceived weaknesses of conventional notions of scientific and social scientific knowledge, in a period when the range and sheer amount of information available to individuals through various media has resulted in greater uncertainty as to what signifies 'knowledge', 'truth' and 'progress'. Language has displaced consciousness as the focus for philosophical and social scientific debate, and science has itself been critiqued as simply another language game rather than a privileged one.

The challenge to traditional science, and by extension to dominant conceptions of knowledge and knowledge production, has therefore taken a number of forms. One long-standing critique of science and of scientific research is that it supports particular interests but masks or mystifies those interests by presenting itself as a neutral and disinterested activity. In other words, the very neutrality of scientific research is already a specific ideological position, a dimension of ideological hegemony. But both the dominant conception of scientific research and its critique share a view of language as a vehicle for transparently conveying meaning. It is the critique of this position that has resulted in the increasing weight being given to the notion of discourse and to forms of discourse analysis within academic study. This in itself can be seen as an aspect of doing research in a postmodern way as well as a way of researching the postmodern.

The turn to discourse has resulted in part from a similar critique in some ways to that offered by an ideological critique. Knowledge is held to be partial and contingent upon the specific factors and contexts within which it is constructed and presented. There is also an emphasis on the oppressive consequences of assuming knowledge to be universal: that is, true for everyone across time and in all settings. Furthermore, there is recognition that there are different kinds of knowledge and different modes of producing knowledge. However, discourse analysis differs from ideological critique in that it does not assume that language conveys a single transparent meaning. The meaning of language is held to be contingent on the specific contexts in which it is constituted. There are constant processes of constructing different meanings from the same texts. The assumptions within such texts, the issues they exclude and marginalise from legitimate debate, and the consequences of the acceptance of what they construct as 'true' become the subject of analysis – hence the emphasis on the work that research does. Which discourses are most powerful, how they come to be powerful, and how they frame practices become significant questions.

In this approach, it is the story-telling capacity of human beings which is held to be fundamental to their being. Increased attention is given to texts and the ways in which discourses construct certain objects as 'knowable' and 'known' and certain perspectives as 'true' – the ways in which they 'tell a tale'. Telling tales carries with it a number of possible meanings and implications. It can mean simply the telling of a story, as we do inevitably in our everyday encounters with other people, or even in the stories we tell ourselves. Some of this story-telling may be more formal and formalised than others – reading a book to someone, chatting in the workplace, giving evidence in an industrial tribunal, or attending a training or appraisal session. While telling tales is a social activity insofar as it always involves narrating to an 'other' (even if this is an 'absent' other), the stories are not necessarily fictions, even though they are not accounts of a single truth. A second notion of telling tales is in the more derogatory sense of talking about other people in a negative or unfounded way. Children are told 'not to tell tales', even when the adults asserting this are often not averse to a 'good gossip'. What this highlights is that the stories told can be normatively powerful – they can privilege some while marginalising and excluding others. There is a third sense to the notion that is also important. This emphasises the *tellingness* of tales: that is, that some stories are more telling, in the sense of more influential and more powerful, than others. Indeed, in the telling of certain tales there are implicit and explicit strategies to make them more or less telling, more or less powerful.

What the notion of 'telling tales' tells us is that all forms of social reality are *textualised*, in the sense that they are represented and inscribed – and thus open to interpretation. The social world is narrated or articulated into being through the discursive practices in which we engage and which constitute our experiences as meaningful. This brings to the fore the place and significance of narrative as a 'world-making' practice. Social practices, including those of the workplace, those of producing knowledge and those of researching the workplace, can be seen as texts – worlds defined, delimited and constituted through narrative processes. A social practice can be multiply 'written' or narrated, it can be 'read' and interpreted with single or multiple meanings, and can be 're-written' or re-presented with different meanings.

Through narratives, selves and worlds are simultaneously and interactively made. The narrator is positioned in relation to events and other selves, and an identity conferred through this. Positioning oneself and being positioned in certain discourses, telling stories and being 'told' by stories, becomes therefore the basis for personal identity. Narratives are unique to individuals, in the sense that each tells their own story, yet at the same time culturally located and therefore trans-individual – we are told by stories. For instance, an employee may tell their own individual stories, but the narrative is itself sedimented in the narrative practices of the workplace and, beyond that, in the narratives of the wider culture and practices in which these are located. Individuals live these stories; through them they construct others and are interactively constructed by them, as active, meaningful, knowable subjects acting in meaningful and knowable ways.

To see things this way is to move from questioning whether or not a discourse gives us a 'true' representation of the 'real world', to an examination of the ways in which a discourse *constructs* 'truth' and what the consequences are of accepting it as true. It is to move *from* a scientific *to* a cultural analysis. Rather than assuming a hierarchy of knowledge with science at the pinnacle giving us 'objective truth' – embedded in the notion of disciplinary knowledge and research in the scientific mode – there is the constant search for the cultural conditions that produce this hierarchy and the recognition of the plurality of knowledge and the diversity of ways of knowledge production. Discourse therefore displaces knowledge as the object of study, as problems and inequalities surrounding notions of the universality of knowledge come to the fore. Meaning can no longer be ascribed simply to human intention or a common language. It is itself a site of contestation and can only be elucidated in the exploration of the particular discourses under consideration. The examination of workplaces and the changes taking place within them are themselves subject to these implications. The focus of research becomes the discourses through which work is narrated and through which those within organisations are positioned and identified. Research at work, therefore, involves researching these discourses while highlighting the work that discourses, including those of research, do.

Discourse analysis is not without its problems and its critics and is not a homogeneous field in itself. Indeed, much research in this area tends to combine discursive and interpretive elements producing hybrid understandings and confusions as to the status of the claims being made. What discourse analysis does is make possible an examination of who is setting the agendas, how they are set, what those agendas are, and where and how they are contested in the workplace. It takes us beyond the ideological critique which tends to become reduced to polarities of 'them' or 'us', 'good' or 'bad', 'emancipation' or 'oppression', offering an opportunity to examine the micro-politics and practices of workplaces even while it enables such understandings to be related to macro-contexts. Here, discourses are:

not once and for all subservient to power or raised up against it, any more than silences are ... Discourses are tactical elements or blocks operating in the field of force relations; there can exist different and even contradictory discourses within the same strategy; they can, on the contrary, circulate without changing their form from one strategy to another, opposing strategy.

(Foucault 1981: 100–2)

Rather than taking discourses – what is said, signed or written – for granted, texts need to be problematised, their neutrality and the knowledge they purport to provide questioned. In the process, the 'truth' is understood as constructed through a discourse that becomes powerful in normalising particular strategies and outcomes. In this way, particular 'regimes of truth' are established. Different circumstances therefore give rise to different discursive possibilities. Within workplaces, this may be even in the very arrangements of seats within a room, the layout of shops, the use of open-plan offices – in other words, in the organisation of space where space itself 'speaks'. Each will affect who speaks and the discourses that workers construct, and are constructed by, providing certain possibilities of 'truth'.

Obviously, there is a range of discourses on most topics. Within the discussion of the workplace, we have, for instance, the discourses of workers, managers, policy-makers, academics, professional bodies, employers, trade unions, awarding bodies, think tanks, journalists and commentators. While these discourses will intersect and overlap, each has their own discourse and it is through the intersection and overlapping of this multiplicity of discourses that the terrain is constructed, contested and challenged. However, as elsewhere, not all discourses are equal. Thus, for example, in a period of financial constraint, the 'truth' of managerial discourses of efficiency will usually win out over employee/trade union discourses of better pay and conditions. In a bringing together of power, knowledge and professional expertise, the power which discourses articulate and concretise means that certain discourses become more 'valid', more 'true', than others.

Research on work

We are now becoming fairly familiar with notions of the workplace as a site of learning, the learning organisation, and with workers as lifelong learners, to the extent that we forget that all this is quite recent. The widespread acceptance of these notions has created a somewhat different space for research on work and research at work. It is not so long ago that research at work would not have been considered possible. There was, of course, a great deal of research on work, but it was done essentially by 'outsiders' – academic researchers who came into the workplace to collect data and then went back to their own workplace to analyse it and present their findings, usually to other academics. What did not happen, and what is now happening, is research on work by those located in that site.

We would argue that the workplace is now being constituted as a discursive domain – a domain of thought and action – where it is understood as a site of learning, knowledge and knowledge production. In other words, the workplace is no longer seen simply as a site to be researched but as a site where research or knowledge production takes place. It is here that the work of Gibbons *et al.* (1994) is significant. In bringing to the fore what they call Mode 2 knowledge production, and defining it in terms of a production of knowledge that is socially distributed, they contribute to the articulation of the workplace as a discursive domain where learning and knowledge production take place. They describe Mode 2 as a new form of knowledge production and one that is opposed to the long-standing Mode 1 form:

> The new mode operates within a context of application in that problems are not set within a disciplinary framework. It is transdisciplinary rather than mono- or multi-disciplinary. It is carried out in non-hierarchical, heterogeneously organised forms which are essentially transient. It is not being institutionalised primarily within university structures. Mode 2 involves the close interaction of many actors throughout the process of knowledge production and this means that knowledge production is becoming more socially accountable. One consequence of these changes is that Mode 2 makes use of a wider range of criteria in judging quality control. Overall, the process of knowledge production is becoming more reflexive and affects at the deepest levels what shall count as 'good science'.
>
> (Gibbons *et al.* 1994: vii)

It could be argued, quite convincingly in our view, that Mode 2 is neither new nor necessarily opposed to Mode 1. Mode 2 has been around for a while, and knowledge production has historically shifted between the two modes. Thus, as we have noted a moment ago, another reading is perhaps possible – one which would see Gibbons *et al.* as not only describing a new mode of knowledge production located in the workplace but also, through their text, contributing to its realisation – in effect, they are helping to create or discursively *constitute* what they describe. The notion of knowledge produced in the workplace by workers becomes, therefore, in an important sense, an artefact of contemporary discourses of human resource management and the forms of governmentality of which the latter is a part. What Gibbons *et al.* articulate, then, as Mode 2 is more than just a way of producing knowledge. Rather, it is perhaps more usefully seen as an aspect of a social technology, a means for bringing together technologies of the self and technologies of power in the contemporary workplace, something which has become a major focus for research on work informed by the work of Foucault (McKinlay and Starkey 1998) and, to a lesser extent, Derrida (Boje 1994).

This notion of constitutive discourse which now plays such a prominent part in much research on the workplace is derived largely from the work of Foucault. In opposition to much 'common-sense' thinking that power and knowledge are separate from one another – that the exercise of power invalidates a claim to knowledge and that knowledge is power-free – Foucault argues that power and knowledge are inseparable. Knowledge is permeated with power and exercises of power are imbued with knowledge. Further, power is not simply oppressive and distorting, but also has a positive and productive role in making things possible. This theorisation of power–knowledge is particularly useful in relation to understanding the discourse of human resource management. Townley (1994: 14) argues that 'personnel practices measure both the physical and subjective dimensions of labour, and offer a technology which aims to render individuals and their behaviour predictable and calculable'. Human resource management can thus be understood as a performative form of knowledge in both senses of 'performative': first, in the sense that its legitimacy is established through its usefulness in enhancing the efficiency and effectiveness of the workplace but, second, in the sense that it performatively constructs the object of which it speaks – the active enterprising subject of the contemporary workplace.

Foucault identified two forms of power – disciplinary and pastoral. Disciplinary power involves those processes through which knowledge about the population is gained by the nation state as a condition for the effective management and governance of 'the people'. These processes are embedded in the knowledgeable (expert) discourses of the human sciences. These discourses constitute the objects of their disciplinary gaze: for example, 'the deviant', 'the prisoner', 'the student', and indeed 'the worker', in the process providing the basis for intervention in the form of programmatic action. Disciplinary knowledge is therefore associated with certain practices or exercises of power which discipline and position people in 'objective' and normative ways and 'produce' certain forms of experience and subjectivity. For Foucault, discipline is exercised through forms of knowledge (expertise), power and subjectivity that are integral to one another. Subjectivity, subjection and becoming a subject are all products of discipline as both knowledge and power, and thus 'the emphasis is on the techniques through which human beings understand themselves and others' (Townley 1994: 12), where these are taken to be aspects of multi-centred identity rather than a false consciousness.

Pastoral power, by contrast, is exercised through 'confession', where the self is constituted as an object of knowledge, self-regulation, self-improvement and self-development (Foucault 1981). This process has become central in the governance of modern society, displacing externally imposed discipline with the self-discipline of an autonomous subjectivity. In other words, confession actively constitutes a productive and autonomous subject already governed through self-regulation and thereby not requiring externally imposed discipline and regulation. In order to participate 'successfully' in the process of confession, subjects need to have already accepted, or be brought to accept, the legitimacy and 'truth' of self-revealing confessional practices and the particular meanings that these invoke. For example, through appraisal and training, employees might be said to become more subjectively aligned with the goals of the organisation, thereby requiring less direct supervision. 'Confession' enables individuals to actively participate in disciplinary regimes by investing their own identity, subjectivity and desires with those ascribed to them through certain knowledgeable discourses such as that of human resource management. Within the contemporary workplace, this might result from, and in, more teamwork and flatter management structures. Here Foucault's work might help explain such trends and also offer strategies through which they might be both pursued and resisted. For instance, in the expert knowledge and practices of human resource development, power is exercised by the attempt to position workers in particular ways: for example, ways where they are engaged affectively, where they are 'empowered' to participate in shaping the organisation's goals and practices, and where there is an alignment between personal goals and the goals of the organisation. In her study of 'Hephaestus', a large manufacturing multi-national in the USA, and drawing in part on the work of Foucault, Casey (1996: 320) argues that 'the archetypal new Hephaestus employee is one who *enthusiastically* manifests the values of dedication, loyalty, self-sacrifice and passion for the product and customer, and who is willing to go the extra mile for his or her team'.

This entails an active subjectivity aligned to organisational goals, producing what Casey refers to as 'designer employees'. Here the alienation of modern industrialisation is displaced by a postmodern enthusiasm for work and a commitment to self-realisation through work. This has been particularly marked in those organisations involved in practices such as employee development schemes, action learning sets, quality circles and the like. The downside of this 'flexibility' for many is an intensification of work and an insecurity of employment. It could be argued that exploitation is actively accepted or reconstructed as stress rather than resented or rejected. Counselling displaces trade union activism. Through certain practices and techniques, such as those of human resource management, people's 'inner' lives are brought into the domain of power – technologies of the self are interlinked with technologies of power. This then is a governmentality where power seeks not only to govern bodies but also to govern subjectivity and intersubjectivity, and to do so not through force and repression, but through 'educating' and 'empowering' people to govern themselves. Here the aim is to displace the regimented and disciplined worker of the industrial age – trained 'docile bodies' (Foucault 1979) – with the active self-motivating autonomous subject, fit to function in the learning organisation and a skilled producer of Mode 2 knowledge.

This engagement with the subjectivities of the workforce is a way of releasing the motivational impact of the 'empowered' and enterprising worker rather than suppressing it through a concentration solely on technical skill or competence. What are called for are kinds of competence centred on the interpersonal, the motivational and the affective. Worker subjectivity is brought forth rather than suppressed and alienated, and becomes subject to training in what some have argued to be the attempt to 'govern the soul' (Miller and Rose 1993). This both stimulates individualisation and reflexivity as aspects of an active subjectivity and also attempts to govern and shape this subjectivity through particular, although never completely successful, strategies of human resource management. It is to an investigation of these dynamics that postmodern perspectives are addressed, and, indeed, through which they are constructed – dynamics which at one and the same time highlight the productivity of postmodern perspectives for research on work, providing an agenda for such research while also pointing to the need to reflexively consider the performative work that such research does in constructing a discursive domain.

Central to postmodern perspectives on the workplace is the view that with changes in the workplace come changes in workplace identities and the ways in which these are constituted. In his study of the retail sector in the UK, du Gay (1996), drawing on Foucault, argues that workplaces are increasingly characterised by forms of governmentality associated with 'an ethos of enterprise'. This ethos is crucial to the development of discourses of flexibility among nations, organisations and individuals in support of economic competitiveness. As well as workplaces, workers are subject to practices of management, appraisal and development that position them as engaged in an 'enterprise of the self'. In this position, no matter what hand circumstances may have dealt a person, he or she remains always continuously engaged … in that one enterprise … In this sense the character of the entrepreneur can no longer be seen as just one among a plurality of ethical personalities but must rather be seen as assuming an ontological priority.

(du Gay 1996: 181)

Exposure to the risks and costs of their activities is constructed as enabling workers to take responsibility for their actions, signifying a form of 'empowerment' and 'success' within the organisation. Nor is this restricted to careers alone, as the whole of life becomes inscribed with the ethos of enterprise, turning the process of biographical formation into an enterprise. Enterprising identity and the self as an enterprise emerges as organisations become subject to measures of performance and quality assessment in the delivery of services and goods. Rather than being governed by bureaucratic and hierarchic procedures wherein decisions are taken elsewhere and handed down to be implemented, workers are given 'responsibility' for achieving certain outcomes efficiently and effectively, but they are then subjected to unprecedented levels of surveillance through processes of monitoring, auditing and performance appraisal. Here, discipline is 'now more immediate and everyday with little overt intervention on the part of the corporate bureaucracy. The employees police themselves. The decentralization and internalisation of discipline deepens the processes of employee identification with the company' (Casey 1996: 326).

Lest this should seem an inescapable determinism, it is important to note that governmentality is never and can never be complete. Indeed, as du Gay argues (1996: 73), the 'very "impossibility" of government justifies and reproduces the attempt to govern'. Its very incompleteness both illustrates and provides the possibly for reflexivity, diversity and resistance, something which is brought forth through an examination of the diversity of workplace practices. Recalcitrance, apathy, resistance and even playfulness remain possible. Even in relatively restricted skill areas such as restaurant-waiting, research indicates that

> service encounters are shown to have a performative character and thus one can think of those kind of workplaces as a stage, as a dramatic setting for certain kinds of performance, involving a mix of mental, manual *and* emotional labour.
>
> (Lash and Urry 1994: 202)

Workers may perform their roles as enterprising and flexible workers as fully as organisations require, but may nonetheless be reflexively conscious that it is a performance. Here the performing self may not always be subsumed by the enterprising self. Casey (1995), for instance, identifies a typology of subjectivities – the defensive self, the colluded self and the capitulated self – emerging in the workplace she researched. The ethos of enterprise is not apparent here, and the performance is not always fully or necessarily in line with the script of the organisation. Other discourses running counter those of the enterprising can position workers in alternative ways. Alternative discourse and knowledges of and in the workplace are possible to those of human resource management and Mode 2 types. The exercise of power is never complete, social technologies are never all-embracing. The point is that postmodern perspectives can open up these multiple practices and diverse discourses to scrutiny and in so doing reveal the micro-political struggles over and surrounding them.

Reflexive tales – research that works

Given the poststructuralist position on language, discourse and text, research practices cannot themselves be said to produce knowledge whose legitimacy is guaranteed by its speaking a universal and transcendental truth. This is something at least which socially distributed knowledge recognises. Our argument, however, is that regardless of the type of knowledge, research or knowledge production is always discursively embedded. Research, whether it is on the workplace or in the workplace, is always a discursive practice, itself reflexively subject to the play of language and meaning as any other discourse, although this reflexivity is rarely acknowledged. While discourses of knowledge production are powerful, with some more powerful than others, they are nonetheless language games. This poses a reflexive difficulty that most 'postmodern' research on workplaces ignores. Postmodern research is also subject to the play of meaning and therefore capable of various constructions. In other words, the work it does may be read and re-read, with many and varied consequences. Research at work can therefore find itself capable of being worked and re-worked in a variety of ways; the work of research is never uniform or simple. Thus, attempts to enhance governmentality through human resource management may be as much a possibility arising from such perspectives as differing forms of individual and collective engagement from workers. Perhaps the only generalization possible is the increased importance given to the discourses at play in workplaces, itself pointed to reflexively by the growth of human resource management practices.

Postmodern research in the workplace therefore produces different approaches to research at work with its focus on the discursive nature of workplace practices, but with uncertain and diverse consequences as to the work such research does. In itself, this points to a form of performativity which goes beyond that suggested by Lyotard, insofar as systemic enhancement is only one among many possibilities in the legitimising of knowledge.

References

Baudrillard, J. (1988) *Selected Works*, Cambridge: Polity Press.

Bauman, Z. (1992) *Intimations of Postmodernity*, London: Routledge.

Beck, U. (1992) *Risk Society: Towards a New Modernity*, London: Sage.

Boje, D. (1994) 'Organizational storytelling: the struggles of pre-modern, modern and postmodern organizational learning discourses', *Management Learning* 25, 3: 433–61.

Burbules, N. (1996) 'Postmodern doubt and philosophy of education', *Philosophy of Education 1995*, Philosophy of Education Society: Urbana, Iu.: 39–48.

Casey, C. (1995) *Work, Self and Society: After Industrialism*, London: Routledge.

Casey, C. (1996) 'Corporate transformations: designer culture, designer employees and "post-occupational" solidarity', *Organisation* 3, 3: 317–39.

Crook, S., Paluski, J. and Waters, M. (1992) *Postmodernization*, London: Sage.

du Gay, P. (1996) *Consumption and Identity at Work*, London: Sage.

Edwards, R. (1997) *Changing Places? Flexibility, Lifelong Learning and a Learning Society*, London: Routledge.

Foucault, M. (1979) *Discipline and Punish: The Birth of the Prison*, Harmondsworth: Penguin.

Foucault, M. (1981) *The History of Sexuality, Volume I: An Introduction*, Harmondsworth: Penguin.

Foucault, M. (1986) 'What is Enlightenment?' in P. Rabinow (ed.) *The Foucault Reader*, Harmondsworth: Peregrine.

Gabriel, Y. and Lang, T. (1995) *The Unmanageable Consumer: Contemporary Consumptions and its Fragmentation*, London: Sage.

Gibbons, M., Limoges, C., Nowotny, H., Schwartzman, S., Scott, P. and Trow, M. (1994) *The New Production of Knowledge: The Dynamics of Science and Research in Contemporary Societies*, London: Sage.

Harvey, D. (1991) *The Condition of Postmodernity*, Oxford: Basil Blackwell.

Kellner, D. (1995) *Media Culture*, London: Routledge.

Lash, S. and Urry, J. (1994) *Economies of Signs and Space*, London: Sage.

Lyotard, J.-F. (1984) *The Postmodern Condition: A Report on Knowledge*, Manchester: Manchester University Press.

Lyotard, J.-F. (1992) *The Postmodern Explained to Children: Correspondence 1982–1985*, Sydney: Power Publications.

McKinlay, A. and Starkey, K. (1998) (eds) *Foucault, Management and Organisation Theory*, London: Sage.

Miller, P. and Rose, N. (1993) 'Governing economic life' in M. Gane and T. Johnson (eds) *Foucault's New Domains*, London: Routledge.

Smart, B. (1992) *Modern Conditions, Postmodern Controversies*, London: Routledge.

Townley, B. (1994) *Reframing Human Resource Management: Power, Ethics and the Subject at Work*, London: Sage.

Usher, R. and Edwards, R. (1994) *Postmodernism and Education: Different Voices, Different Worlds*, London: Routledge.

4 The crisis of scientific research

Christine Ewan and Dennis Calvert

The title of this chapter claims a state of crisis for scientific research. This is a dramatic claim which would have lacked credibility even a few years ago, yet many of those engaged in scientific research today would have little trouble identifying elements of crisis in their chosen vocation. What kind of crisis is this? Why have we arrived at this point? There are no simple answers, nor is there a need to despair. In developed economies scientific research has, during this century, achieved the status of a cultural icon and has challenged traditional belief systems which evolved over millennia. In our lifetimes we have seen miracles become commonplace, we have seen scientists idolised, mythologised and vilified, we have progressively increased our ability to control or at least predict nature, paradoxically while watching aspects of our environment deteriorate. At some point in the course of this turbulent recent history, the balance between research in pursuit of knowledge and research in pursuit of economic returns has changed. We now speak openly and commonly of the 'knowledge industry' and the 'information economy'. The first proposition which needs to be examined to better understand the origins of the 'crisis' we face is that the process of knowledge creation has been transformed into a commodity and is therefore shifted fundamentally to the province of productive work rather than of academic discourse. That the scientific community lacks the socio-political and historical perspective that will allow it to analyse and transform this development in constructive ways is the second major proposition.

This chapter examines the multiple facets of altruism, pragmatism and economic rationalism which will make research in the next century more complex, as well as reviewing the implications this complexity has for research workers in a shrinking global environment. Key points are illustrated by examples from health and medical research which has recently been the subject of a major national review in Australia (Wills 1998). We examine changing definitions and locations of research work and perceptions of what constitutes research, and how it is supported, the training of the research workforce and preparation for the future.

Economic imperatives and the knowledge industry

The traditional view of research is that it results either in accumulation of knowledge for its own sake, or in production of knowledge which is instrumental to some other activity or economic indicator. Within this framework, researchers (usually academics) and the users of the knowledge they produce (usually workers in industry or service professions) often inhabit different worlds and even different generations. This uncoupling of the research process from the commercial or social development of the knowledge it produces has been overtaken by the notion of information as a tradable commodity in its own right, with enormous potential strategic value to the economic well-being of nations. Research outcomes with immediate commercial or strategic value alter the relationships between researchers and their communities of interest. As Johnston (1998) points out, commerce in information results in expanded roles for knowledge workers which extend beyond those traditionally associated with researchers. The roles comprise not only problem identification and solution but also brokerage – the ability to recognise and exploit the value of the knowledge produced in the research and development process.

This reformulation of the place of information in the economic sphere is accompanied by a growing concern that pursuit of knowledge for its own sake is a luxury which may no longer be taken for granted. Sites of commercial activity, usually workplaces, come to be seen as more legitimate venues for research than academic venues, which are perceived to be lacking in 'real world experience'. Weber (1996: 53), in a talk on the future of the university, warns:

> It would be a grievous mistake to see the tendency of the economically 'developed' countries to reduce state support to education and research as merely a quantitative and temporary adjustment. Rather what seems to be involved is a fundamental and political redefinition of the social value of public services in general, and of universities and education in particular. Social and political values are today increasingly subordinated to economic values, that of producing profit, of operating efficiently. Notions such as 'accountability',

'responsibility', and 'transparency' are all being redefined so as to assume a direct fiduciary significance.

In an information-based global economic system, all knowledge has potential economic value and the production of that knowledge necessarily becomes a matter of national interest which extends beyond the intellectual curiosity or control of the scientific researcher or even of the university. Universities, research centres and scientific researchers no longer control the definition and production of knowledge – they are simply actors in a multi-sectoral social and political, as well as scientific and technological, enterprise. In an effort to convince politicians and Treasury officials that research is a good investment, many reports have appeared in recent years which attempt to quantify economic spin-off from even basic research. For example, a review conducted by Turpin *et al.* (1996: 109) concluded that:

> In some cases Australian industrial enterprises have been built, quite directly, from fundamental advances in science. At the same time other important connections between basic research and socio-economic activities rely more on the national scientific infrastructure that provides for research training and a scientific environment conducive to solving problems and promoting innovation.

While this approach may be necessary and appropriate, it is also seen by many researchers as risky in that it capitulates to the economic rather than intrinsic valuing of academic knowledge and collaborates in the appropriation of the academy to a market model.

Where knowledge is a commodity, the university becomes part of the

> arena in which the new high-tech wars of economic advantage are waged … But the knowledge industry is now crowded with rivals to the universities, often operating in its most dynamic sectors. In the process higher education's autonomous space has been invaded.
>
> (Scott 1997: 24)

As several other chapters in this book illustrate, the workplace is a principal invader of that space. For researchers in some of the traditional academic disciplines, this invasion by the workplace is a culture shock; for researchers in some of the longer-standing academic professions, such as engineering and medicine, the workplace has always been a venue for research. In these professions, research began in the workplace – the hospital or the mine – and only retreated to the laboratories when the problems began to require specialised technological support. Ironically, a reversion to the workplace is now evident as laboratories which can afford such technological support are increasingly linked with workplaces.

As Barnett has alluded in Chapter 2, perhaps more damaging potentially than invasion of the institution's autonomous space is invasion of the researcher's intellectual and creative space by pressures towards accountability in terms of cost-effective outcomes. For many years academic researchers were protected from these pressures – researchers in the workplace rarely are. Sir Peter Medawar, renowned for laying the foundations for cellular immunology, said in a 1968 public speech: 'Nearly all scientific research leads nowhere – or, if it does lead somewhere, then not in the direction it started off with. I reckon that for all the use it has been to science about four-fifths of my time has been wasted.' Thirty years on, it would be a brave researcher who would admit to such a thought in public for fear that he would be regarded as non-productive and unworthy of continued funding or continued employment. Research tied to workplace goals and targets for productivity enjoys no such luxury.

The changing research environment: from cottage industry to global economy

Scientific research used to be carried out by a limited number of researchers, often working as individuals in a limited number of centres or even within their own home laboratories or small businesses. Many of these early researchers were researching at work and preoccupied with intensely applied problems such as communication, infection control or agricultural or industrial productivity. As knowledge increased on the bases of these applied endeavours, opportunities for more fundamental research became more apparent and more exciting. Universities developed a research industry outside the practical or industrial domain and offered researchers a protected and structured environment in which to train and work, without concern for the patronage of benefactors – thus the ivory tower was built, largely in the twentieth century.

Prior to this century, universities were predominantly centres of teaching and learning, established for the intellectual pursuit and transmission of understanding rather than the empirical or scientific pursuit of knowledge. As we reach the end of this century, the scale and expense of much scientific research extends beyond the resources of most universities, and the patronage of benefactors is once again critical. In some societies, notably the USA and UK, research benefaction, especially for medical research, is an established cultural tradition and provides considerable financial support. Private non-profit support for health and medical research in the 1995 to 1997 period averaged $9.4 per capita in the UK, due mainly to the existence of the Wellcome Foundation, which disbursed over $450 million in 1997, compared with $3 per capita in Australia (Wills 1998: 152). In most developed countries, including Australia and much of Europe, research benefaction is not a strongly established tradition and government support of research is the norm.

The research environment has grown increasingly more complex, more expensive and more competitive. Kanigel's (1993) narrative of the development of some of the most significant biomedical research laboratories in the US post World War II gives some insight into just how much more complex and competitive the environment has become. Kanigel (ibid.: 11) remarks that in 1941 research was 'the province of a few gentlemen investigators' and reports that the National Institutes of Health (NIH) awarded 12 grants in 1941 for a total of $78,000; in 1970 it awarded 11,339 grants valued at more than $600 million. In 1997 the the NIH had an annual budget of approximately $13 billion, of which more than 90 per cent was used to support research directly – each year the NIH receives 24,000 research project grant applications, of which 28 per cent are successful (National Institutes of Health 1997). In such a climate, the NIH has developed explicit processes to allow it to set priorities and to evaluate and judge areas in which to invest research dollars. The United Kingdom and several European nations, as well as Australia, have also grappled with the need to allocate research funds selectively and strategically (Black 1997; Wills 1998).

Close government interest in strategic allocation of research funds is at the root of another element of the perceived 'crisis' in scientific research: the researchers' anxieties about continuity of public funding for investigator-driven or 'pure' research in a political environment which appears to value only economic objectives and strategic outcomes. There is genuine and perhaps justified fear that research will be driven increasingly into instrumental questions and workplace environments, where the imperative for economic returns will direct priorities principally to short-term gains in knowledge with an immediate or predictable pay-off.

The voracious appetite of the gigantic modern global research enterprise which can transform national economies outstrips government resources and is increasingly reliant upon commercial investment sources that expect a financial return on their investment. Notably, in medical research, multi-national pharmaceutical companies have recognised the commercial value of the vast research enterprise in biotechnology and are investing heavily in selected areas of research which have greatest potential for financial payoff, but perhaps not always for social equity or community health. Capturing some of this investment is important for governments, who try to ensure that they are net exporters of the resultant pharmaceutical products. Sweden has been very effective in this strategy (Wills 1998: 115). Australia, with a comparable population, is at significant risk of remaining a net importer. This situation is made more critical since lack of research and development investment by companies within Australia means that the intellectual property rights in Australian scientific discovery are often sold off-shore, and the downward spiral as a significant player in the global research enterprise is begun.

Commercial and industry drivers have redefined the research enterprise and created the need for a more strategic overview of the total research endeavour, whether workplace or academy based, to ensure that fundamental intellectual goals and social goals as well as economic ones are addressed. But who claims the right to maintain that strategic overview and, even more, to make decisions about whether a desirable balance has been achieved in directions for research?

An Australian report (Australian Science and Technology Council 1990), considering the case for setting national research priorities, drew a helpful distinction between priorities at policy level, which concern politicians and communities, and at operational level, which concern the scientific researchers, and the need to balance socio-political and scientific agendas while acknowledging that the boundaries can be blurred. The report warned that Australia must join the global move to focus the national research endeavour more sharply

> since the consequences of not doing so are obvious; our performance will become relatively worse, and to the extent that research and development are linked with our competitive edge as a trading nation, the longed-for transformation of the Australian economy will be delayed.
>
> (ibid.: 9)

Another recent report by the Australian Academy of Technological Sciences and Engineering (Tegart *et al.* 1998) outlines ten principles for Australia's response to the emergence of the global knowledge economy. Among them is the recommendation to strengthen science and technology through policy initiatives which provide incentives for investment and innovation – in the absence of such policy initiatives, the scientific output of Australian researchers will be necessarily constrained.

More recently, the peak Australian body for scientists and technologists, the Federation of Australian Scientific and Technological Societies (FASTS), identified as one of its top ten policies for 1999 the urging of scientists to 'think commercially' and to commercialise their work (Higher

Education Supplement 1999). The British government has reportedly pledged to put the commercialisation of scientific knowledge at the heart of its industrial policy, which includes a new national venture capital fund to help finance small businesses and a higher education Reach Out fund to reward universities that work with businesses (Masood 1998). Clearly, this signals a significant move into research linked more closely with work and work linked more closely with research.

An editorial in a recent issue of *Nature* (*Nature* 1999) points out that one of the greatest risks of a knowledge-based economy is the growing knowledge gap between knowledge-rich and knowledge-poor countries, and the resultant social disparities and unrest. The editorial argues that there is a need to combine commitment to both scientific excellence and social equity and that government's role is to provide a sound underpinning for excellence in knowledge-creation and to compensate for market failures and weaknesses. This can be done partly by ensuring that social needs are catered for on as sound a scientific footing as are wealth-generating activities.

Many social as well as economic issues come to the fore, especially in the public service or non-profit service and related sectors. Increasingly, accountability measures call for service planning and provision in these sectors to be 'evidence-based'. At the same time, however, core staff with professional and research skills are being lost as budgets are trimmed and research often has to be 'outsourced', increasingly to large multi-national consulting companies whose independence and social accountability, by their very nature, must be open to question. In those workplaces which produce social services rather than economic commodities, the diminished capacity to do rigorous independent research or to evaluate rigorously the research done by consultants is a crisis in its own right.

Science as art, craft or industrial enterprise?

Investment, incentive, venture capital and commercialisation are recent additions to the lexicon of science, whose mainstream culture, until relatively recently, has held itself aloof from such worldly concepts. Science has celebrated its practitioners' dedication to altruistic goals: to the relief of human suffering and greater understanding of the universe and its contents. The pursuit of profit is left to others who draw on the information output of that altruistic quest. In a culture with altruism at its core, the notions of cost-benefit, efficiency gains and corporate management styles are anathema. Ways of 'doing science' have, in reality, changed greatly over the past few decades, but the mythologies which guide the scientific profession's self-concept and identity have not yet caught up with the reality of everyday life.

Scientific research, its proponents believe, results in progressive accumulation of knowledge, each breakthrough becoming the departure point for new ventures of discovery and creation of new disciplines. Possibilities are bounded only by the limits of imagination and in the virtually boundless field of these possibilities, hierarchies form and the focus of scientific research undergoes constant renegotiation. In this century alone, the drivers of research activity have spiralled from problems in the external environment to the intrinsic curiosity of scientists, and back again. For example, the discovery of effective anti-malarial drugs was the result of a need to solve the practical problem of debilitated troops in tropical war zones, and the space race during the cold war spawned large numbers of technological innovations now in use in daily life. The new knowledge developed as a by-product of solving practical problems opens up new avenues of enquiry, which are then pursued for their intrinsic interest as 'pure' rather than applied research; pure and applied research efforts provide complementary forms of stimulus. The pressures towards accountability for investment outcomes cause some to predict a growing disequilibrium in the pure/applied oscillation, a disequilibrium which will tip the balance towards research outcomes with obvious or immediate extrinsic value rather than intrinsic value.

In spite, or perhaps because, of the changing context of research work, some threads of stability persist. The cult of the individual researcher pursuing intellectual curiosity in splendid isolation remains strong in spite of the lack of genuine evidence for the pre-eminence of this model of science over the past fifty years. Kanigel's (1993) descriptions of the work of science during the 1930s to the 1950s in the US, Latour and Woolgar's (1979) description of laboratory life in the 1970s in the US, Goldberg's (1989) story of research into endorphins which crossed national boundaries in the 1970s, Charlesworth and co-authors' (1989) description of science work in Australia in the 1980s, and many other similar accounts, all portray vibrant scientific teams whose creativity was sparked by interaction and an urgency of purpose.

There appears to be a pattern of association between research competitiveness (international comparisons based mainly on publication data) and the structure of research management (Adams 1998). Adams' analysis shows that research economies which are typically more directed (for example, through mission-led institutes) tend to have positive associations between research output and the impact of that research as measured by citations. The success of research teams is hardly surprising. Teams contain specialists, full-time researchers and, in some cases, full-time managers or even fundraisers (Wills 1998).

Yet appointments and promotions committees in universities continue to require applicants to analyse in detail their particular contribution to a grant or a published paper, even sometimes down to percentage points of 'ownership'. Thus, individualism and even competitiveness is prized and rewarded, when the successful practice of modern science requires skilled and creative collaborators who can not only deliver their own best efforts but help others to maximise their potential. Quantifying individual inputs to creative teamwork is a self-contradictory exercise. All of these contradictory practices shape our appreciation of what is *valid* science.

Research in the workplace is more likely to be perceived as a team enterprise because the research has a life of its own – if the scientist moves on, the research stays put and is carried on by the team. Often, in an academic environment if the principal scientist moves on the team moves, too. If research can be thus depersonalised, is it still legitimate in mainstream scientific culture or is it merely another industrial process subject to corruption? These questions need to be worked through as part of this transition in scientific research cultures.

Modern science is a sophisticated business, no longer a cottage industry. Like it or not, the reality of research practice is being transformed from inspired art or dedicated craft to global industrial enterprise where researchers may replace the anonymous cohorts of factory workers of earlier times. The research work force is undergoing significant expansion as elite education systems become mass education, even at the doctoral level, where the global increase in doctoral graduates is evidence enough of a ready work force for the mass industrial research enterprise.

Although graduate destinations are difficult to identify with precision, a survey of Australian research groups in 1995 (Turpin *et al.* 1996) elicited the response that about 59 per cent of total PhD graduates go into academic positions, 15 per cent annually go into government appointments and around 19 per cent are initially employed in the non-government sector, with considerable variation across disciplines. In the United States 20 to 40 per cent of science and engineering graduates are estimated to go into academia, with the majority going into industry (LaPidus 1997). In Australia, too, according to Turpin's study, general engineering, applied science and chemistry graduates find employment in industry in greater proportion than other disciplines. The number of students in research higher degrees in Australia increased from 12,586 in 1988 to 31,092 in 1997 (a 147 per cent increase), while total undergraduate enrolments increased by only 40 per cent (Higher Education Division 1998). Since most of these graduates are trained within a narrow field of endeavour focused on scientific objectivity to the exclusion of social curiosity or contextual analysis, they are ready-made to be anonymous cogs in the industrial research machine, and relatively few will assume leadership roles without further training or experience in other disciplines.

Will the history of the industrial revolution be repeated in the information revolution? Will scientific craftsmen and artists become production workers in a mass industrial enterprise driven by economic goals rather than social or personal enrichment? This question represents the 'crisis'; the answer depends on whether the culture of science can evolve adaptive responses. Pessimism is justified, given the tendency of the scientific research community to adopt an inward-looking, divided and defensive stance, rather than to focus outwards to better influence the broader context which will dictate the terms of its prosperity.

Research in the workplace is not new. It has a long and established tradition in many disciplines, some of whom have forgotten their ancestral roots. Re-emergence of its salience offers opportunity for growth rather than threat to the established order, if it can be comprehended in its full complexity and if research can be valued as a diverse and complex enterprise rather than an ideological icon.

Research as ideological battleground

Science, as every other field of human endeavour, is a complex social enterprise governed by rules and conventions and controlled ultimately by a powerful elite. The objectives and characteristics of the elite change over time but, inevitably, adherents to some disciplines, some philosophies, some investigative paradigms, some organisational patterns, attain ascendancy for a time before being superseded by a new elite which has won a power base arising from forces at work in the wider social context.

Snow first drew attention to *the two cultures* of intellectual life in 1959 in his famous Rede lecture at Cambridge, in which he pointed out the difficulties which the 'intellectual' sector of the academy and the natural science sector had in interacting. Snow described 'traditional intellectuals' as 'natural Luddites' and lamented the failure of academics to take part in the industrial revolution. Snow also anticipated the philosophical schism between pure and applied scientific research when he said:

> It is permissible to lump pure and applied scientists into the same scientific culture but the gaps are wide … Pure scientists have by and large been dim-witted about engineers and applied science. They couldn't get interested. They wouldn't recognise that many of the problems were as intellectually exacting as pure problems and that

many of the solutions were as satisfying and beautiful. Their instinct ... was to take it for granted that applied science was an occupation for second-rate minds. The climate of thought of young research workers in Cambridge then was not to our credit. We prided ourselves that the science we were doing could not, in any conceivable circumstances, have any practical use.

(Snow 1993: 31–2)

These difficulties persist today, although the relative power base within the academy has shifted. World War II stimulated a huge growth in the influence and activity of the natural and applied sciences. In the US, arts and humanities accounted for 20 per cent of all doctorates awarded prior to the war but only 11 per cent in the 1950s, while engineering and natural science grew to one third of all degrees by 1990. Resource allocation accompanied, or perhaps caused, these trends, with the US National Endowment for the Humanities declining by 20 per cent between 1979 and 1991 while the National Science Foundation doubled in the same period (Keller 1996).

For practical reasons of funding, of organisational politics, of professional and scientific power struggles, it has proven necessary to categorise and define research effort in ways which not only deny the oscillating continuum of pure and applied research focus but generate discontinuity in or, more regrettable still, competition between the concepts, processes, methods and cultures of research work. It is perhaps symptomatic of the crisis in scientific research that we feel the need for such compartmentalisation – the anthropological constructs of purity and pollution apply in science as they do in religion. Purity is attained in monasteries (universities), pollution is at large in the world (global industry and the workplace).

Johnston (1998) provides a comprehensive summary of the various systems which have been proposed to classify research activity, perhaps to better distinguish the sacred and profane.

In some discipline areas internecine struggle for the right to define the dominant or 'sacred' paradigm for research is endemic. A dispassionate observer might assume, quite reasonably, that a struggle for supremacy between fundamental and applied or between qualitative and quantitative research is fruitless since all types of research are evidently valuable if applied rigorously. Why, then, do highly intelligent groups of people invest considerable energy in debating an apparently non-contentious issue? The answer is that, in a scientific world of infinite possibilities but finite resources, members of different 'tribes' of researchers are in competition with each other for resources, for political attention and community support. Each tribe draws on its own mythologies and history to support its claim to supremacy. While such debates are not peculiar to the latter half of this century, they have increased in intensity and significance because the size of the global research enterprise and its competitiveness has increased many thousandfold.

In the debate about who controls the research agenda and its strategic direction, researchers as well as governments claim the right by virtue of their specialist knowledge and skills. Arguments invoked to support this claim sound, to sceptics, alarmingly like religious dogma. Objectivity and 'proper' scientific method is the central creed, maintained by the monasticism of a scientific vocation, the purity of funding sources and the unquestionable sanctity of the individual researcher judged solely by 'peer review'. Little wonder that this dogma has drawn criticism in the latter half of this century, when idealism is at a low ebb and pragmatism and economic rationalism are in the ascendancy. It can expect to draw a great deal more criticism as the imperatives of the workplace intrude more forcefully into the debate.

Critiques of science spawn efforts to improve its image

Volumes have been published in the literature of the history and philosophy of science challenging the articles of faith which sustain scientific research and deconstruct concepts such as objectivity (for a classic example refer to Latour and Woolgar 1979). Paraphrasing Keller (1996), the principal point that emerges from three decades of careful historical and sociological analysis is that, on every level, choices are made – of what it is that we want to know, of how we proceed, of what counts as knowledge – and that these choices are social even as they are cognitive and experimental.

Even the scientists themselves are 'discovering' flaws in the doctrine of science. As Vandenbroucke (1998) points out, subjectivity creeps into the way in which we accept (or reject) various scientific findings, and in the way in which scientific findings are selected or rejected for publication. Unfortunately, we would argue that there is little evidence of broader awareness or genuine engagement with these issues among practising scientific researchers. At the same time, the critics of scientific endeavour, embroidered with words such as phenomenology, positivism, relativism, postmodernism, hermeneutics, and so forth, are too often locked in their own mutually reinforcing power-plays to offer opportunities for constructive dialogue with scientists. Keller (1996) claims that the failure to engage in this dialogue is marked not only by an absence of respect between the 'two cultures' but by the cultivation of active disrespect. It would appear almost self-evident that if scientific researchers are to prosper in the new environment, to turn crisis to opportunity, and to influence the research agenda in workplaces and elsewhere, they will need more sophisticated capacities for self-awareness, self-criticism and self-determination.

The scientific community is aware that planned efforts must be made to better inform the community and politicians of the benefits that science can bring. It is at this point that research in the workplace assumes considerable significance. Research which is close to the 'point of sale' of consumer goods or services has relevance and salience, and its benefits are more easily promoted. The downside of this consumer focus is that overzealous marketing can also ensure that the results of research are oversold or overstated, resulting in eventual disillusionment. One of the facets of the postulated crisis is the degree to which communication of scientific success can be trusted to industrial or commercial communications frameworks, which in service to their own goals both over-promote and restrict access to information.

Although annual reports of the major public research funding agencies are beginning to pay more attention to professional promotion of the benefits of research, reliance in communicating research outcomes has been traditionally upon 'star researchers' and dramatic breakthroughs. The cult of the Nobel prize-winner is an interesting one. Scientific heroes are needed as icons for public reference, and a mythology of the solitary saviour single-mindedly labouring to unlock scientific secrets is perpetuated. Popular media assist in this cult of the individual, and the public is educated by the retelling of stories which rely heavily on the charisma of the scientist and (usually) his achievement (for example, Christian Barnard who performed the first heart transplant), or on the romance of the serendipity of unexpected discovery (for example, Fleming's discovery of the bactericidal effects of the penicillium mould).

These mythic accounts of the fortunate circumstance of the dedicated individual who brings about a revolution fail to highlight adequately the influence of the social and work-related context in which such discoveries are made, or the large teams of researchers, clinicians, technicians and financiers who create the conditions for the breakthrough to happen. Without the political desire of a pariah apartheid government to attract world acclaim, the immense resources required for the first heart transplant in South Africa might not have been made available. Fleming's observation of penicillium's action on bacteria sat unused for more than ten years until the urgent need for infection control was generated during war. World War II created the impetus for the government and industry investment needed to extract and produce the active agent, penicillin.

The mythology of the brilliant individual unfettered by political, economic or social imperatives impedes progress towards a more socially, politically and industrially effective scientific establishment principally because a large segment of the scientific community itself believes in it and uses it to support conservatism and adherence to a false memory of a Utopian past. A more positive option is to recognise and engage with the challenge of constructing a visionary scientific future grounded in social realities such as the limitations and opportunities offered by workplace research and research funded by investors seeking economic returns.

The daily work of science

It is easy to offer such criticisms, but in the day-to-day Darwinian struggle to practise their craft, most researchers have little time for a broader perspective. They are focused, of necessity, on an endless cycle of dead-lines for grant applications, quotas for published papers, grant income or achievement of production targets. The process in academia is driven by funding formulae and reward structures based in a philosophical stance which asserts that competition, frequent review of funding by peers, and formulae based on quantitative performance indicators are a guaranteed strategy for excellence and value for money. (For examples of the effort which has been and continues to be expended in developing such perfor-mance indicators in Australia alone, see NBEET 1993; Hill and Murphy 1994; Turpin *et al.* 1996; Bourke and Butler 1998.)

An alternative proposition which recognises that one's peers are increas-ingly one's competitors, and that quantitative indicators are often those which are simple to measure but lacking in discriminative power or real significance to social or economic objectives, is rarely advanced effectively by researchers themselves. When it is advanced, the evident lack of conceptual depth or even conviction in the argument condemns it to inter-pretation as self-serving excuse.

Corridor gossip among scientists recognises the limitations of peer review, but the orthodoxy is too fragile to withstand a critical examination of its continued use as the cornerstone for judging research merit well beyond the era when one's peers could necessarily afford to be supportive and objective. The current framework for research funding is a relatively recent phenomenon which originated with the formation of the National Science Foundation in the US in 1950. The NSF was to:

> provide funds for the best scientists who would compete by setting out what each proposed to do if successful; these proposals would be judged by experts in the field, who would by doing so exercise peer

review. There would in principle be no fixed sums or proportions for
this discipline or that one: excellence would rule, wherever it led.
(Australian Science and Technology Council 1990: 2)

The core of this model remains current in many national research
funding agencies; however, the pressure to introduce criteria beyond excellence has grown dramatically following the exponential growth of scientific
activity and the levelling off of funds available to support it.

The problematic of peer review in a cross-disciplinary, strategic or
applied research environment, especially in the workplace, is an important
one given the core function which peer review performs in maintaining the
scientific social order. Finch (1997: 152) has described the centrality of
peer review in this context: 'the social order of academic life does depend
upon each of us accepting the legitimacy of judgements made about us
and it is our academic peers in whom we have collectively vested the right
to make those judgements'. There is considerable scope to argue that
today's academic research environment, entwined as it is with the
economic well-being of nations (Turpin *et al.* 1996) and businesses engaged
in a global knowledge industry, can no longer trust so implicitly in the
objective neutrality of peers.

The rules of engagement for academics participating in the global
college, whose common objective is the pursuit of knowledge for its own
sake, did not evolve to cope with the demands of an environment where
knowledge is readily transferable to the national balance of payments, the
company's bottom line or the researcher's performance bonus. This
problem is deeper and more serious than that which is acknowledged
traditionally in relation to industry-commissioned or partnership research.
In that arena there has been a longstanding recognition of the need to
clarify ownership of intellectual property and publication rights, and to
negotiate codified mechanisms for ensuring the integrity of the research
process. Academic institutions and industry should now be sufficiently
experienced in handling these issues that serious problems should not often
arise. The more serious problem, however, is not so easily resolved,
because it relates to the cultural shift in definition of the purposes and
outputs of higher education institutions, and to the shifting shape of
society itself and how it constructs its priorities around social and
economic objectives. An objective analysis of the current situation
surrounding the status of peers in the academy must reveal that conflicts of
interest are emerging as the academic enterprise is co-opted more strongly
into an economic model for national or corporate development.

Another core concept which merits closer attention is 'competition'.
Researchers embrace the concept of academic competition in the sense

that it maintains research effort at the cutting edge and guarantees excellence through maintaining the esteem of one's peers. However, the commercial definition of competition, the one which is applied in most workplaces, has more to do with survival in the market-place and is based on the ability to meet demand for a certain commodity within a certain price range by a specified time, and supported by a sophisticated marketing effort.

These two definitions of competition are not necessarily compatible and certainly require reconciliation if excellence is to be maintained in a research environment with economic objectives. For example, there is genuine reluctance in some fields of research to submit to international peer review, for fear that peers with greater resources offshore will be able to develop the ideas they are asked to review faster than those who are proposing them. Most researchers are aware of instances in which this is suspected to have happened. Processes for peer review of research proposals fail to deal adequately with protecting the ownership of the intellectual property embodied in a proposal or an idea. In a smaller research world, where one's peers may also be one's friends, colleagues and collaborators, these issues were controlled by professional ethics and mutual self-interest. In a global research enterprise involving thousands of researchers with billions of dollars at stake, ethical and personal bonds are loosened or replaced by 'commercial in confidence' conditions.

In the publication process, stakes are also high – publications and citations earn reputation, further funding and approaches from industry partners, and competition for publication in top-quality journals is keen. Researchers have to rely heavily on trust – the following example indicates how much trust may be required. An Australian researcher sends a report of a clinical study involving dietary behaviour to an international journal. The journal rejects the report on the recommendation of the international peer reviewers, whose substantive comments are that the results of the study are unexpected and the data must therefore be incorrect – so much for objectivity and discovery of new knowledge. The problem with trust, however, emerges the following week, when the Australian researcher sees a television report of a major, essentially identical, study being conducted by a prominent research group in the country from which the reviews came. The Australian researcher can hardly be blamed for wondering whether the peers who reviewed his study are involved with the study reported on TV and not anxious to see his study published before theirs. How objective can a peer be if confronted with a paper which will essentially upstage years of his or her own work and perhaps put an end to contracts with a local industry partner?

The other end of the spectrum of limitation of this orthodoxy of peer review is the tendency which peer review has to inhibit innovation – the tendency to ensure that the well-recognised researcher working in the well-trodden paths of established disciplines has a higher chance of success in funding and publication than the new researcher working in unbroken ground at the intersection of disciplines where there are no true peers to judge. Many granting bodies institutionalise this conservatism by making 'track record' a major criterion. This ensures that new researchers can only break into the cycle of success by collaborating with an established researcher in an established field – Catch-22. Funding bodies have good reason for relying on such criteria, since they operate in an environment in which there is strong competition for scarce resources and considerable pressure to produce demonstrable outcomes from funding. For this reason, granting bodies are risk averse. Researchers are also risk averse because they need to maximise the chances of their research being published. It has long been recognised that negative research findings or hypotheses which fail to be proven are under-reported in the literature, although negative findings advance knowledge as much as positive ones. Journal editors tend to discriminate against negative findings, and researchers are so strongly pressed to produce publishable outcomes that they are subtly shifted towards low-risk, high-yield research. One submission to the Wills review commented on the pressure for outcomes:

> The typical one to three year funding window in Australian grants, with inadequate budgets, is a recipe for conservative research. The only way you can be confident of getting funded is to apply to do work you have already done, so that you have results to present at interview to show that the project is feasible.
>
> (Wills 1998: 22)

Contrast this statement with the following excerpt from an interview of a worker in the lab of George Wallace, a leading pharmacologist at New York University medical school in the 1940s:

> Wallace taught Brodie about the role of intuition in science and stressed the creative freedom granted by a tentative working hypothesis: You don't have to be sure you're right about an idea. You don't even have to be pretty sure. Rather it's enough to go in with a good hunch, see what experiment it suggests, then test it out.
>
> (Kanigel 1993: 38)

In today's world, working on these principles, Wallace would probably be among the 75 per cent of grant applicants who are not funded. In this

regard, research generated in workplaces may help to advance the process
– successful businesses know how to manage risk so that innovation is
encouraged, not stifled. Academic science can learn from this experience.

If not, if we lose the ability to 'go in with a good hunch', have we lost
the excitement that drives the creativity of the very best? The data indicate that perhaps we have. Citations are an indication of the extent to
which one's published work gives rise to other published work and is
therefore at the leading edge. In the field of pharmacology, Australia's
relative citation impact – that is the proportion of citations divided by the
proportion of papers published internationally – is only 1.06 compared
with 1.51 for Switzerland, 1.37 for the UK and 1.30 for the US (Wills
1998: 23). Young researchers are understandably nervous about giving
free rein to their creativity and proposing risky cutting-edge ideas if their
jobs depend on them being among the successful 25 per cent of grant
applicants. They recognise this crisis in their career prospects, their salary
levels and the high attrition rate among their colleagues, but they see the
solution largely in simplistic terms of more money for research. Few
experienced mentors are available who are capable of creating research
environments where risk is managed as part of the total enterprise.
Partnerships with the world of work and 'professionalisation' of research
teams can create this environment.

Lacking the conceptual tools, or even the time, to critically analyse this
situation beyond the simple solution of more money and to re-invent the
culture of research, the scientific community frequently draws easy criticism because of the lack of insight and apparent self-interest with which it
states its case. It is an exaggeration, but only a slight one, to describe the
case scientific researchers offer in their own defence in the following terms:
'We need more money, because we do good things which are too complex
to explain easily and therefore not readily judged by outsiders such as
political decision-makers. Therefore you must trust us, appreciate our
value and double the research budget.'

It is doubtful whether this was ever an effective strategy, but in the age
of economic rationalism, free markets, anti-competition policy and privatisation of public services its chances of sustained success are slim indeed. In
a normal workplace environment, it won't get to first base. Researchers
learning to work outside the academy have to come to grips with these
realities. The experienced R and D arms of industry understand the
controlled elasticity which is required in research budgets where breakthroughs may be elusive, but developing researchers who can realistically
engage with that environment is a challenge yet to be faced effectively by
universities' research training programmes.

Shaping the future

To move beyond this impasse, the research community will need a more sophisticated analytical understanding of the parameters of the enterprise in which it is engaged and where it is headed. Given the sheer impossibility of ever providing enough money, from whatever source, to fund all the good ideas or 'hunches', ways have to be found so that at least some hunches in areas which are most likely to yield social and economic benefit are adequately supported. Given also the heavy reliance of funding bodies on peer review, and on the advice of the scientific community, it is already well within their sphere of influence to bring about the changes in mindset and methods which can reintroduce at least some of that excitement of being engaged in science, rather than only in the endless pursuit of grant funds.

What is needed is for the scientific research community, through all of its levels, to become more conversant and comfortable with conceptual models which describe the business of knowledge production in method-ologically defensible but more comprehensive terms than they have encountered in their laboratory-based training. Johnston (1998) summarises a model proposed by Gibbons *et al.* (1994) in which knowledge production and application is divided into two complementary modes. Mode 1 is essentially the mode which most would recognise currently as standard university-based scientific practice and standard doctoral training. Mode 2 is characterised by problems being addressed in the context of application through transdisciplinary approaches by heterogeneous and transient research teams assembled for the problem at hand – quality control is not only through peer review but by judgement against criteria reflecting a wider group of stakeholders.

Leaving aside the inevitably forced nature of such constructed dichotomies Mode 2 is unquestionably the underlying structure of many of the 'special' co-operative and industry-based schemes which funding bodies such as the Australian Research Council have introduced in recent years, but its application needs to be broadened and deepened. The President of the Federation of Australian Scientific and Technological Societies (FASTS), Professor Peter Cullen, is quoted as saying, 'There's a real cultural gap between scientists and industry. While things like CRCs [Co-operative Research Centres] are helping bridge that, they still don't really talk the same language in terms of risk, money and management and marketing' (Higher Education Supplement 1999). The ability of scien-tific researchers to embrace these new modes of working genuinely and confidently without compromising scientific integrity will be the most significant sign that the crisis is manageable.

Without doubt, scientific research will increase in importance as an economic commodity, whatever its other social outcomes. This means inevitably that the relationship between scientific researchers and society will assume a different trajectory from the one it has undergone this century. In the twentieth century, the goals of science have been predominantly pursuit of knowledge for its own sake and for the betterment of human life, and, more recently, environmental quality. In the twenty-first century, these goals will remain but will create a different set of demands for scientists as technological and economic conditions change the way we organise society and its institutions.

Much of the current debate in academic forums concerning the future of scientific research centres on micro-level concerns such as government policies for allocating funds to researchers. Relatively minor adjustments in government research funding policy can have profound effects on the shape of the Australian university sector, but ultimately they are unlikely to be more than a blip on the radar screen of the national research effort. Significant impact will result from complex interacting scenarios at the level of taxation and investment policy. While Australian researchers argue the merits of 'block funding' or concentration of effort, billions of dollars are invested in research in other countries where capital gains tax is less punitive. A sense of perspective is warranted.

The community of researchers can have most impact where they recognise and harness research talent, provide conditions which generate flexibility to work in various sectors, and nurture, excite and support creativity rather than smother it under the weight of annual proposal writing and production line publication targets.

Developing innovative ways to allocate funds most effectively, to judge excellence and, acknowledging economic and commercial realities, to maintain a strong international competitive edge within a co-operative framework is a job that only researchers can do. Incorporating within scientific value structures a commitment to all kinds of science, in all kinds of milieu including the applied and strategic, will be necessary to allow genuine mutual engagement in industrial research and development – if engagement is not achieved, scientists will be the servants of the industrial process rather than agents in its development.

Research training, structures and processes which achieve these higher-order objectives are the concerns which should be exercising research communities. If the debate remains at the level of whether setting research priorities is or is not appropriate, whether individuals or groups are more productive, how government funding should be carved up between pure, applied or strategic purposes, or whether funding decisions for small grants should be centralised or decentralised, then the scientific research community will remain on the sidelines while the main game is played elsewhere. All of these are important issues which deserve to be resolved by the scientific community, but they are not the core issue. The core issue is the need to recognise that the world has changed and that some of the cherished truisms of scientific research no longer serve the purpose for which they evolved. Like it or not, modern scientific research depends on the individual researcher having access to a creative team and to significant technological, managerial, logistical, sometimes industrial and often political support. Success in the new environment requires researchers who understand that environment and who can manipulate it to the benefit of science and the community.

A critical assessment of the need for change can probably only be carried out by a new generation whose training will have been broadened to encompass abilities in context analysis and social problem solution as well as experimental methods. Increasingly, research occurs not at the bench but in cyberspace and boardrooms, and is supported not by government grants but by government policies which create investment incentives. The average scientist and PhD graduate has few tools to master this environment, and is arguably selectively disadvantaged in comparison with colleagues who have a broader education and appreciation of the way the world works. This is beginning to be recognised in formal national reports on research and research training. For example, in the US the Committee on Science, Engineering, and Public Policy (COSEPUP 1995) recommended, among other things, that graduate education be broadened to include courses and experiences beyond dissertation research, and the Wills Report in Australia (1998) recommended broader training for health research PhDs, including such areas as finance, journalism and patent law. The job market for highly specialised PhDs in science and engineering is probably healthy in the longer term, but in the shorter term fewer jobs in academia and related areas are available, and external factors such as reduced defence budgets after the end of the Cold War decrease job opportunities in other areas. Osborn (1997) notes, however, the conclusion by COSEPUP (1995) that opportunities are emerging in interdisciplinary fields such as healthcare policy, patent law, industrial ecology and technology-related areas of government. The COSEPUP report also found that both academic and non-academic employers were unanimous in their description of the ideal PhD graduate. He or she is:

- able to think and solve problems;
- broadly based rather than narrowly oriented to a specific technology;
- able to communicate effectively to non-experts as well as peers;

- able to understand technology transfer and develop as well as initiate ideas;
- able to work comfortably in a collaborative group environment and have respect for the employment milieu and their place within it.

Sadly, many graduate research programmes fail to offer this breadth of experience, fearful of diluting their specialist academic mission and failing to recognise that such skills are increasingly mainstream within the academy as well as in more applied careers.

If scientific research is indeed in crisis it is a crisis of our own making. We have refined our research education and practice to such a pinnacle of excellence, to such purity of mission and method, that it is enfeebled in any environment whose parameters it cannot predict and does not control.

The global information economy offers unparalleled opportunity to reverse this risk – it offers and requires trans-discipline, trans-workplace, trans-paradigm and trans-national scientific research – these are the new frontiers. It also offers new ways of doing, appreciating, using and communicating science, and thus ways of renewing the excitement that brought us successfully to this point. The next generation of scientists can lament the passing of an organisational and cultural pattern which served science well in the twentieth century, or it can participate creatively and with strength of purpose in the definition and construction of a research environment for the next century. The outcome depends on the leadership we provide. The ability of the current generation to unravel the messages in the current 'crisis' may well be limited, but its preparedness to provide leadership which exemplifies the defining characteristic of the scientist – an open mind – will be a significant forward step.

References

Adams, J. (1998) 'Benchmarking international research', *Nature* 396: 615–18.
Australian Science and Technology Council (1990) *Setting Directions for Australian Research. A Report to the Prime Minister by the Australian Science and Technology Council in association with the Australian Research Council,* Canberra: Australian Government Publishing Service.
Black, N. (1997) 'A national strategy for research and development: lessons from England', *Annual Review of Public Health* 18: 485–505.
Bourke, P. and Butler, L. (1998) *The Concentration of Research in Australian Universities: Six Measures of Activity and Impact,* Higher Education Series, Report No. 32, Canberra: Department of Employment, Education, Training and Youth Affairs.

Charlesworth, M., Farrall, L., Stokes, T. and Turnbull, D. (1989) *Life among the Scientists. An Anthropological Study of an Australian Scientific Community*, Melbourne: Oxford University Press.

Committee on Science, Engineering, and Public Policy (COSEPUP) of the National Academy of Sciences, the National Academy of Engineering and the Institute of Medicine (1995) *Reshaping the Graduate Education of Scientists and Engineers*, Washington DC: National Academy Press.

Finch, J. (1997) 'Power, legitimacy and academic standards', Chapter 10 in J. Brennan, P. de Vries and R. Williams (eds) *Standards and Quality in Higher Education*, London: Jessica Kingsley Publishers.

Gibbons, M., Limoges, C., Nowotny, H., Schwartzman, S., Scott, P. and Trow, M. (1994) *The New Production of Knowledge: The Dynamics of Science and Research in Contemporary Societies*, London: Sage.

Goldberg, J. (1989) *Anatomy of a Scientific Discovery*, New York: Bantam Books.

Higher Education Division (1998) *Higher Education Students Time Series Tables*, Canberra: Department of Employment, Education, Training and Youth Affairs.

Higher Education Supplement (1999) 'Scientists told to commercialise', *The Australian*, 14 January.

Hill, S. and Murphy, P. (1994) *Quantitative Indicators of Australian Academic Research, Commissioned Report No. 27*, Canberra: National Board of Employment, Education and Training, Australian Research Council.

Johnston, R. (1998) *The Changing Nature and Forms of Knowledge: A Review*, Canberra: Evaluations and Investigations Programme, Higher Education Division, Department of Employment, Education, Training and Youth Affairs.

Kanigel, R. (1993) *Apprentice to Genius: The Making of a Scientific Discovery*, Baltimore: Johns Hopkins University Press.

Keller, E.F. (1996) 'Science and its critics' in L. Menand (ed.) *The Future of Academic Freedom*, Chicago: University of Chicago Press.

LaPidus, J.B. (1997) 'Issues and themes in postgraduate education in the United States' in R.G. Burgess (ed.) *Beyond the First Degree. Graduate Education, Lifelong Learning and Careers*, Buckingham: Society for Research into Higher Education and Open University Press.

Latour, B. and Woolgar, S. (1979) *Laboratory Life. The Social Construction of Scientific Facts*, vol. 80, Sage Library of Social Research, Beverly Hills: Sage Publications.

Masood, E. (1998) 'Britain embraces "knowledge economy"', *Nature* 396: 714–15.

Medawar, P. (1969) *Induction and Intuition in Scientific Thought*, Jayne Lectures for 1968, Philadelphia: American Philosophical Society.

National Institutes of Health Working Group on Priority Setting (1997) *Setting Research Priorities at the National Institutes of Health*, Bethesda: NIH. Updates on NIH home page at http://www.nih.gov/

Nature (1999) 'Promises and threats of the knowledge-based economy', editorial, *Nature* 397: 1.

NBEET (1993) *Research Performance Indicators Survey*, Commissioned Report No. 21, Canberra: National Board of Employment, Education and Training.

Osborn, M.J. (1997) 'A note on reshaping the graduate education of scientists and engineers' in R.G. Burgess (ed.) *Beyond the First Degree: Graduate Education, Lifelong Learning and Careers*, Buckingham: Society for Research into Higher Education and Open University Press.

Scott, P. (1997) 'The crisis of knowledge and the massification of higher education', Chapter 2 in R. Barnett and A. Griffin (eds) *The End of Knowledge in Higher Education*, London: Cassell.

Snow, C.P. (1993) *The Two Cultures*, Cambridge: Cambridge University Press.

Tegart, G., Johnston, R. and Sheehan, P. (1998) *Working for the Future*, special report, Australia: Academy of Technological Sciences and Engineering.

Turpin, T., Garrett-Jones, S., Rankin, N. and Aylward, D. (1996) *Using Basic Research*. Commissioned Report No. 45, Canberra: National Board of Employment, Education and Training, Australian Research Council.

Vandenbroucke, J.P. (1998) 'Medical journals and the shaping of medical knowledge', *Lancet* 19–26 December, 352: 2001–6.

Weber, S. (1996) 'The future of the university: the cutting edge' in T. Smith (ed.) *Ideas of the University*, Sydney: Research Institute for the Humanities and Social Sciences, University of Sydney.

Wills, P. (1998) 'The virtuous cycle. Working together for health and medical research. Health and medical research strategic review', discussion document, Commonwealth of Australia.

Part II

Whose knowledge?
Collaboration and research in and around work

5 Globalising the intelligent organisation

Stewart Clegg

This chapter contrasts exploratory with exploitative learning, in order to argue for the importance of both – not just the latter. It considers three case studies briefly: Microsoft, Berlei and Patricks. While Microsoft may often be thought of as the epitome of an 'intelligent' organisation, the company has a reputation for unreliable products. Although the employees at the Lithgow plant of Berlei achieved world's best practice, their jobs were exported offshore, on the basis of the learning that they had achieved for the company. In the case of Patricks, we can see the effect of managerial cleverness (advised by some of the best legal and accounting expertise available) producing fundamentally flawed attempts at reorganisation that failed to consider the social, political or organisational dimensions or consequences of the type of learning unleashed. At the same time, this paper argues a particular case for organisation studies that situates itself within a classical tradition of sociology stretching from Max Weber, through C. Wright Mills, to the present.

> Nowadays people often feel that their private lives are a series of traps. They sense that within their everyday worlds, they cannot overcome their troubles, and in this feeling, they are often quite correct: what ordinary people are directly aware of and what they try to do are bounded by the private orbits in which they live; their visions and their powers are limited to the close-up scenes of job, family, neighbourhood; in other milieux they move vicariously and remain spectators. And the more aware they become, however vaguely, of ambitions and of threats which transcend their immediate locales, the more trapped they seem to feel.
>
> (adapted from the opening paragraph of Mills 1970)

The many facets of power, knowledge and learning

I am a hybrid management-sociological social scientist, concerned with the 'reflexive representation and reconstruction of organizations' to use Martin Albrow's (1997: 1) terms. Organisational reconstruction, in an era of global change, has become the norm, and organisations typically generate myriad representations on a routine basis. One thinks of balance sheets and boardroom reports, for instance. However, I want to start from the presupposition that the 'reality of organizations is neither boardroom nor balance sheet but people's practices and encounters, capacities and aspirations inscribed in social patterns' (Albrow 1997: 3). What provide the patterns are the diverse rationalities that members of organisations and those who affect them typically use, thus configuring differential relations of power and knowledge in organisations.

In seeking to understand organisational practices one is not beholden to any specific organisational interest: not to management as a whole, nor to sectional interests within management, nor the owners of capital that hire it, nor those defined by its actions as employed or unemployed. This is not to say that one is uninterested in, or indifferent to, the sentiments of different stakeholders or community interests. In Zygmunt Bauman's (1987) terms, one is simply one among many interpreters of the organisational condition – not a legislator upon it. One does not tell people what they should do – there are churches and pulpits and pundits aplenty, as well as consultants, to fulfil that function. One merely researches and seeks to understand what it is that people do when they are doing organisation, when they are in and around organisations, when they are being organised and when they are organising. The diverse rationalities, the projects that they inform and the strategies that express them, are the stuff one studies. Then, like any good academic, one produces theory, concepts, books, papers, research grants and graduates in the same way that others may produce profits – from diverse projects.

Note the plural use of rationalities. What one seeks to do is to relativise people's practical experiences against universal themes, such as, in my case, that of power, 'reflecting on practice, revising its ways of thinking as a result' (Albrow 1997: 9), constructing a 'learning discipline' par excellence. And it is the many facets of power, knowledge and learning that will provide the themes for this paper.

Learning

Generally, learning can take many forms: it may involve accelerating learning curves through the institutionalisation of personal knowledge into widespread organisational knowledge, through quality circles that seek to build a shared and integrated knowledge of organisational practices. It may introduce behavioural change through trial and error, where actions are checked against their outcomes in order to make subsequent adjustments to the actions. It is this type of learning that is the basis of continuous adjustment to improve quality or reduce cycle time. Here, the employee is subject to an eternal exhortation to improve his or her performance – and thus that of the organisation. Improved performance may come from enhanced adaptation to stimuli in the organisational environment through attending systematically to end-user and customer concerns. These then become incorporated into changed search rules, attention rules and organisational goals (Cyert and March 1963). All of these kinds of learning may involve people changing not only their routines but also their rationalities: the ways that they make sense of what they do, who they are and who they are not in an organisation. Sometimes, as in business process re-engineering, the changes may be extremely dramatic – as old routines are made redundant, so too may be the positions formally associated with them.

Learning always implies remembering and forgetting. At any given time, that which one remembers, and that which one forgets, shapes what one takes to be rational. What is it that one is obliged to remember? What is it that one is allowed to forget? And who or what is it, organisationally, that obliges and allows? In other words, in learning, how does power constitute what is taken to be relevant and appropriate knowledge, and how does knowledge constitute power? These questions will frame what follows.

Substantial areas of agreement exist among scholars of organisational learning. These areas stress the role of environmental adaptation, the distinctiveness of organisational (as opposed to individual) learning, and the identification of culture, strategy, structure and the environment as the major sources of innovation. While it is innovation that creates and reinforces learning, there is also recognition that there are two distinct ways in which organisations strive for this advantage: through exploitative or through exploratory learning. Different emphases in the literature favour each of these modes.

Exploitative learning

The model of exploitative learning emerges, initially, from the classical management school of Taylor (1911). Detailed research conducted by Adler (1993) and Adler and Cole (1993) of knowledge-workers at NUMMI (the acronym for 'New United Motor Manufacturing Inc.', coined as a name for a joint Japanese–American venture in automobile manufacturing in the USA) continues the tradition of research into modern times. Adler and his associates argue that detailed prescription of tasks, arising from learning, is the best basis for production efficiency. Knowledge-based workers learn as they work and thus enhance the organisation.

Exploitative learning is focused on making tasks explicit and task cycles short and routine. At NUMMI, teams of four or five workers perform tasks of relatively short duration, are highly specialised, have detailed work procedures and a modest degree of job rotation. The emphasis is on quality through continuous improvement. The system lends itself to rapid learning. Workers at NUMMI learn from making an explicit model of what they already know, applied to relatively short, focused tasks, in quality circles. In this model, learning is best accomplished through explicitness about rules – the core of much organisational theory since F.W. Taylor (1911).

Explicitness about rules may restrict organisational practices, in the familiar punitive sense of rule-implementation as a way of preventing people from doing things that they might otherwise do, or it may enable innovation – the sense that Adler and his colleagues identify. In rule-enabling settings, continuous improvement develops through the structuring of desire, understanding and trust:

- Workers learn to share with managers a 'desire' to achieve excellence and to work towards a job well done.
- Workers come to 'understand' that their jobs depend on the competitive success of the organisation and the best way to protect their jobs is to constantly improve the way that they do them, and thus continuously improve the competitive position of their employers.
- Managers and workers develop 'trust' in each other – that is, they have confident expectations about future patterns of behaviour and vocabularies of motive – and this trust is amplified through the commitment that the workers show.

Exploratory learning

At the heart of exploitative learning is an explicitness about routines – it is only then that one can identify precisely what it is that is innovative in a specific organisational practice. By contrast, exploratory learning allows for a different type of learning than learning simply from existing routines. It is associated with complex search, basic research, innovation, variation, risk-taking and more relaxed controls. The stress is on flexibility, investments in learning and the creation of new capabilities. It may be thought of in terms of coaching or improvisation, and its articulation as training, advice and creative interaction. One might think of a sports team and the role of the coach in continuously improving both individual and team performance, or a great jazz group, like the Miles Davis group that recorded 'Kind of Blue' in one take of spontaneous improvisation in the studio. Exploratory learning that is exploited successfully characterises organisations where innovation, rather than refining what already exists, produces creative discontinuities in practices.

Exploratory learning offers distant time horizons and uncertain benefits as its vision. While it offers the chance of increasing performance levels significantly beyond trend-lines, there is also the risk that performance might be significantly lower if risky ventures fail. When it works, one might think of it as 'intelligent organisation' – organisation that successfully trades off the intelligence that it employs, using it to deepen and distinguish its capacities. At its most extreme, exploratory learning can capture and learn from fleeting, flexible moments within the overall orderly flow. Take humour: its role in relieving tension in organisational settings, or of surfacing criticism in a way that is socially acceptable, is well known, but it can also be an occasion for learning. Humour allows for the expression of criticism, contradiction, ambiguity and contrary worldviews in a classically improvisational form. Usually formally unscripted and informally contextualised, although it can become informally routinised (Roy 1958), humour has a capacity to be highly creative and potentially code-breaking.

Improvisations pose unique opportunities for insight and innovation among routines as they break on through to the other side of structure. Action-oriented organisations in the heat of action, like firefighters (Weick 1996) or combat units (Janowitz 1959), provide an organisational model of improvisation over, above, beyond, around, sometimes in harmony and sometimes in counterpoint with the script that steers normality. All organisations have moments of improvisation; not all organisations seem capable of capturing these and making them work for their future. In many, structure strives to overwhelm novelty rather than to feel the shock of the new. Rules effectively constrain innovation in such organisations. Of course, this may be effective, especially where great disparities of power or socially agreed rights are concerned – such as in rules regarding police procedures for the taking of evidence. In other instances, where the rules do not constrain in order to protect some fundamentally agreed right, constraint may be somewhat more protective of organisational practices, protecting organisational members rather than those with whom they come into contact. We shall return to such a situation later.

It has been proposed that the survival of any organisation depends upon being sufficiently exploitative to insure current viability and sufficiently exploratory to insure future viability (Levinthal and March 1993: 105). From the managerial point of view, too much exploitation risks organisational survival by creating a 'competency trap', where increasingly obsolescent capabilities continue to be elaborated; equally, too much exploration insufficiently linked to its exploitation leads to 'too many undeveloped ideas and too little distinctive competence' (ibid.). What is determined as a rational balance of 'exploitative' and 'exploratory' learning, in any organisation, will depend on the distribution and relations of power and knowledge constituting that organisation. It is not an objective or an academic post hoc decision. So learning is never detached from power. On this reckoning, more intelligent organisations are not more intelligent because they by-pass power relations but because they are characterised by power relations that foster innovation. Power is immutable; how it is configured is not.

High learning quality problems: probability, efficiency and representation

Let's try and make things more specific: think of Microsoft, the very model of a cybercorp that seems to have exploited exploratory learning to the full. Despite all the positive things that one can say about Microsoft's achievements, it is hardly a total quality organisation – there have been too many infamously bugged or late product launches for anyone to claim that, although it is undoubtedly an organisation in which a great deal of learning occurs. Microsoft is somewhat like its figurehead, Bill Gates – a slapstick organisation with pie on its face. If firms in some other industries, such as the auto industry, were to achieve the level of 'reliability' and 'efficiency' of Microsoft, they would probably end up like the British auto industry: non-existent, out of business. Microsoft may be a very powerful monopolist and marketer, and, in large part as a consequence, an extremely wealthy company, but it is not a reliable or efficient organisation in the way that quality management would recommend.

Traditionally, the exploitative tradition of organisational learning has been oriented towards issues of stochastic event *probability* and continuous event *efficiency*. Managing probability focuses on the management of stochastic events, premised on sampling from a pool of products, while the management of continuous events focuses on efficiency. Firms like Microsoft do not deal with issues of efficiency and reliability as their core concerns. Microsoft's key focus is on the innovation of representations – or abstract codes. Signs, rather than highly tangible machined objects, are the stuff of their innovation. And one cannot sample a sign or measure its continuous flow.

One can consider reliability, efficiency and representation as three decisive and, at certain moments, novel, organising principles, each characterising a specific organisational era and its concerns. Note that the notion of organisational era refers not to temporal progression so much as to the characteristics imprinted organisationally: a small machine shop in the 1990s might still be embedded in the industrial era, even while the prevailing epoch might not be. Organisations are sedimented in a complex relation of epochs, rather like the great cities of Europe where majestic cathedrals from the Middle Ages jostle for supremacy on the skyline with the icons of later, more materialist, times. Thus, organisational principles are sedimented deeply into organisations, so that novel principles do not obliterate previous ones: they simply overlie and exist in potential tension with them as they organise more current aspects of the realities in which different agents within these organisations constitute themselves and their organisation.

Organisationally, each era frames a different principle for exploratory learning. And, since the industrial era at least, with each shift, exploitation of learning becomes dependent on recovering ever more abstract and intangible aspects of social action, in terms of the critical issues attended to. Table 5.1 represents the argument.

'Stochastic events' form the essence of an organisation's exploratory learning about *reliability*, the hallmark of the industrial era (Roberts and Grabowski 1996: 412). Most recent management fashions founder on the reef of stochastic events. For instance, if an organisation trained its members rigorously and prescriptively in one-best-way processes, it would not be designed for explorative learning. Organisations always require more skills than they know. The repertoire of skills that must be maintained if that organisation is to learn, if it is to be intelligent, must be larger than the skill-set in use at any time. Error must be allowable. This is particularly the case where a new procedure or technology is introduced, and especially where diagnosis is required to make the start-up work smoothly. In these circumstances, learning occurs through error and its rectification: if an organisation knew already there would be no error and no learning. Employees should be able to offer more skills than, vocation-

Table 5.1   Organising principles for different eras

Novel organising principle	Critical workflow issues	Organisational era	Exemplar
Reliability	Stochastic events	Industrial era	Machine production – ensuring the accuracy and reliability of the machined parts through sampling
Efficiency	Continuity of flow	Post-industrial era	Flow-production – maintaining the continuity of the process
Representation	Reflexive diagnosis and recovery	Postmodern era	Software production – interpretation of 'crashes', 'freezes' and incompatibilities

ally, they need right now, and much of Microsoft's unorthodox selection procedures (such as asking candidates impossible questions and studying the processes that they go through in trying to answer them) seeks to identify people who do have these surplus skills.

In the post-industrial era, where continuous events tie together disparate geographical spaces, *efficiency* has become the hallmark of quality. Here, exploratory learning arises not so much from learning how to avoid the error of unanticipated or random events but in learning from disorderly interruptions to the order of due process and its management. The emphasis is on rapid responses to emergencies, the ability to keep cool while managing tense environments and on early detection of malfunctions in continuous systems. Much of the 'bug-testing' that occurs in Microsoft is of this order: processes are in simultaneous development and, as existing bugs may be resolved in one application, they may simultaneously introduce errors in another. In Microsoft this has led to several disastrous or late product launches, as Cusamano and Selby (1996) detail.

In the management of tense technical environments 'supervisors often pay more attention to processes and products than to people' (Roberts and Grabowski 1996: 412). Microsoft is typical; while the technical management skills are excellent, the people-management skills have not been so well developed. Over-attention to process and under-attention to people produce particular management problems. Process does not encourage causal analysis: when an event flows seamlessly, it is much more difficult to work out what is responsible for what, or who is responsible for what. One consequence is that as supervisors pay more attention to processes than to people, and people working closely with the processes pay less attention to their 'naive' conception of the causal linkages at work in sound and unsound operation. Instead they rely on reading the technical instruments measuring the processes and ignore any other stimuli that contradict the instrumentation, thus compounding error and the inability to learn exploitatively from the process. Thus, the cognitive interactive capacities of people working close to continuous processes in intelligent organisations may routinely produce dumber learning capacities, unless closely monitored.

Increasingly, technology in the postmodern era is a source of abstract events, for which the hallmark is neither reliability nor efficiency, but their *representation*. One aspect of new technologies is the essentially invisible material process that unfolds in their application. Nonetheless, despite this unavailability, we all try to construct socially a sense of the world in which we live and work; as it becomes ever more remote and inaccessible technologically, the less are we able to learn what to attend to. Operating a lathe through feel, rhythm and visual cues as extensive sensory data is a very different operation to reading from a computer graphic applied to an automatic process where the usual sense data are absent. One result may be 'inadequate sampling of displayed information, inattention to information on the periphery, and distractions when building problem representations' (Roberts and Grabowski 1996: 412). Abstract events require a kind of learning without environmental stimuli as cues. Hence, organisations that make use of technologies premised on the abstraction of events require learning capacities that are equally abstract but that 'can intervene at any time, pick up the process and assemble a recovery' (Roberts and Grabowski 1996: 412). Consequently, diagnosis and monitoring, as much as operation, become crucial skill-sets in work that deals in representations (Weick 1996: 4).

Knowing so little about what may go wrong, where and when, or how to effect a recovery means that to be intelligent under these circumstances organisations must be smart enough to know that they can never know all of what they need to know. That is why they need people to work in them who are smart enough to know that they need to know more than they do (the definition that determined Socrates to be the wisest man in ancient Athens). Learning in organisations of the postmodern era is thus sufficiently abstract as to be tacit, ineffable or not capable of being caught in a programme. Even if the ineffable can subsequently be translated into the do-able, through learning from the captured image, as Microsoft developers have done in trying to transmit tacit learning, this will, with great difficulty, capture the initial exploratory breakthroughs that rendered the ineffable into the knowable. Exploitative learning is extremely limited in its innovative capacities for organisations of the postmodern era. Cognitive capacities rather than physical effort characterise most work in an organisation such as Microsoft. Much intelligent organisational work relates to technologies conceived as codes to produce outputs, as in abstract representations (scans, medical imaging, X-rays, etc.). Codes may be produced as by-products of functioning, in terms of interpretative devices that make sense of the functioning of the technology from the signs that it emits and that process operators pick up. One thinks of sounds, smells and touch, or the interpretive modes that we develop, for instance, with respect to narrative styles in video. Often it is mastery of these codes that is essential for organisational functioning; learning to read a script or a narrative style is, in this respect, not too different from learning to read an X-ray.

When these new technologies are applied to more orthodox organisa-tional settings, one effect of their representations may be to circumvent existing codes; thus, they transform the existing circuits of power in organ-isations. For instance, as representational devices capture processes that were previously managed with a degree of indeterminacy through profes-sionally tacit knowledge as data, then claims to autonomy and power based on this indeterminacy are not as easy to sustain. Think of the impact of electronic data processing on conveyancing, once the backbone of most suburban solicitors' practices. Not any more, though.[1] Now it is largely the preserve of less expensive legal semi-professionals. Hence, even powerful organisational professionals are not immune to the effects of new representational technologies, although they are better equipped to with-stand them by ensuring implementation through their professionally mandated terms.

Strategies for organisational learning and their national implications

Strategies for achieving linkage between exploratory and exploitative learning characterise the latest managerial developments. Essentially, managerial perspectives are optimistic about the linkage. However, when we study some of the learning implications that can take place in more detail we find that there are some aspects that picture a less opti-mistic scenario, at least from the point of view of national considerations. What is excellent managerially may not be so nationally, in terms of the host nations within which these organisations are embedded, or in terms of the employees of these organisations. By asking questions about these different levels, we may illuminate some of the power aspects of organisational learning that have been overlooked in the past.

Rawlinson and Wells (1996: 203) identified a situation in an auto plant in the UK where work teams problem-solved under lean production. The learning that was generated from problem solution did not stay within the team but became an input to manufacturing engineers who took suggestions for making work smarter or faster and re-coded them into standard job sheets or operating procedures. These became the benchmark for work within the plant. But such a process need not stop there.

The benchmark, once achieved within one team and one plant, can be virtually circulated throughout the entire organisation, world-wide. The interlinkage of plants by Electronic Data Interchange (EDI), or through the World Wide Web (www) and web-based technologies, allows for the learning to be distributed globally, immediately and virtually. Imagine an improved process being exploratively innovated in a plant. How could management make this improved process virtual, distribute it freely and widely? (The consequences of doing so are another matter – one where the political and ethical implications outweigh the technical issues.) As a technical managerial problem there are two dimensions: portability and embeddedness.

Portability

The first dimension is that of portability, defined as the ability to materially translate innovative learning from one locale to any other locale. It includes three aspects:

1   The exploratory learning must be standardised, made more exploitative. This means that the moment of insight, disorder, in the orderly routine, must be codified into standardised terms that all can understand.

2   Exploratory insight depends on the individuals who produced it: to eliminate this dependence, tacit knowledge requires commodifying. Standardised information must be commodified. It must be rendered as something that any person could do, not something that one person might have done. If management can reduce their dependency on individuals as the bearers of knowledge and skills by rendering these skills into computer-based artifacts, it is possible to manipulate and combine these with other factors of production in ways that are

impossible if these skills remain a human possession. The commodity status of knowledge clearly involves power: who retains what rights, to what knowledge, under what conditions, will be crucial.

3   Abstract properties need to be developed for the phenomenon that has been standardised and commodified. Examples include the registration of a house or land title: the title allows for the property to be alienated, to be exchanged across time and space in a recognisable commodity form. Abstract property rights simplify the preservation of assets over time and their movement through space.

Embeddedness

The second dimension, that of embeddedness, flows directly from the digital properties of technologies such as EDI and the web. Exploratory learning embedded in innovation becomes tangible when embedded in a computer program. It is easy to transmit this throughout the world. But a program may not capture the tacit knowledge that is involved in making the exploratory innovation work. It is here that EDI or the web can assist. The work process can be video-taped, scanned on to computer and downloaded instantly by the globally networked corporation. Management thus attempts to incorporate the tacit knowledge that created an exploratory breakthrough in one plant as part of the strategy of competitive advantage of global, digitised, intelligent corporations. As Rawlinson and Wells (1996: 203) conclude, 'the pace of work is no longer controlled and defined on a plant basis but on a global basis'. However, while they may expropriate the tacit knowledge of the innovative explorers they cannot dictate how it will be received, culturally, politically or existentially.

It was such a conjuncture that sealed the fate of the employees of the Berlei bra factory in Lithgow, just over the Blue Mountains from Sydney, Australia. The plant was originally developed under an older political regime of protection and regional development that no longer exists today. The work practices of the employees there, recognised as world class in their standards, were video-taped and benchmarked and used to configure and train a new factory and employees overseas. And the Australian plant closed down – it was no longer 'competitive': under Australian industrial relations conditions it would not have been possible for it to be so. The skills and intelligence of its employees were expropriated and incorporated into routines of the overseas plant, at a fraction of the previous wage costs. Wage-competitiveness alone would be very attractive for capital: the addition of intelligence derived from elsewhere proved even more so. However, the chief factors in this story were cost considerations: the rates of exploitation, or of wage-payment (from certain perspectives, opposite sides of the same thing), allowed as a minimum in Australia, are way above the maximum of any third world economy.

Notwithstanding factors of simple economic calculation, certain implications may be drawn. The intelligence that intelligent organisations claim, one might say, must always be the expropriation of tacit knowledge and power. Whether its progenitors can retain patent rights or intellectual copyright is itself an index of market power. Microsoft has been able to. The Berlei bra workers could not. Because they lacked this power, the jobs they had held were literally disembedded and the workers literally alienated.

Power/knowledge and globalising organisation

It should not be thought that the argument thus far is one that advocates old-style constraining, or protectionist, rules. Nationally, the arguments that countries such as Australia can no longer afford to be substantially involved in low-value-added and relatively unskilled industries are quite compelling. Yet little sense attaches to developing organisational best practices on the back of national education and training schemes and regional competencies. At least, that is, not if these are then used systematically to destroy the competencies that made them possible in the first place. To do so in the absence of any systematic policies for creating more intelligent organisations where they are needed merely compounds the initial foolishness. There is room here for policy innovation, one might suggest. Additionally, it is unlikely that a sustainable basis for shared *desire, understanding* and *trust* will be generalised in communities that learn, only too well, from injurious past practice.

The implications of portable embeddedness are massive in the age of the smart machine (Zuboff 1988). Innovation premised on the tacit learning and embedded skills of the work forces of the more developed countries can rapidly be standardised, commodified and abstracted into organisational processes anywhere. Workers with lower standards of schooling and education can be organisationally tooled-up to match the competencies of more creative employees elsewhere. At least, for a short while – but then one would expect that exploratory learning might stop as it runs up against the system-effects of the national framework within which it is embedded, and the organisation will flounder in its learning capacities. There may be a limit to this process, however. While the exploitative utilisation of exploratory learning that occurs in a sophisticated system may be generalised as a portable standardised, commodified and abstracted process, the socio-technical conditions that gave rise to the exploratory learning in the first place, by definition, cannot. They are unique and highly contingent upon the sophisticated system conditions that produced them. Global firms should thus ensure that portable processes do not cut them off from sources of exploratory learning in the first place. Important socio-technical system properties attach to these initial exploratory opportunities; certain systems of education and training, and education/training/work articulation, will offer greater opportunities for exploratory creativity to develop. Managers ignore these fundamental sources of intelligence at their peril.

It is, of course, not only organisations that may be intelligent – countries can be clever, too. Once upon a time, in the late 1980s, the Labor government of the day had pretensions of turning Australia into a 'clever country'; the rhetoric was associated with an expansion of tertiary education into a mass education system. Yet it is not in the universities alone that clever countries are made; it is in the workplace and organisational practices in which the products of the education system are employed. Sometimes, as in the case of the Berlei bra workers, these produce portable best practices – and sometimes, what is transported are the jobs of the people whose intelligence made them best practice in the first place. Here, while managerial writers would say that virtuous organisation learning had occurred, the results were vicious. Vicious learning implies diminished efficiency – in this case a deliberately restricted circuit of innovation and intelligence, for the national and regional level, impoverishing regional and national resources as organisational resources are enriched, but, in the long term, impoverished. There is a global dimension to the issue of learning organisations that is not fully incorporated by the management literature. For what reasons should employees rationally *desire* excellence, *understand* management imperatives and *trust* their employers, when the total organisation may prosper but their place in it is globalised away?

Other jobs are less portable – they are fixed in a particular space, such as a dock, where ships are loaded and unloaded. However, these fixed spaces are not exempt from globalising pressures any more than portable ones are. Recent events and commentaries in Australia suggest that where jobs are spatially fixed, necessarily *here*, in a specific organisational locale, it may not be so much organisational intelligence or even the clever country that prevails. Instead, what prevails is a peculiar and extraordinary form of viciousness.

The employees of Australia appear to be trapped between the globalising pressures of intelligent organisation and the resistant responses of traditional labourism. The Berlei bra workers fell victim to the former. They did everything that they could to lift productivity and improve working arrangements so that they became, literally, world's best practice. Then they lost their jobs because they had done so – but of course, they may well have lost their jobs anyway. What is the nature of the resistant responses of traditional labourism? They are not difficult to identify. An important example comes from Australia which, for much of 1999, was locked into a bitter and divisive struggle centring on the waterfront.

Employment relations on the docks have a long and bitter history, dating from the great strikes of the 1890s. Over the years the employers collectively agreed to bargains with the Maritime Union of Australia (MUA), enshrined in contracts and their associated effort-bargain. The union won comparatively favourable employment conditions, largely because the employers settled conflicts with the unions through the cash-nexus. Sweetheart deals on conditions and terms of employment were then passed on to the clients of the stevedoring firms through higher costs that the market simply had to bear. State governments compounded the problems by regarding port authorities as 'cash cows' that could be taxed at will, as did shippers, who were more concerned with unloading cargo than the costs of doing so – they encouraged the stevedoring companies to settle rather than prolong disputes. Costs escalated and productivity failed to keep pace with 'best practice' elsewhere. Management effectively abrogated the right to manage to the union. The union used the normal procedures of collective bargaining to incorporate many 'small wins' over conditions and terms of employment. In time, these small wins transformed the docks from a highly exploitative 'casual' system to one in which a disciplined union maintained a closed shop to ensure that the benefits that the union's effort-bargain had gained through the industrial agreements and their interpretation flowed through only to union members.

While the union members prospered, the costs of them doing so were still being passed on to the broader community. By the late 1980s and early 1990s, a Maritime Reform Board had been established by the federal Labor government of the day to try to hasten waterfront reform, at the urging, especially, of primary producer interests. Productivity increases and shedding of labour resulted from the reforms implemented. At the same time, in line with the 'Accord' politics of the day, union mergers occurred – resulting in the creation of the MUA as a national waterfront union. Productivity increased throughout the country, approaching best practice elsewhere, according to the National Productivity Commission – except in Sydney. One reason, undoubtedly, for this failure to achieve 'best practice' was the deficit in capital investment on the Sydney wharves. But there are other factors as well. On the Sydney waterfront labour–management relations have been characterised by a workplace culture that exists in a state of 'virtual running warfare':

> The legacies are extremely high levels of industrial disputation, poor
> occupational health and safety performance, limited communication
> between managers and employees ... The lack of trust leads to high
> prescriptive and inflexible workplace arrangements – out of place with
> modern bargaining techniques.
>
> (Millett 1998: 21)

Not only were the workplace arrangements and the loyalties of the
employees to their union suggested as being 'out of place with modern
bargaining techniques' but also as out of place with the priorities of a new
government, unimpressed with the previous government's Maritime
Reform Board and its improvements to productivity.

One of the strategic objectives of the conservative Liberal–National
Coalition when it took office in 1996 (after thirteen years of 'Accord' politics; see Clegg *et al.* 1984) was 'cleaning-up' the wharves: in the terms that
the government used this meant breaking the monopoly power of the
MUA rather than effecting any compromise with it. With what appears to
have been government support, as well as that of the National Farmers
Federation (NFF), Patricks, one of the duopoly of employers on the
wharves, secretly trained ex- and current servicemen in Dubai in stevedoring techniques around Christmas of 1997. In the early months of
1998, Patricks leased one of its Melbourne docks to the NFF, who then
employed non-unionised labour – principally the servicemen trained in
Dubai. The MUA immediately declared a strike against the Melbourne
branch of Patricks and withdrew its labour.

On the night of 7 April, at midnight, masked security men with dogs
moved on to all the wharves that Patricks operated around Australia, and
locked out the suddenly dismissed employees. The morning newspapers
and television news had shots of IRA-like terrorists, the security men, in
balaclavas with just their eyes peeping out of the black – a chilling spec-
tacle and a defining moment in the semiotics of power in the dispute.

Consequently, the MUA began to picket the locked-out sites and the
non-unionised labour that had been immediately smuggled in by water.
Meanwhile, as a result of some secret corporate restructuring that had
occurred in the latter part of the previous year, Patricks disclosed that they
were no longer the employers on the wharves. Patricks secretly had created
four 'labour-hire' sub-contract companies that now held all the contracts
with the MUA. Through corporate acts yet to be exposed fully in the law
courts, they stripped these companies of assets such that they declared
themselves bankrupt – this being the trigger for the dismissal of the union
labour. The government immediately rushed through legislation within

hours of the dismissals, agreeing to an extraordinary set of severance payments to the MUA workforce. The MUA appealed to the courts for wrongful dismissal and reinstatement under legislation. On 4 May the Full Bench of the High Court of Australia found, 6 to 1, in favour of the judgment that the dismissal of the MUA members had, in the first place, been unlawful. Additionally, grounds were found for the MUA to proceed to trial with charges of conspiracy between the employer, Patricks, the government and the NFF. So far, three courts have found with the MUA, including this Full Bench of the High Court. The administrators of the Patrick labour-hire companies were obliged to reinstate the workers, but under conditions of commercial considerations. At the end of their judgment the High Court noted that:

> The courts do not – indeed they cannot – resolve disputes that involve issues wider than legal rights and obligations. They are confined to the ascertainment and declaration of legal rights and obligations and when legal rights are in competition, the courts do no more than define which rights take priority over others.

In other words, the law court is not the appropriate means to achieve a settlement of complex organisational issues.

We may note that none of the sorry story was necessary. It was all an effect of too much cleverness and too little intelligence, one might say, if one will accept the semantic distinction between the two terms. The end was improved efficiency on the docks, according to some accounts. The means, however, were something else. It is not too difficult to see it as a victory for viciousness all round (as well, of course, for the legal industry), and a considerable loss to Australia. Especially when one considers that there are more managerially intelligent ways of doing things.

Patricks depicted the obstacles to change as the agreements that they had formally entered into in the past with the union. While it takes two sides to make a contract, it takes only one to break it. In this case, each side accused the other of being the contract breaker. Irrespective of the veracity of these claims, one may ask the counterfactual question: what would have had to happen for things to have been otherwise? A strategy for organisations which realise that they have to change to survive, otherwise they will cease to trade, could have been tried on the waterfront, as a managerially more intelligent way of handling the dispute (Burack *et al.* 1994). It wasn't – the change of government in 1996 and the determination of Patricks to be rid of the union effectively put paid to that prospect, emboldening a tough management style both in politics and in certain areas of business close to the government parties.

It is impossible to conceive either managing and being managed, or learning and forgetting, as about anything so much other than the use of power. Thus, power always implicates knowledge: that which is learnt, that which is known, that which is forgotten and that which is remembered. It is not that Patricks and the MUA (and the government) exercised rationalities that chose *for* a crude exercise of power and *against* learning. Each chose to remember and forget some things – although the dominant memory and knowledge which each of them privileged differed greatly.

The dominant coalition in each organisation (Patricks and the MUA) used a confrontational and weak strategy of power – one based on resource mobilisation designed to make the other dependent on what each could supply: capital and labour, respectively. If the power that was mobilised by the owners of capital and the framers of procedural rules – Patricks and the government – was massive, it was also ineffective. One should not think that this is merely because of the resistance of the MUA.

Throughout the waterfront dispute the use of power by all the parties has been strategically misguided. Note that none of the wielders of power realised their goals: neither the government, nor the employer, nor the union. The end game became one where the means quite overwhelmed the initial ends, and where the power unleashed spun out of the control of all the participants, into the law courts. Despite strategic claims made by various participants, it is a situation where knowledge has not been transformed positively, and, as far as one can see, little virtuous learning has occurred anywhere. Organisationally, one must conclude that the situation and the dispute were hardly intelligent at all.

Had government, management and the union chosen another strategy, such as that advised by Burack *et al.* (1994), it would still have involved power, as well as learning. But it would have been a different strategy of power – one that would have meant that both sides would have had to *manage* power rather than merely mobilise it in a disturbing theatre of the absurd. But to do so would have meant abandoning, in each case, protective rules. In the case of the MUA members, there was a commitment to maintaining work practices premised on their knowledge of constraining rules. These rules were protective of organisational practices for the members of the union. Adopting a protective role is what, traditionally, union organisations have based their legitimacy upon.

But it was not just the union that was protectionist in this dispute. Patricks, as a duopoly, had benefited from the traditional reliance of Australian industry on government protection. The pending charges of criminal conspiracy suggest that nothing much may have changed. The government seemed to regard industrial war as another means of power. If warfare is diplomacy by other means, then recourse to war by protected proxy was regarded, and encouraged, as appropriate politics.

Conclusion

Notwithstanding recent events on the Australian waterfront and past events at plants such as the Lithgow Berlei factory, there are many organisations that undoubtedly do strive to achieve learning capacities more intelligently. They have learnt from the Karpin Report on *Enterprising Nation* (1995) that 'one-best-way' solutions and confrontation, as well as the espousal of a rationality that denies other rationalities, are not how one best learns to do better. For others, however, stuck in the structural weaknesses of a small economy, accustomed in the past to management by government through protection and centralised industrial relations, the effort may just be too hard. It is so much easier to blame the workers rather than to attempt reform dialogue with legitimate trade unions. The MUA monopoly of labour should not have been a sufficient reason to foreclose dialogue and resort to force. For some organisations, among which one would venture to include Patricks and their advisors, being too clever was insufficiently intelligent.

Do organisations (and governments) have to be clever – can't they be intelligent? Two contrasting intellectual scenarios suggest not. I shall discuss these and then reject them. The first scenario derives from economic rationalism; the second scenario draws on old-style labourism.

Some economically rationalist pessimistic intellectual observers – new class warriors of corporate and political interests as well as old-style class warriors of labourism – in an unholy alliance, may remain undeterred by the stupidity presently evident in our country. A class confrontation, they would argue, is the preferable outcome of a bargaining situation where labour's organisational resources are well developed. Of course, one strategy seeks to smash these capacities, the other to mobilise them.

For the realist right, only power can break power. Hence, there is no point bargaining power away – better a confrontation that seeks to rewrite the rules of the game rather than to become embroiled in any 'intelligent organisation game'. Some on the left agree, in an odd alliance of strange bedfellows. For both camps, the prospect of more intelligent organisation is wholly negative. It seems a dystopian situation reflecting a totalitarian nightmare of total control through total surveillance, one in which jobs will not even be ensured. From such perspectives, what attempts at intelligent organisation offer would be a simulacrum of positive power; at the end of the day one group of people would still own and control the means of production and the majority would own and control only their own labour-power. Thus, everything crucial about the organisation could be read off from the terms under which the ownership of labour and capital are deployed.

Those who do not accept class premises might be equally pessimistic. It is not too difficult to see the strength of intelligent organisations as being the effortless incorporation of the creativity of employees, without resistance, for future corporate use. Managerialist commentators, inspired by the prospect of 'positive power', would see such a scenario as a good thing, one that allows for the exercise of enhanced individual discretion. Hence, virtuous learning (seen from the point of view of the organisation's management, the class warriors would no doubt add) will characterise the future.

I have my doubts about both scenarios. Instead, I propose that, for the future, the trick will be to facilitate organisational learning that is not so embedded in past memory and constraining rules that it cannot learn, which is to say that it cannot remember to forget. Systematic and negotiated remembering and forgetting involve dialogue and reform between stakeholders and members; it involves, as we have seen, configuring desire, understanding and trust in reciprocal relations.

Organisation must always be built from those flows of power and knowledge, of memory, of remembering and forgetting, which link diverse understandings that fuse around technologies, and other artefacts that carry past designs and future applications. Thus, practical organisational learning always involves imagination, the insight that can enable people to be more than clever, to be intelligent, in the sense that the Maquarie Dictionary defines, as 'having the faculty of understanding'. Perhaps, as suggested by the great German intellectual, Max Weber (1978, 1948), managers and management academics require training in those skills of interpretative understanding that he termed *verstehende Soziologie*?

C. Wright Mills, whose words began this paper, said of such an imagination that it 'enables its possessor to understand the larger historical scene in terms of its meaning for the inner life and the external career of a variety of individuals' (Mills 1970: 11). Such an imagination provides a capacity to connect with and understand the rationalities that others use to configure their sense, of their organisation, their organising and those organisations that structure their lives. It is in the tensions between public rhetoric and private anxieties, the 'personal troubles of milieu' and the 'public issues of social structure' (Mills 1970: 14), that such an imagination might work, as revealed in the case of the MUA dispute.

Where sociological imagination is absent, it is all too easy for a singular conception of rationality to rule. On the one hand, ordinary men and women can be easily trapped in their organisations by populist political imaginations. In Australia we know this as 'Hansonism' (after the right-wing politician, Pauline Hanson), imagining transcendence through memories of organisational life protected by the policies of White Australia and McEwanism: protectionist rules come flooding back, like repressed memories, in the form of nightmares weighing on the imagination of the present, remembering more than they forget.

On the other hand, organisational elites can be easily restricted in their imagination by the consultancy advice that they rent on the market. Typically, in such cases, consulting cleverness can leave important questions implicitly hanging in the margin of its recommendations, like a dangling participle that does not specify those persons or specific subjects that comprise its subject – the organisation. The stakeholders are all too often implicitly limited only to 'the shareholders'. When diverse practices are reduced to best practice, for instance, the question of 'best for whom?' may remain silent. It is assumed that what is best for short-term shareholder value will be good for the organisation long term. When social reality is reduced only to accounting fictions, the question of how and what these fictions do, when they do what they do, remains implicit. Organising is too easily imagined only as a project of an elite. Through such reductions and replacements, those aspects of their organisational lives that trouble ordinary women and men can become sacrificed to the issues of the day – as the rich and powerful see them.

Note that I am not arguing against the search by others for quality, learning and excellence in organisations. I just don't think that singular designs for, and conceptions of, organisational reality can provide them. I would go further and suggest that it would be an unwise organisation that subordinated itself only to techniques that *prescribed* exploitative learning just as much as it would be to one that *proscribed* the rationality inherent in any such techniques. Either option would threaten organisational intelligence and diminish opportunities for exploratory learning – not only for those being organised and those organising, but also for those researching them.

Perhaps, by way of a conclusion, I should spell out in clear terms some of the implications of my position. I do not think it is the academic's task to become a partisan. 'Scientists are much more in the position of seeking to understand how people are succeeding in making sense of the contemporary situation, rather than being able to supply answers to their problems', as Albrow (1997: 7) suggests. A wise academic, one whose premises are agnostic, would not affirm a particular mode of rationality, taking sides, as it were, from the lectern or in the lecture theatre, irrespective of their convictions. Other platforms serve that end. It is not correspondence with the specific realities that particular interests represent that constitutes good theory, but the quality of its imagination – especially, as I have argued elsewhere, the degree of reflexivity of that imagination in being able to account for its own practices (Clegg and Hardy 1996). And it is this sense of vocation that forms the keystone of that which I profess.

Notes

1   Except, in Australia, the state of Queensland, where the politics of continuing protection of legal interests ensure that conveyancing still remains a fiefdom for solicitors.

References

Adler, P.S. (1993) 'The learning bureaucracy: New United Motor Manufacturing, Inc.', *Research in Organisation Behaviour* 15: 111–94.

Adler, P.S. and Cole, R.E. (1993) 'Designed for learning: a tale of two plants', *Sloan Management Review* 34, 3: 85–94.

Albrow, M. (1997) *Do Organisations Have Feelings?* London: Routledge.

Bauman, Z. (1987) *Legislators and Interpreters*, Cambridge: Polity Press.

Burack, E.R., Burack, M.D., Miller, D.M. and Morgan, K. (1994) 'New paradigm approaches in strategic human resource management', *Group and Organisation Management* 19, 2: 141–59.

Clegg, S.R. and Hardy, C. (1996) 'Representations' in S.R. Clegg, C. Hardy and W.R. Nord (eds) *Handbook of Organization Studies*, London: Sage (pp. 676–708).

Clegg, S.R., Boreham, P. and Dow, G. (1984) 'From the politics of production to the production of politics', *Thesis Eleven* 9: 16–32.

Cusamano, M.A. and Selby, R.W. (1996) *Microsoft Secrets – How the World's Most Powerful Software Company Creates Technology, Shapes Markets, and Manages People*, New York: HarperCollinsBusiness.

Cyert, R.M. and March, J.G. (1963) *A Behavioural Theory of the Firm*, Englewood Cliffs: Prentice-Hall.

Janowitz, M. (1959) 'Changing patterns of organisational authority: the military establishment', *Administrative Science Quarterly* 3, 4: 473–93.

Karpin Report (1995) *Enterprising Nation: Renewing Australia's Managers to Meet the Challenges of the Asia-Pacific Century: Report of the Industry Task Force on Leadership and Management Skills*, Canberra: AGPS.

Levinthal, D.A. and March, J.G. (1993) 'The myopia of learning', *Strategic Management Journal* 14: 95–112.

Millett, M. (1998) 'And the culprit is … Sydney', *Sydney Morning Herald*, Friday 1 May: 21.

Mills, C.W. (1940) 'Situated actions and vocabularies of motive', *American Sociological Review* 5: 904–13.

Mills, C.W. (1970) [1959] *The Sociological Imagination*, Harmondsworth: Penguin.

Rawlinson, M. and Wells, P. (1996) 'Taylorism, lean production and the automotive industry', *Asia Pacific Business Review* 2, 4: 189–204.

Roberts, K.H. and Grabowski, M. (1996) 'Organisations, technology and structuring', in S.R. Clegg, C. Hardy and W. Nord (eds) *Handbook of Organisation Studies*, London: Sage.

Roy, D. (1958) ' "Banana time": job satisfaction and informal interaction', *Human Organisation* 18: 158–68.

Taylor, F.W. (1911) *Principles of Scientific Management*, New York: Harper.

Weber, M. (1948) *From Max Weber: Essays in Sociology*, London: Routledge and Kegan Paul.

Weber, M. (1978) *Economy and Society*, Berkeley: University of California Press.

Weick, K.E. (1996) 'Drop your tools: an allegory for organisation studies', *Administrative Science Quarterly* 41, 2: 301–13.

Williamson, O.E. (1985) *The Economic Institutions of Capitalism*, New York: Free Press.

Zuboff, S. (1988) *In the Age of the Smart Machine*, London: Heinemann.

6 Knowledge and control in the Japanese workplace

Keiko Morita

Japanese management systems and economic power

Evaluations of the Japanese management system and its various practices seem to have swung from one extreme to the other. When Japan's doors were forcibly opened by the West over a century ago, subsequent industrialisation took place in the context of external threats and the urgent need for technological development. The political economy of Japan shifted rapidly in favour of fostering special skills and capabilities needed to compete on equal terms with its Western counterparts. During the 1950s and 1960s, the growth of the Japanese economy was less visible than it was to become over the ensuing thirty years. Not surprisingly, the 'real' interest in Japanese industrial and managerial practices came when Japan's economic power became highly visible. The gaze of the West, particularly the US, turned towards Japan's hitherto unknown methods of capital accumulation, its intercorporate alliance structures and its managerial practices. For many Western observers, Japan's post-war economic development has been impressive. Its management system has produced continuous, highly productive processes. This chapter examines critically the Japanese industrial scene with a particular emphasis on workplace management methods, considering some of the unforeseen consequences of the Western world's uncritical appropriation of these methods for the new production of knowledge at work.

Japan's management system is, or more accurately was, often praised. It is also often implied that Japan's work force lives and works as if in an 'iron cage', a concept borrowed from Max Weber. This chapter elucidates some of the dynamics of Japanese workplaces. It begins with a brief account of Weber's notion of the 'iron cage', and then continues with a two-level analysis of the Japanese industrial scene. The first considers the hierarchical structure of Japanese industry at the national level. The second examines the labour relations practices of leading companies and how these practices shape the 'mental state' of the workforce. In particular, quality control activities are used to illustrate how continuous daily controls influence that mental state. Also discussed are reported cases of 'death from overwork', as a recent phenomenon that is suggestive of a distortion of lives in the work force and arguably reinforcing Weber's concerns about the darker sides of modernisation.

Weber's concept of capitalism and the 'iron cage'

In Weber's seminal work *The Protestant Ethic and the Spirit of Capitalism*, he set out a possible explanation for the origin of the spirit of capitalism with its moralistic view of work and its determination to rationalise all aspects of life. The question Weber raised was: what had provided the initial motivation for capitalist activity? According to Weber, the source of the motivation was to be found in the transformation of religious ideas brought about by the Reformation, particularly the impact of Calvinism. There was, he argued, a resemblance between the capitalist spirit and the attitudes of Protestants towards hard work and wealth, for the latter also emphasised duty and austerity, encouraged economic diligence, condemned laziness and wastefulness, and spread the virtues of thrift and productivity. It was his hypothesis that the spirit of capitalism is the secularised successor of the Protestant ethic, and that the latter was a cause of the former.

The vital feature of the Protestant ethic, Weber emphasised, was the idea of 'the calling': that is, the idea that people have been 'called by God' to the position that they occupy in this world. The concept of 'the calling' as an obligation of individuals in their everyday life turned the task of earning a living into a religious duty. What was striking about the effects of Lutheranism and Calvinism was that they brought into the lives of ordinary religious believers demands for self-monitoring and self-control that had, hitherto, been asked only of the most advanced of religious practitioners. What the Protestant sects collectively created was a new mentality, which involved the thorough disciplining of every detail of practical life. Weber held that it was through the formation of this stringently managed attitude to everyday activity that the Protestant ethic helped create the spirit of capitalism. It was a further feature of that spirit that it encouraged the extensive rationalisation of life, the extension of calculation and control to all its sectors, and in particular, to the sphere of economic action.

Calvinism manifested that God's world gives to people opportunities to add to God's greatness by doing well in their calling. It would therefore be sinful to fail to take even the smallest opportunity that God gives. There was no reason to regard oneself as being prevented by the obligations of tradition from taking whatever economic opportunity life offered. On the contrary, to do so would be to reject something that God had given. Accordingly, the inevitable result of such remorseless profit-seeking would be the prosperity of the business:

> As far as the influence of the Puritan outlook extended, under all circumstances – and this is, of course, much more important than the mere encouragement of capital accumulation – if it favoured the development of a rational bourgeois economic life; it was the most important, and above all the only consistent influence in the development of that life. It stood at the cradle of the modern economic man.
>
> (Weber 1996: 174)

Weber did not expect that modern capitalism could directly achieve the emancipation of humankind. Instead, he foresaw the tragedy of modernity. The advancement of capitalism, in his eyes, contributes much to the meaninglessness of modern life. Within its vast administrative structures, the individual becomes increasingly a mere cog in an impersonal machine. Life becomes conducted within an 'iron cage' of regulation and oppression.

For Weber, the Puritan wanted to work in a 'calling'; we are forced to do so. For when asceticism was carried out of monastic cells into everyday life and began to dominate worldly morality, it did its part in building the tremendous cosmos of the modern economic order. The care for external goods should only lie on the shoulders of:

> the saint like a light cloak, which can be thrown aside at any moment …
> But fate decreed that the cloak should become an iron cage … No one knows who will live in this cage in the future, or whether at the end of this tremendous development entirely new prophets will arise, or there will be a great rebirth of old ideas and ideals, or, if neither, mechanized petrifaction, embellished with a sort of convulsive self-importance.
>
> (Weber 1996: 181)

Here, the ethos of capitalism itself became the 'iron cage' of modernity. Weber continued to express this tragedy of modernity in this way: 'For of the last stage of this cultural development, it might well be truly said: Specialists without spirit, sensualists without heart; this nullity imagines that it has attained a level of civilization never before achieved' (Weber 1996: 182).

Japan's industrial relations environment

Based on Weber's discussion of capitalism, this section examines the control system in Japanese industry in order to reveal the extent to which an 'iron cage' has developed. At the national level, the hierarchical structure of the industry which maintains and reproduces the shape of the 'iron cage' is discussed. At the organisational level, the industrial relations practices which shape the 'mental approach' of the work force in leading companies is outlined.

The hierarchical structure of Japanese industry

Despite an image of homogeneity, Japan's industry is characterised by a distinct differentiation. The powerful corporate sector of large companies co-exists with a marginalised sector of small and medium enterprises. Many of the latter play the role of being subcontractors, small suppliers and distributors. Yet these small and medium-sized enterprises are related to the small number of big companies in a hierarchical manner (with the 'big' companies at the top of the hierarchy) (Hein 1993).

According to the *Ministry of Labor White Book* (1993), over 99 per cent of offices/factories have fewer than 300 full-time employees. Over 80 per cent of the full-time employed population work in small and medium-sized companies, of which 55 per cent employ fewer than 100 full-time workers. The number of Japanese offices/factories with more than 1,000 full-time employees in the manufacturing industry is only 0.2 per cent and these employ around 14 per cent of the country's workers. By comparison, in the UK 40 per cent of employees work in offices/factories with over 1,000 full-time employees.

The hierarchical industrial system works effectively for the larger companies. For structural reasons, the parent company need control only the first layer of subcontractors. The countless numbers of small and medium-sized companies absorb any general economic shocks, such as a sudden rise in the value of the yen or other monetary crises. These small and medium-sized companies grow dramatically during boom periods, but equally drastically they are the first-line victims of any downturn in the economy, often representing over 99 per cent of Japanese enterprise bankruptcies. As a consequence of these companies 'absorbing' the shock, the large corporate sector has been able to introduce innovative systems of industrial manufacturing and management as the large corporate bodies have, in the past, been less vulnerable. For instance, the philosophy of total quality control with zero defects – as the only acceptable quality level – works to download the risks of defective parts from the manufacturer to the (marginalised) suppliers. As a consequence, suppliers can become 'captive' to a specific manufacturer. Similarly, 'just in time' production systems download the burden of holding work-in-process inventories until needed for production processes in the factory.

The development and maintenance of this industrial structure owes much to the workings of the nexus of government and big business, wherein politics and economics are intimately fused. The underlying belief in the value of this interdependency is that, on the one hand, business is the lifeblood and the essence of the nation's life; on the other hand, without solid connections to those wielding political powers, no business can survive, grow and prosper (Eccleston 1995: 47–9).

The bureaucracy has been working to help, protect and promote Japanese business. 'Administrative guidance' comes from government ministries in the form of government initiatives that define the direction and shape of Japan's industry (Johnson 1986; Prestowitz 1988). Certain industries, seen as having potential, become actively promoted as 'strategic'. These industries are given access to debt capital on easy terms under a government-supported banking system. With the knowledge that it is ultimately the government (or, rather, the entire nation) that bears the risks, such industries can incur debt to a level that elsewhere would be considered financially suicidal.

Consequently, the labour market has also been separated into an elite group that works for big business and the civil service, and a marginalised group that works in the small business sector or as part-timers in the large sector (Eccleston 1995: 234–8). Although the great majority of the Japanese labour force do not work in big companies, they are nevertheless working for and under them and, ultimately, in the interest of the state. While the captive elite group of the work force is 'normalised' and appears loyal and committed to the organisation, their behaviour may represent not intrinsic obedience, but a compromise between the opportunities, desired goals, and possible alternatives available (Marsh and Mannari 1977; Morita 1995). I shall explain some of the consequences of this 'captivity' for individual workers later in this chapter.

Industrial relations practices

Recruitment practices

Joining a leading company in Japan is a process full of symbolism and ritual. A 'mainstream' worker will attend the company entrance ceremonies held on 1 April every year. Entry into the company is treated as an employee becoming an 'adopted' child of the 'company family'. Each recruitment batch identifies itself by the year of recruitment and progresses through the company as a group. The group identity is used to assist a new recruit to forge a strong sense of kinship within the company. When these new recruits come to work, they are sometimes placed in company dormitories, where they live and which are considered not only part of the company's employee welfare but also a place for employee education and socialisation.

Recruitment into the leading companies is highly selective. It is not on the basis of skills, competence or even what an individual has learnt in school, but rather on the ultimate criterion as to whether the prospective employee will be able to fit into the company as a loyal member. Docility, adaptability, discipline and the ability to develop loyalty and commitment to the company are the overriding requirements (Lu 1989).

The principle of long-service seniority has dominated the employment scene for much of the post-war period. The common practice at that time for companies was to resort to in-house training of their own hand-picked workers because of the lack of a skilled labour force. The primary quality required was therefore not skill or competence for a particular job, but rather a docile attitude. Out of this recruitment philosophy grew the practice of preferring people fresh from school/colleges. Those who might have gained experience elsewhere, but were changing jobs, were seen as potential misfits – their commitment and undivided loyalty would remain suspect.

The growth in the service industry since the early 1970s has promoted companies to hire more flexible workers to meet their changing needs. These flexible workers were initially employed part-time, on a contract or temporary basis, and supplied by staff placement agencies. From the 1990s, since rapid technological change has widened the diversity of customer needs and due to increasing globalisation, companies have started to employ some specialists directly from the external labour market. According to the Ministry of Labour's basic wage structure statistics for 1995, over 10 per cent of Japanese corporations have institutionalised the hiring of outside workers on a regular basis. Among the companies with over 3,000 employees, almost 20 per cent utilise these casual employees. Nevertheless, the mainstream methods of employment remain unchanged.

Lifetime employment

'Lifetime employment' is a second feature of the industrial labour process. This phrase must be interpreted as being somewhat imprecise. First, employment contracts never state that the individual concerned is to be employed until retirement. Second, even the majority of workers in the established companies do not work at the same company until they retire. It is common for an employee to be transferred among companies within a group under an umbrella company (Eccleston 1995: 61–7).

In the post-war years, governments at both national and local levels and private industries required an organised and stratified work force. Corporations needed to secure a body of skilled workers as well as younger and cheaper new recruits in order to grow. As a result, lifetime employment became a general practice of major corporations. While lifetime employment is deemed desirable, it is not a reality for the majority of workers in Japan. During the high growth period throughout the 1960s and into the beginning of the 1970s, less than one third of Japanese workers were employed by well-established companies, or in the public sector, and enjoyed this type of employment. It is commonly believed by smaller companies that such an approach reinforces worker productivity and company loyalty, and through this device they look for a higher quality working force.

Job rotation

A third feature of industrial relations is the practice of job rotation that moves the workers in one company from one section to other sections continuously. According to the statistics from a national survey conducted by the Institute for Research on Labour Management and Government Policies, for college graduate Japanese 'salary men' (a term generally referring to white-collar employees), the frequency of job rotation at different hierarchical levels displayed the general pattern shown in Table 6.1.

Job rotation has an advantage in cutting across the maze of bureaucracy in larger companies. It is deemed important in preparing employees to become future middle-level or top managers. For future managers in mid-career, job rotation provides opportunities for the company to observe

Table 6.1   Patterns of job rotation at different hierarchical levels

Hierarchical position	Entry age	Number of job rotations at that hierarchical level
Non-titled position (*Hira shain*)	22	4 to 6 times[*]
Sub-section chief (*Kakari cho*)	35	2.7 times
Section chief (*Kacho*)	45	4.5 times
Manager (*Bucho*)	55	6.2 times

Source   Based on Shimada (1994)

[*]Estimated

their suitability for higher positions. While most managers and regular employees undergo job rotation, only a handful finally emerge as directors. If the cost of the system were viewed strictly, the expense would be prohibitive. The rationale, however, is that incurring a great expense to produce only a few directors still leaves a cadre of committed middle-level executives who have a full knowledge of the whole company.

Seniority

A fourth characteristic feature of industrial management is the seniority system. The core of the seniority system relates to the use of promotions so that they do not to create too much difference between different people's promotion and income levels. That is, if there is a small difference in promotions or salary rises, the victor is happy, but the loser also sees a chance to overtake and therefore works even harder. The implications of this equal practice could be a system devised to keep as many people as possible in the race for promotion as long as possible.

Even in companies where seniority-based salary is the norm, there have always been salary disparities among the workers who joined the company in the same year. This was because their monthly pay was based upon two components: those determined by individual characteristics, and those related to the nature of the work and therefore the capabilities required. The individual's characteristics are independent of year-by-year perform-ance factors such as age, seniority (length of continuous service with the company), education and special qualifications related to the individual's educational background. The job-related factors are the type of job one holds, the level of performance and efficiency, and required skills and abili-ties. All these components contribute to salary differentials among employees.

Current salary structures exhibit some revisions made over the past fifteen years. The salaries do not increase the way they used to. The decline in actual salaries among those with only high school degrees over the age of 55 suggests that they may be outliving their usefulness in the eyes of management. In many companies, salaries stop increasing after 55, and in some cases salaries actually decrease between 55 and 60.

According to the Ministry of Labour's statistics, in the 1970s the mandatory retirement age in most companies was 55 or younger. In 1980, approximately half of the Japanese corporations had their mandatory retirement age set at 55 and the other half at 60. By 1991, over 70 per cent of all companies had raised their mandatory retirement age to 60 or over. Ninety-five per cent of large companies with over 5,000 employees but only 67 per cent of companies with fewer than 100 employees had set their mandatory retirement age at 60 or over. In 1980, 30 per cent of those companies with more than 5,000 workers were offering early retirement plans as an option. By 1991, 20 per cent were offering their workers the option to retire from the job before they reached 50, while 40 per cent offered early retirement to those between 50 and 55. Generally, the larger the corporation, the earlier they offered the option of retirement. This has meant that while corporations have extended their mandatory retirement age to 60 as a system, they have given themselves as many opportunities as they require to shed older workers in order to cut costs (Shimada 1994).

The workers who follow this industrial labour process are what can be called 'company-holics'. While it can be argued that a company-holic mentality is related to a workaholic mentality, the two phenomena represent distinct behavioural patterns. On the one hand, addiction to work does not preclude labour mobility across different companies. On the other hand, addiction to one particular company does not guarantee a workaholic attitude automatically. A company-holic worker sets their boundary of knowledge and their mind only on matters related to their company.

'Quality circles' and cases of continuous control

From a management perspective, a company-holic approach is not regarded as dysfunctional. Moreover, through quality control activities the industrial relations system ensures the maintenance of a total work perspective that emphasises continuous control, or, as Weber put it, the 'iron cage'. One of the features in Japanese management often praised as an essential part of the 'economic miracle' has been its ability to ensure quality control. In adopting Western-style industrial management and production control, the Japanese went a step further by mobilising the work force into focusing on quality and productivity improvements. *Jishu Kanri* (JK) (self-control) became widespread as the vehicle for quality control (QC), zero defects (ZD), suggestion system and other similar quality improvement activities undertaken in small groups.

The ZD and QC activities were introduced in heavy industries from the first half of 1960s. But their popularity got a tremendous boost when Nippon Electric Corporation (NEC) introduced ZD activities in 1965. In 1969, the Japan Federation of Employers' Associations wrote a report entitled *Ability-Based Control*, and presented it as the definitive blueprint for what they termed 'small group activity' schemes.

QC activities in Japan are in principle a voluntary activity with no extra pay, but in fact often the main purpose behind being a member of a QC circle is to achieve a promotion or incremental assessment. When the

QC circle is set up at the workplace, with the foreman as one of the members, few workers can be so brave as not to participate if the foreman has the power to recommend workers' promotions and increments. When a circle with five to eight workers is selected for presentation of their QC report, circle members go to great lengths to prepare for their speech in front of managers and colleagues. One worker at Nippon Steel wrote:

> The foreman encouraged me to make a presentation. He told me that it was a good opportunity for me for a future promotion and to become future chairman of meetings. But it was stressful. I had to prepare transparencies, the drafts of my speech, and put everything in my mind. Then I had to practice my speech in front of my wife and children every night ... We could not dream of going on any holidays. When all was almost ready, I had to do the rehearsal at my work place and invite technical officers to check up on me.
>
> (Saito 1990: 207–8)

Another worker found he could not sleep after being selected as QC leader. He started taking sleeping pills and finally suffered from neurosis. In the Sumitomo Chemical Company, a worker committed suicide. He had reportedly been under painful stress because he had not presented well in a QC circle meeting and was anxious about his delayed promotion. One day he drank agricultural pesticide and killed himself. He was 43 years old.

ZD activity can be seen as a way of making workers feel guilty about mistakes. In banks, for example, mistakes by individuals and by sections are checked every day and recorded on graphs. These graphs are put on the notice-board of the company dining corner. The number and frequency of mistakes are summarised at head office, and this influences the formal assessment of the leaders at the branch level. In these circumstances, it is no wonder that some workers report being terribly scared of making mistakes and start dreaming of running away from the job, or, even worse, committing suicide (see Totsuka and Ueyanagi 1991). An individual's mistake is not only their *own* mistake, but is also considered a sectional or branch-wide mistake. This sense of fear and guilt is pervasive. As one worker declared, 'I really do not know whether this is Quality Control of "products" or Quality Control of "human beings"' (Saito 1990: 291–2). Total quality control does not mean total quality control on products/services, but on the totality of the worker's mind and sense of humanity. This all-embracing control starts from the very beginning of a worker's life, and it certainly affects the knowledge formation of workers (Kumazawa 1986).

The use of small group activities spread more widely after the oil crisis in the 1970s under the pressure of restructuring the industry from mass production to value-added production. Their use spread from production divisions to secretariat divisions, and to research and development divisions. In the 1980s, the use of small group activities spread into small and medium enterprises through the subcontracting processes of big companies (Gordon 1993). In addition to the small group activities, most big companies have many kinds of company-supported activities such as sports clubs and cultural classes. These activities constitute one of the components of the so-called 'company welfare system', which a number of scholars have praised as a human-centred tendency or a humanistic approach by Japanese management. For example, Toyota has thirty-one sports groups and forty hobby–cultural groups throughout the company, and workers can participate in them almost free of charge. Also, at each job place, many recreation activities are available, such as baseball games, volleyball tournaments, golf competitions and chess games. Officially, participation in these activities is voluntary. Those groups supported by the company seem to unify and promote workers' feelings and to improve the working morale in accordance with the company dictates. In addition, when viewed through the Weberian lens of bureaucratic rationality, the groups serve to regulate workers' free time and dominate their mentality – without employees even being fully aware of the extent of such regulation and domination.

Under this type of control, the company can programme as well as schedule the worker's life. At the end of one year of working in Toyota after finishing high school, workers can get a loan for a new Toyota car at the age of 19 to 20. Three years later, when they have cleared their car loans, they are expected to marry (at around 23 to 25 years of age). For the next ten years, they can stay in company flats with their families. Meanwhile, they start saving to buy their own houses. They can get a 12-year Toyota home loan, and later upgrade by asking for another 25-year loan for a 'special' Toyota home in specially fenced Toyota housing estates. Since the prices of Japanese houses and land are extraordinarily expensive, many workers have no choice but to buy a special Toyota home. Thus, if a worker stays in the company's flat for ten years and gets a special Toyota home with a 25-year loan, they will only be free from the company's loan commitments when they are about 58 years old. While clearing these loans, they would not be able to quit their job unless they can forgo both their job and their house. All this time, whether in the company dormitory or flat or in their own house, all their neighbours will be company colleagues. Their entire community is under the net of company control (Kamata 1983). Under this type of continuous control, workers are not only in a physical 'cage' but are also mentally caged.

Karoshi – death from overwork

Karoshi, meaning literally 'death from overwork', signifies death from the over-exertion and stress due to working too much. The term has been used in the social medicine field since the 1980s, but it is now commonly used in general conversations. Karoshi has spread to nearly all industries and job types, regardless of age, sex or position in the company. In June 1988, when lawyers, physicians and labour campaigners set up the 'Karoshi Hotline' national network, it was inundated by inquiries from widows and other survivors. This triggered the rapid spread of the word 'karoshi' and the term has come into broad use to describe the dark side of Japan at a time when it was considered to be one of the economic giants.

> Defined in more technical terms, it is a condition in which psychologically unsound work processes are allowed to continue in a way that disrupts the worker's normal work and life rhythms, leading to a build-up of fatigue in the body and a chronic condition of overwork, accompanied by a worsening of pre-existent high blood pressure and hardening of the arteries, and finally resulting in a fatal breakdown [i.e. outright death].
>
> (National Institute of Public Health, quoted in Ueyanagi 1988: 2)

The causes of fatigue build-up in Japanese workplaces are well documented and include:

- heavy physical labour;
- long hours of overtime;
- working without days off;
- late-night work (and other factors that obstruct biological rhythms);
- excessive stress (resulting from factors like over-intense work responsibilities);
- solitary job transfers (for instance, being transferred to a different and distant workplace, a different locality, town, city or country);
- undesired job assignments or transfers.

To illustrate the everyday reality of the karoshi phenomenon, a case study follows, which the Karoshi Hotline reported in detail (Ueyanagi 1988).

Alpha Restaurants is one of three major chains in Japan. Its 1985 sales revenue amounted to about 48 million yen. Alpha is listed on the Tokyo stock exchange. It is one of the key companies of Omega Group, which is a large retail outlet group made up of discount stores, convenience stores and supermarkets. Alpha Restaurants was established in 1973 through a technical affiliation with an American company.

Mr A, an employee of Alpha Restaurants who was 20 years old at the time, was a healthy young man of average build and normal blood pressure, with no previous symptoms or past history of illness. When one looks at the events leading up to the onset of Mr A's symptoms, what become clear are the horrifying working conditions in this top-ranking company, which boasted of having 'American technology and service and Japanese spirit'.

The company had 310 outlets, 1,510 full-time employees (including 66 women) with an average age of 27, and 5 years' average length of service. The monthly average number of part-time workers was 5,575 (this average is based on an 8-hour working day). As is evident, there was an exceptionally high reliance on part-time workers. Based on simple calculations using these figures, this would mean that one outlet would employ 4 to 5 full-time employees and about 18 part-time employees. Since part-time workers work only 4 to 6 hours per day, the actual number of part-time workers could have been as many as 30 to 50 per restaurant, ten times the number of full-time employees. Since the average age of the full-time employees was only 27, it also means that the salaries of these workers were low.

Mr A, born in 1963, had worked for over a year with a wood products company after high school graduation. When he joined Alpha Restaurants in Osaka, his conscientious character was appreciated even among the small number of full-time employees. As a rising star, he was gradually promoted and sent from one new restaurant to another. In his fourth year, in March 1988, he was made an assistant manager of the ABC Restaurant, the oldest and the largest outlet in Osaka. If he were to gain a reputation for his work at this restaurant, it was conceivable that he would be assigned to a new outlet somewhere else as manager.

There were approximately 60 employees at the ABC Restaurant. Besides the manager and two or three cooks, the rest of workers were part-time temporary staff. ABC Restaurant's manager was in overall control, but at night it was the assistant managers who had full responsibility for running the restaurant. As will be described later, most of Mr A's responsibilities were at night. He was in name an assistant manager, but his work included managerial responsibilities as well as responsibility for part-timers' work. In other words, he was involved in every aspect of running the restaurant.

Mr A started working at the ABC Restaurant on 4 March 1988. He then started suffering from symptoms of cerebral infarction in August of the same year. During this period, Mr A's work schedule was as follows: for the five-month period from March to July, his working hours, as recorded on his time card alone, added up to 1,523 hours, making an average of 3,305 hours per month or a daily average of 13 to 15 hours. In addition, he commuted an hour each way to and from work, which meant he was spending up to 17 hours per day on the job. As a result, he often had fewer than 5 hours of sleep a day. In order to ensure extra sleep, he would often skip meals at home. When he was on the night shift his daily pattern was to come home about noon and go straight to bed, wake up in the late afternoon and, after having a meal around 5 p.m., leave for work around 6 p.m. In April 1988, he fell asleep at the steering wheel of his car and crashed into an ornamental rock in his neighbour's garden.

Mr A's actual working hours were in fact much longer than those calculated above. Although the time cards from March to August show 45 holidays and days off, 13 of these days were spent at work when 3 to 8 hours a day were spent in tallying the sales and production control records. Also not included are the weekly 2-hour managers' meetings. Of the remaining days off, 14 were spent between the times when his shift changed from nights to days and again from days to nights. The result was that because these days off were spent adjusting to the shift changes, he had no chance to recover from fatigue. The astonishing fact is that in five months he had only five days of rest.

Around 20 July, students started their summer vacation and there was a sudden increase in customers. The annual festival at a nearby shrine followed this from 30 July to 1 August. That year, business reached a peak on 31 July, when there were 1,872 customers, twice the normal number.

On 6 August, Mr A got home at 2 a.m. and went to bed at 3 a.m. Unable to sleep because of the heat, he got up at 10 a.m., had some breakfast, and went back to bed at 1 p.m. He drifted in and out of sleep, with the oppressive feeling that he should get back to work as soon as possible because of the rush that would come with the annual All Souls Festival, which started on the 7th. At 2 p.m. he got up to go to the bathroom and collapsed.

At the hospital it was found that Mr A was paralysed on his right side and was having difficulty speaking. About a week later, he manifested symptoms of extreme psychological disturbance: loss of self-control, hyperactivity, disturbed consciousness and hysterical laughter. For days he ran about the hospital, shouting. At about the time when the night shift at the restaurant would begin, he would get out of bed and 'go to work', heading toward the nurses' station. He would sit at the nurses' desk, which for him had become the restaurant counter, and shout at the startled nurses, 'Hey! No slacking off, you guys!' and later, when his brother came to visit him, Mr A grabbed his brother's bag and tried to leave the hospital.

When asked where he was going, he became unruly and said, 'I have to go to the restaurant now.' A short time later that same month (August 1988), Mr A died, at the age of 25. One may say this is a very extreme case. But from the report of Karoshi Hotline, karoshi is a spreading phenomenon in almost all industries. On 18 June 1988, Karoshi Hotline counters were opened in seven major urban centres around Japan: Sapporo, Sendai, Tokyo, Kyoto, Osaka, Kobe and Fukuoka. The number of consultations phoned in about karoshi victims far exceeded the organisers' expectations, with 135 calls coming in nationwide on the first day alone. The calls came from family members, relatives, fellow workers, labour unions and others. Karoshi Hotline received some 4,150 calls, mostly from widows of workers who had died from overwork between 1988 and 1996 (Karoshi Hotline 1996). In the same period, 185 cases of suicide from overwork were reported. Yet because of social prejudice about suicide, many relatives, especially wives and children, would not dare to open cases on behalf of the overworked-deceased.

According to Totsuka and Ueyanagi (1991), each year nearly 1,000 victims of overwork apply for workers' compensation; 5 to 10 per cent are awarded such grants. Almost all workers are covered by the government-managed insurance system under the Workers' Compensation Insurance law. All employers are obliged to pay an insurance premium. Insurance benefits are paid to victims who file claims with the Labour Standards Office and have their claim approved as a work-related injury. In the 1989 fiscal year, 777 claims for workers' compensation for cardiovascular disease were filed. Of these, 110 were awarded; 30 were for non-accidental disease (karoshi) and the others were for cardiovascular diseases resulting from physical accidents such as head bruises. Unfortunately, but not surprisingly, it is almost impossible to obtain up-to-the-minute data on this phenomenon.

Escaping the cage?

Is it possible for the Japanese industrial relations system to free itself from the 'iron cage' and return to work under a 'cloak of enlightenment'? Several scenarios could be envisaged. One would be that the marginalised majority of the Japanese work force would gradually stop adopting the value system of the elite work force. They would then need to create new values and mentalities for themselves. Instead of being subject to the dominant elite value system in the work force, they would help create greater value diversity in society.

Another possibility is that Japan's social and political elite decides, largely for functional reasons, to change the nature of the 'iron cage' by altering work practices and values for the elite group of employees. As a result of the 1990s financial crises, a number of financial institutions and governmental organisations involved in the productive sector found their power and influence declining rapidly. The members of the work-force elite may no longer have long-term expectations of permanency, even if they are prepared to run the risk of dying from overwork. Some will refuse to continue and others will be forced to leave the 'iron cage'.

Although new leading industries and companies may emerge, and they too may have their new replacement elite work force, the dynamics of control will not be same. Under the acceleration of changes in the world economy and, particularly, increasing international competition, maintaining the protectionism of the 'iron cage' will be increasingly less feasible. In particular, it is my argument that the mental control that has been imposed through industrial relations practices, and which lies at the heart of Japanese quality control measures, will become increasingly untenable. The current 'iron cage' will become rusty and collapse from lack of maintenance. The new knowledge produced under such conditions is connected to a labyrinth of 'technologies', and in time we shall see if the work force leaves the 'iron cage', only to find some form of new super-alloy or perhaps even 'virtual' cage awaiting it.

References

Eccleston, B. (1995) *State and Society in Post-War Japan*, Cambridge: Polity Press.

Gordon, A. (1993) 'Contests for the workplace' in A. Gordon (ed.) *Postwar Japan as History*, Berkeley: University of California Press (pp. 373–94).

Hein, L.E. (1993) 'Growth versus success: Japan's economic policy in historical perspective' in A. Gordon (ed.) *Postwar Japan as History*, Berkeley: University of California Press (pp. 99–122).

Johnson, D. (1986) *MITI and the Japanese Miracle: The Growth of Industrial Policy, 1925–1975*, Stanford: Stanford University Press.

Kamata, S. (1983), *Jidosha Zetsubo Kōjyo: Aru Kisetsuko no Nikki (Hopeless Auto Factory: A Diary by One Seasonal Worker)*, Tokyo: Kodansha.

Karoshi Hotline (1996) 'Karoshi Hotline results', National Defence Council for Victims of KAROSHI, http://www.bekkoame.or.jp/i.karoshi/EnglishIndex/Emeeting/etotalreport.html

Kumazawa, M. (1986) *Shokubashi no Shura ni Ikitel (A Pandemonium of Job-Spot History)*, Tokyo: Chikuma Shobo.

Lu, D.J. (1989) *Inside Corporate Japan: The Art of Fumble-Free Management*, Tokyo: Charles E. Tuttle.

Marsh, R.M. and Mannari, H. (1977) *Modernization and the Japanese Factory*, Princeton: Princeton University Press.

Ministry of Labor, Japan (1993) *Labor White Book*, Tokyo: Ministry of Labor.

Morita, K. (1995) 'Power, ideology, and the Japanese state: with special reference to the control systems in the Japanese post-war industrial labour process', PhD thesis, University of Hull, UK.

Prestowitz, C.V. (1988) *Trading Places*, New York: Basic Books.

Saito, S. (1990) *Waganakiatoni Kozui wa Kitare! (After My Death, the Worst that Happens Would Not Matter!)*, Tokyo: Gendaishi Shuppankai.

Shimada, H. (1994) *Nihon no Koyo: 21seikiheno Saisekkei (Japanese Employment: Redesigning for the 21st Century)*, Tokyo: Chikuma Shinsho.

Totsuka, E. and Ueyanagi, T. (1991) 'Prevention of death from overwork and remedies for its victims', *National Defence Council for Victims of KAROSHI*, http://www.bekkoame.or.jp/i/karoshi/EnglishIndex/kokuren.html

Ueyanagi, T. (1988) '*Kaoshi 110ban no keka to kadai* (Progress and limitation of Karoshi Hotline)', *Rodo Horitsu Jyunpo* 1206 (December).

Weber, M. (1996) *The Protestant Ethic and the Spirit of Capitalism*, translated by T. Parsons, Los Angeles: Roxbury Publications.

7 Organisational knowledge, professional practice and the professional doctorate at work

Alison Lee, Bill Green and Marie Brennan

The relationship between what might be termed 'organisational knowledge' and higher education has always been complex, dynamic and contested. The university, primary institution for the formal accreditation of knowledge and higher learning during most of this century, has at the same time faced extensive critique for its consistent privileging of disciplinary and formal modes of knowledge production over the more situated knowledges and practices of knowledge production within workplaces (a canonical text in this regard being Schön 1983). In recent times, the rapid development of what has been termed the 'knowledge society' (Gibbons *et al.* 1994; Stehr 1994) has placed new demands on higher education. The university has come under pressure from a number of angles with regard to its role in the production of the new populations of 'knowledge workers' required by the 'new work order' of late capitalism (Gee *et al.* 1996). In the 1980s, education increasingly became linked to economic development in the context of globalised capitalism. Higher education, in particular, has been under major redefinition in its relation to the economy and work. Indeed, as Scott (1997: 36) notes, this relationship, while 'always latently dominant, … is now seen as the key determinant of the university's future development'. As funding pressures impact upon universities, they have responded by attempting to turn themselves into quasi-businesses. Such developments have had important effects on their external relationships, as well as their internal dynamics.

Arguably, the university is becoming displaced in its 'traditional' position of pre-eminence as the primary site for the production of knowledge (Gibbons *et al.* 1994; Scott 1995). Gibbons *et al.* produce a persuasive account of what they describe as a new mode of knowledge production; by this account, knowledge is produced, not in the enclosed space of the disciplinary university, but in 'the context of application'. This situation is predicated in turn upon the massive expansion of higher education after the Second World War and the emergence of a large population of highly educated workers. According to this account, and to those of analysts of 'fast capitalism' generally (e.g. Gee *et al.* 1996), new kinds of organisational structures and practices are emerging, ones which deploy the labour of 'knowledge workers'. These new 'knowledge workers' characteristically do not reproduce the forms of academic and professional socialisation, as typically in the universities but, rather, produce contextualised knowledge, fast, in other than formal, disciplinary ways, for competitive advantage. Scott's (1997: 41) naming of such organisations as 'knowledge institutions' signals the extent of the displacement of the modern idea of the university in this scenario.

Whatever the nature of the changes in the relationship of the university to its environment, though, it is clear that its role in the formal credentialling of knowledge workers remains, for the moment, central, and indeed is increasing, based at least on documented levels of participation (OECD 1995; Burgess 1998; Pearson and Ford 1996). More people are gaining higher levels of educational qualification, with the massive expansion of graduate study being one striking marker of the increasing search for advanced knowledge and skills. This is a situation of expansion, in terms of both supply and demand for specialist knowledge (Gibbons *et al.* 1994).

Doctoral education in particular has for more than a century been a major site for the training and credentialling of researchers within the university. As the modern university developed its contemporary focus on research in the nineteenth century (Wittrock 1993; Lee and Green 1997), the PhD, as an explicitly research-oriented degree, emerged to train new generations of researchers and to induct them into the new disciplinary knowledges. Since the introduction of the PhD in Germany in the mid-nineteenth century and its importation into the US in 1848, the research-based doctorate has grown internationally to assume primary importance during this century as the highest form of educational provision that the university offers. The possession of a PhD has been, at least since the end of the Second World War, the university's licence for independent, discipline-based research. The PhD has become so naturalised and entrenched in the story of the university and its modes of knowledge production that it is easy to overlook how recently it arrived. In the light of the recent rapid change and debate in higher education, however, it is hardly surprising that the PhD, and research training more generally, have come under intense scrutiny. This chapter is concerned with one outcome of such scrutiny in Australia – the emergence of an alternative form of doctoral education, the 'professional doctorate'.

In what follows, we discuss some of the salient conceptual and structural features of professional doctorates in Australia, understanding them to be in the business of producing both new and hybrid forms of knowledge, as well as new kinds of knowing subjects – professionals with formal research skills, along with specific understandings and dispositions, undertaking advanced research in the specific context of their workplaces. After a brief description of the emerging scene, we turn to a consideration of recent work on new modes of knowledge production, and hence return to discuss some of the implications of these new modes for research education, with specific reference to the professional doctorate. Our aim in this chapter, then, is twofold. First, we want to introduce and outline the new 'professional doctorate' as a distinctive innovation in doctoral research education, and to explore some of its implications and challenges. Second, we want to propose a necessary, albeit reconceptualised and changed, role for the university in this newly reconfigured research and advanced training scene – in so doing, and despite arguing here and elsewhere for its displacement, to bring the university 'back in', so to speak.

The emergence of the professional doctorate in Australia

The Australian federal government's Higher Education Council recommended in 1989 the introduction of 'doctoral programs more suited to professional settings in fields such as engineering, accounting, law, education and nursing' (NBEET 1989: 28). At the time, this recommendation was entirely consistent with the strong national policy emphasis on vocational education and the service role of universities in the production of useful knowledge so as to provide Australia with economic advantage in a global economy. In response to this, many new doctorates have been developed and offered in different fields throughout the 1990s. In 1989 there were only two such doctorates; in 1998 at least 63 different programmes were offered, in 19 discipline areas, with 13 new ones in 1996, 16 in 1997 and at least 6 in 1997 (Grichting 1998). In 1998, in the 31 participating universities, there were 1,162 professional doctorate students, with over half of these in the Doctor of Education (EdD) (Grichting 1998). The next largest group was the Doctor of Business Administration (DBA), with 9 offerings, then juridical science (8) and psychology (4) (Jongeling 1996). In addition to these, there are also professional doctorates in architecture, creative arts, environmental design, health services management, nursing, organisational dynamics, public administration, public health, science education, teaching, technology and the visual arts (Jongeling 1996). Still others, such as midwifery, have been introduced in 1999.

Professional doctorates are distinguished structurally from the PhD in Australia through the offering of coursework and other formal activity such as seminars, as well as in some cases a practicum component. (The Australian PhD, by contrast, almost exclusively consists only of a single extended written dissertation.) As well, the different professional doctorates are also diverse. This diversity is not only in terms of the different fields of study in which they are located, but also in terms of the extraordinary variation in what *counts* as a professional doctorate, within and across disciplines and within and across universities. It is worth detailing some of this diversity, which is in marked contrast to what appears to be the structural simplicity and stability of the PhD. The point here is not so much to suggest that there is not a great deal of complexity and diversity in actual offerings and practices of PhD education, as it is to suggest that the overt proliferation of differences in professional doctorates functions as a clear sign of the volatility and 'flexibility' of the doctoral education environment more generally (Pearson and Ford 1996; Evans 1998).

Variations in offerings that appear across the award cover a variety of significant features. There is a considerable divergence in the extent to which these doctorates count as research degrees, with just over half of existing professional doctorates meeting the formal government requirements (that is, 67 per cent of the programme must be 'research' for the degree to count as a research degree). Some professional doctorates are 100 per cent research based (such as the Doctor of Education at Deakin University), while some are 100 per cent coursework. Between these two extremes, the percentage of coursework ranges from 17 per cent to 67 per cent (Trigwell *et al.* 1997). In relation to enrolment patterns, three-quarters are part-time (Grichting 1998), with the majority of candidates being in full-time employment. Further, there is some variation in entrance requirements compared to the PhD. These degrees differ also in terms of the amount of clinical/field work required, in terms of formal relationships with industry bodies and professional groups, and in terms of the 'products' or outcomes of the degree candidature (e.g. portfolio, performance, thesis, assignments, workplace activities). Finally, a picture of variation in examination and supervision is emerging, with various in-house, academic-only and professional and industry forms of examination being practised and debated (Grichting 1998; Maxwell and Shanahan 1996).

In light of the emergence of the professional doctorate, as outlined above, the particular focus in what follows is on how this relates to the question of knowledge production *per se*. In a context, where disciplinary forms of knowledge and modes of knowledge production are fragmenting and where the locus of knowledge production has made a major general shift from the university to the workplace, such a focus is clearly necessary as a way of situating the significance of professional doctorates. Discussion in the international literature on postgraduate education focuses to a considerable extent on tensions between an 'education/training' binary (Noble 1997; Burgess *et al.* 1998), as the system's response to policy-driven pressures to link doctorates to labour-market demands or 'man-power requirements' (Burgess 1998: 141). Yet an examination of some of the emerging literature on the sociology of scientific knowledge requires doctoral education to be subjected to questioning in terms of its participation in broader shifts in epistemology.

Modes of knowledge production and changing research contexts

As we indicated in the introduction to this chapter, the university is being displaced in some sense from its primary place in the production of the world's knowledge. This is often represented as a radical departure from an almost timeless tradition in European history. Yet according to Scott (1995), a major research role for the university was really established in its contemporary, recognisable form in Britain only after the Second World War, although the importance of scientific research began to become apparent to government decision-makers, and hence became part of the new mission of universities, after the shocks sustained by the experience of the First World War. This emergence of a scientific research mission for universities coincided with the introduction of the PhD in Britain in 1917, 'borrowed' from Germany with its more than half a century head-start in the research stakes. The PhD, understood as an advanced form of research education, was developed in response to the need for basic research in the economic and strategic political advancement of the British nation. This coincidence had a significant effect on what came in British universities to count as a new model for knowledge production, and hence for research training, at the time. Much of the university's prestige during the remainder of this century has been predicated upon this assumption of its primacy. Other countries have had very different organisational structures for the production of research and the training of researchers. The British example is salutary here, in terms of the long-term influence of British education policy in Australia (not to mention more direct forms of influence in colonial times).

Scott questions, however, whether what came to be the 'standard account' of knowledge production in twentieth-century English universities was in fact an accurate account – or was it, as he puts it, always 'university-centric and anachronistic' (Scott 1995: 142)? These questions, and Scott's historical analysis, assume a particular significance at the present moment where the conditions under which knowledge is produced are being 'radically revised' (Scott 1995: 142) – this revision being in response both to the contemporary reordering of the economy and to shifts in intellectual culture, where the role of the university is much less clear. Scott describes these shifts, drawing on the extensive analysis of the team of scholars headed by Michael Gibbons (Gibbons *et al.* 1994). The Gibbons team identify two major and distinct narratives of knowledge production. We draw here first on Scott's own subsequent account of this analysis, reading it against the original discussion, which differs somewhat in point of emphasis, although in fact they are usefully read together. The first of these modes (called by the team 'Mode 1') is a narrative of knowledge production in which the university as a modern disciplinary enclosure has prime position; the second ('Mode 2') is one in which that position is not only usurped but where the dominance and accuracy of the first narrative ever to have accounted for the material conditions of knowledge production are challenged.

According to Scott, the Mode 1 narrative had four broad characteristics. First, the production process was seen as linear, causal and cumulative. Knowledge (and we are here talking about 'scientific' knowledge, arguably still the dominant frame within which research practices are imagined) was generated within universities or other research establishments and 'applied' to solve practical problems, whether social or commercial. Scientific discoveries were 'transferred' into or through technology that was the source of innovation. According to Scott (1995: 142):

> [T]he language of application and transfer was, and is, revealing because it suggested that scientific creativity was seen as the prime mover in the process of knowledge production. Paradoxically it was also asserted that science was autonomous. Although it might help eventually to solve practical problems, scientific problems were initially defined within and by the scientific community.

Second, science in Mode 1 is seen as a closed system, in that only scientists could define what was and was not science and what counted as 'good' science. Because 'pure science' was seen as the 'start of the chain' of knowledge production, and hence as the 'ultimate source' of innovation, scientists' authority was not confined to their disciplinary specialisms but extended to the application of their research findings. Third, Mode 1 is also 'inherently reductionist'. In the quintessential expression of disciplinarity, Mode 1 is characterised by what has elsewhere been identified as 'differentiation – the generation of grids of specification and practices of specialisation' (Lee and Green 1997: 11). With increasing reliance on sophisticated technologies, of instrumentation, for example, the trend towards reductionism has inevitably led to regarding more holistic and interdisciplinary endeavours as a risk to the necessary conditions for 'expertise'. Finally, Mode 1 science has been publicly funded as an autonomous enterprise, a 'guardian of the public interest', rather than as a 'client' for research 'services'. The university played a key role in the maintenance of the practices and narratives of autonomy, its own autonomy mirroring that of science's (Scott 1995: 142–3).

What is important to note here, however, is that the university's position as pre-eminent knowledge producer according to the Mode 1 narrative is essentially a post-1945, if not a post-1960s, phenomenon, and hence its position is much less secure even historically than it might have looked. Gibbons *et al.*'s historical analysis reveals that, even during this time, much university research had practical beginnings, and 'pure' sciences evolved out of their applied varieties and not the other way around. Yet, as Scott notes, despite its empirical inaccuracy the Mode 1 narrative probably still accurately reflects the assumptions made by many scientists. What is further important is the role assumed by the university in the formation and training of researchers, as particular kinds of persons who occupied the positions of 'knowers' within the Mode 1 narrative.

Mode 2 knowledge, in contrast to Mode 1, is more varied, less systematic and even anti-coherent. It too has four key characteristics. First, sources of innovation for Mode 2 knowledge are as likely to be found in the dynamics of the market-place or in broader socio-economic changes as in the laboratory. Importantly, as Scott (1995: 144) notes: '[Change] is most likely to arise in the often contested borderland between the university and the market/society.' This understanding of innovation places technology not as derivative of, or dependent upon, science, but rather as autonomous from it. Hence the language of application and transfer breaks down, as does the metaphor of the 'chain of innovation' with its linear assumptions of cause and effect (Scott 1995: 144). While this is putatively the territory of the engineer rather than the scientist, it has profound and disruptive effects upon the foundational narratives of disciplinary preeminence in knowledge production within the disciplinary formations of the university.

The second characteristic of Mode 2 is that it is an open system, with different parts for the different participants in the production process to play. Crucially, 'users' are not 'passive beneficiaries' but 'creative agents', not only in determining scientific priorities but also in defining the research problems for science. Experience in innovation matters as much as disciplinary expertise, and a privileged group of 'knowledge brokers', who are able to cross disciplinary and logistical boundaries, become preeminent.

Third, Mode 2 is 'synoptic rather than reductionist'. By this is meant that the focus shifts from micro concerns of the disciplinary scientist to the management of the 'whole process of innovation'. This requires the formation of multi-disciplinary teams and even the shift beyond disciplinarity, because of the problems of internally generated 'affinities and self-referential norms' in the frames of disciplinary discourses (Scott 1995: 145). Finally, Mode 2 takes place largely in what he terms 'the market', rather than the enclosure of the laboratory.

The account of these narratives of knowledge production in the text produced by the original Gibbons team elaborates Mode 2 in ways that are of particular relevance to the professional doctorate. Contrasting 'culturally concentrated' knowledge (Mode 1) with 'socially distributed' knowledge (Mode 2), they enable the imagining of new forms of research practice carried out in places far from the university and judged by, and communicated to, communities other than academic–disciplinary ones. Knowledge production is driven by demand within an open system that requires local and multi-variant forms of problem-solving. The key features of the Gibbons team's initial characterisation of Modes 1 and 2 are summarised in Table 7.1.

It is important to note, at this point, that a simple binary polarised 'before-and-after' scenario of knowledge production is not being suggested here. Mode 1 and Mode 2, as both the Gibbons and the Scott accounts indicate, overlap significantly; elements of both have always existed and they are mutually dependent. In local sites of Mode 2 knowledge production, the tools of disciplinary knowledge are strategically deployed. The Gibbons team's claim that transdisciplinary research is 'unsystematic' appears to refer to the departure from strict adherence to disciplinary–methodological

Table 7.1　Modes of knowledge

Mode 1	Mode 2
Problems set and solved in context governed by academic interests of specific communities	Knowledge produced in context of application
Disciplinary	Transdisciplinary
Homogeneous	Heterogeneous
Hierarchical and form-preserving	Heterarchical and transient
Accountable to discipline-based notions of methodologically 'sound' research practice	Socially accountable and reflexive, including a wider and more temporary and heterogeneous set of practitioners, collaborating on problems defined in specific and localised contexts

protocols, and the replacement of these by local assemblages of 'strategic information' geared to specific contexts of application.

A related conceptual issue with Mode 1–Mode 2 analysis is that its very formulation actively produces the binary that the team then seeks to displace and dismantle. Despite disclaimers, the Gibbons team proceed in their account as though Modes 1 and 2 were 'things-in-the-world' rather than discursive constructs and artefacts of the team's categorisation practices. Further, as Fuller (1995) notes in reviewing this and related work, there is a problem in the very term 'knowledge' itself, which leads to reductionisms as well as contradictions of one kind or another. Gibbons *et al.* acknowledge that the definition of 'knowledge' itself has expanded beyond the control or recognition of disciplines and academic communities. Fuller (1995: 164), in response, wonders whether 'knowledge' is being made to do 'too much semantic work in contemporary English usage'. Certainly, the reductionism of the Gibbons account, while not detracting from its suggestiveness for our purposes here, does raise important questions for further empirical investigation. As Fuller notes, for example, Mode 1 is little more than an 'ideal type, one whose likelihood of being superseded is only matched by its unlikelihood of ever having existed' (Fuller 1995: 166).

While recognising these conceptual issues, professional doctorates can be seen, in the light of these developments, to represent an emerging form of knowledge production and practice of research within a Mode 2 environment. There is accordingly a need to engage carefully in exploring the particular practices of knowledge generation in these degrees – practices that emerge as doctoral candidates in different professional doctoral programmes negotiate relationships with the practice sites in which their research will be carried out, and to which it will in important ways be referenced; with the profession of which they are a member; with the idea of professionalism itself; and with the university, still the primary credentialling body and still the custodian of the doctoral enterprise.

Conceptual implications and a case example

In this section, we consider some questions of the conceptual underpinnings of the new professional doctorates, taking as an example management education. Our reference is specifically to two existing doctoral programmes in Australia, namely the Doctor of Business Administration (DBA) programme at RMIT in Melbourne,[1] and the Professional Doctorate in Organisation Dynamics at Swinburne University of Technology.[2] It should be noted that institutions such as RMIT and Swinburne have historically had strong links with industry and also with professional and vocational education, and hence they appear to be exemplary sites for the development of these new forms of doctoral education.

The DBA at RMIT has been conceptualised as a 'professional doctorate that can meet the requirements of candidates, the business community and the university' (Morley and Priest 1998: 23). Having established that the programme operates 'at a doctoral level', Morley and Priest go on to note that:

> professional practice is the key to the nature of the doctorate. The complexity of professional practice in business provides the milieu within which the program operates and enforces the level of sophistication necessary to obtain results. It requires the coursework and research to be relevant to professional practice and the assessment and outcomes also to be related to professional practice. Candidates' research should make a real contribution to the development of practice in their profession.
>
> (ibid.)

The RMIT Doctor of Business Administration programme involves coursework and supervised research, resulting in a thesis 'with reflection on professional practice and the linkages between knowledge, research and practice'. The research is supported by both an academic and a business 'mentor'. The doctoral thesis is expected 'to make an original and significant contribution to the advancement of professional practice in strategic management, as well as demonstrating a level of competence appropriate for a doctoral award' (Morley and Priest 1998: 25). A key principle guiding the development of curriculum and pedagogical practice in the DBA is 'reflection'. In this way the programme:

> impels the candidates to develop a deeper awareness of themselves as managers and leaders, through a series of revisiting of such ideas, planned opportunities to reflect and systematic consideration of the self as a professional in the context of discussion and analysis of leadership, decision making, etc.
>
> (Morley and Priest 1998: 25)

Morley and Priest go on to elaborate a 'model for the improvement of reflective-practice skill', which is framed in terms of a complementarity of what they call 'modern' and 'postmodern' orientations to reflection. While beyond the scope of this discussion to elaborate on their argument, the example should suffice to demonstrate that, within the emerging scene of the professional doctorate as an educational field, there is conceptual space for the explicit re-imagining of a curriculum and pedagogy for research education and organisational learning. The DBA, as it is represented in the paper on which we are drawing here, is exemplary of the imagining and practice of what we call the 'hybrid curriculum' of the professional doctorate (Green 1997; Lee *et al.* 1999).

The hybrid curriculum of the professional doctorate is one which takes explicitly into account that, in the intersections between the university and the organisation in which typically a doctoral research project will be undertaken, new kinds of knowledge and new ways of producing knowledge will be developed, involving new relationships among participants and new kinds of research writing. We imagine, indeed, a three-way model, where the university, the candidate's profession and the particular work-site of the research meet and intersect in specific and local ways, in the context of a specific organisation (see Figure 7.1). The task of the doctoral candidate, together with her academic and workplace supervisors, is to conceptualise and reflexively represent the nature of that space, in relation to the knowledge that is to be produced through the research process. Indeed, in our own teaching in professional doctoral courses, we ask students to explicitly work with such a model in developing their research proposals.

At issue in such explorations, crucially, are interanimating questions of professional practice, organisational dynamics and new kinds of textual practices. We explicitly conceptualise the latter as 'research literacies' and see them, in the context of professional doctorates, as including academic literacies, professional literacies and workplace literacies, in complex interaction. The notion of *literacy* is a central conceptual organiser for developing research practices in professional doctorates, largely because of what has been termed the growing 'textualisation' of the workplace. The

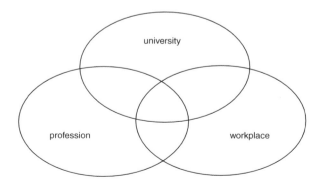

Figure 7.1 The hybrid curriculum of the professional doctorate

128 *Alison Lee* et al.

increasing social complexity of workplaces and their increasing reliance on knowledge production and communication mean that the practice of professionals and 'knowledge workers' has in large part become the 'symbolic analytic work' involved in 'higher-order problem solving' (Gee *et al.* 1996, paraphrasing Reich 1992). In this account, in the increasingly open and distributed, unpredictable and rapidly changing environments of professional work, there is an inevitable collapsing of learning and doing (Gee *et al.*1996 : 67).

The professional doctoral researcher formalises a relationship of work as learning, and of the workplace as both site for the production of new knowledge and as object for reflexive analysis. The conceptual space of the 'hybrid curriculum' is therefore a space where the workplace, work practice and the professional self come into a new and reflexive relationship with the academy. It is this reflexivity which we see projected in the figure of the 'executive–scholar', the imagined subject of the RMIT DBA on this account:

> It is certainly intended that the DBA graduates will have taken on some of the positive attributes of the scholar. The particular scholarly attributes that are aimed for include familiarity with advanced knowledge and analytical skills, an easy facility in the use of academic research and literature (that is relevant to the practising executive), rigor and care in judging and deciding, and a reflective, informed self.
>
> (Morley and Priest 1998: 25)

Swinburne's Professional Doctorate in Organisation Dynamics is similarly oriented to professional practice in context. Taking explicit account of 'the dynamic nature of the modern workplace and its environment' (Long *et al.* 1996: 157), it seeks to bring together practice-referenced scholarly inquiry and improved practice in management, leadership and organisation(al) behaviour. Three issues informed the initial development of the programme (Long *et al.* 1996: 154–5):

- Organisations are perceived to be operating in a highly turbulent environment where change is occurring at chaotic rates now and in the foreseeable future.
- Senior managers were perceived as needing to more fully develop those skills and capacities that could respond to such an environment.
- Management education should be developed to facilitate learning from experience and personal development, and to be directly relevant to the workplace and 'bottom line' considerations.

These issues derived from exploratory 'market' research conducted with stakeholders, who emerged as 'very interested in new forms of [postgraduate] education to stimulate and shape management, leadership and consultancy appropriate to the problems currently facing Australian organisations and society' (Long *et al.* 1996: 155). Significantly, various criticisms emerged of existing programmes in postgraduate education, and perhaps particularly of their other- and un-worldliness, largely due, it would seem, to their traditional links with universities:

> [graduate] managers do not seem to be learning how to 'work in uncertainty' nor to have the capacity or confidence to think about the uniquely Australian dimensions of their organisational dynamics. This is so much the case that many organisations are now suspicious of university credentials and are turning to consultants and in-house programs.
>
> (Long *et al.* 1996: 155–6)

What characterises the programme is a focus on informed, reflective practice, as realised through a combination of 'action learning' and 'action research': 'a strong emphasis on the practicum (action learning) and on applied action research (a possible research method for an organisationally focused dissertation) ... developed to meet the needs of practising managers' (Long *et al.* 1996: 158).

Moreover, the view taken from the outset is that managers characteristically 'tend to learn through direct experience and in a cyclical analogic manner rather than in a strictly logical or analytic fashion' (Long *et al.* 1996: 159). They note the particular difficulties and challenges associated with professional development in the context of the university, linked to doctoral education and research training, and concede that '[w]hether or not this is possible within the institution of the university is something to be explored and evaluated as the program develops' (Long *et al.* 1996: 160). The emergent subject of the programme is projected as follows: 'Overall, graduates of the program ... will be equipped with highly developed professional skills that include the ability to research organisational dynamics and evaluate organisational change' (Long *et al.* 1996: 166).

Once again, however, there is some ambivalence about the relationship between professional practice and research education, with the university's role still appearing to be superordinate with regard to knowledge production in organisational context. Moreover, there would appear to be a certain ambivalence as well regarding the role and significance of knowledge, with the emphasis possibly falling more on skills development, albeit in 'learning', 'reflection', 'evaluation' and 'research'. The programme, as

represented, is, however, clearly oriented towards the curriculum production of skilled, reflective practitioners.

As a further succinct and telling example of all this, it is worth pointing
to the quite fascinating account of 'crisis', reflection and representation
that Morley and Priest (1998: 28–9) offer, with regard to the DBA
programme at RMIT – a good instance, in fact, of the professional
doctorate at work, as it were. In this example, there was clearly a breakdown in communication – and more generally, a discursive mismatch –
between the academic staff in the programme and the students, who are
presented as senior managers, precisely over the question of reflection as
practice and as representation. The student cohort apparently rejected the
staff's attempts to incorporate reflection into the practice of the
programme itself, rather than simply thematising it, in the usual
'academic' fashion. As Morley and Priest (1998: 29) write:

> With some exceptions, the candidates rejected reflection at the time
> as unnecessary and unwarranted. This was despite the program
> being based on reflection as an important mechanism for learning,
> and all candidates being aware of this aspect of the program from
> the beginning.

Moreover, '[T]he resistance to reflection among senior managers in a
public way in the seminar room raised queries about the use and role of
reflection amongst senior managers in a learning context' (ibid.). Morley
and Priest note various characteristics of such a group:

> They tend to value efficiency and clarity in their work and interactions
> with others. They are focused, particularly task focused, and time
> alert. The saying that 'time is money', or at least it is very valuable, is
> how any of the candidates felt. They are alert to and intolerant of
> incompetence or ineffectualness, and prepared to judge and label it
> when they perceive it. They do not want to be 'stuffed around'.
>
> (ibid.)

What this suggests is, first, that more explicit account needs to be taken,
in the theory and practice of the professional doctorate, of the ideological–
discursive character of professionalism and professional practice, and
second, that it remains important to be properly sceptical about the
'Enlightenment' assumptions of the rhetoric of 'reflective practice'.
Examples such as these constitute significant 'critical incidents' and symptomatic moments in the discourse and development of the professional
doctorate, as it currently operates in the Australian higher education

context. Furthermore, the problems that they generate are likely to be evident across the range of available professional doctorates and participating fields of praxis and inquiry; they are by no means unique to business and management education.

What can be said about programmes such as these, in the light of our earlier discussion of new forms of knowledge and production and new relationships and articulations between universities, professions, workplaces and organisations? One of these concerns the question of *reflection* itself, and hence raises issues to do with the notions of 'reflective practice' and the 'reflective practitioner', which would seem to be important rhetorical and epistemological categories for the professional doctorate, as it is emerging in Australia and elsewhere. As one commentator writes (Parker 1997), there are metaphysical problems in such formulations, and these may need to be tackled – at the very least acknowledged – if some of the dilemmas generated by them are to be adequately engaged. Moreover, broader epistemic shifts from modernity to postmodernity, or increasingly complex relations between the two, as social conditions and prevailing orders of contemporary existence, need to be reckoned into account. This is partly a matter of drawing on new theoretical resources, such as those associated with post-structuralism and postmodernism. To do that is to acknowledge the significance of the so-called 'linguistic turn' for professional education and doctoral studies alike, which clearly has important implications for the construction and cultivation of 'research literacies' – hence the value of strategies and attitudes such as those associated with 'deconstruction' (Garrick and Rhodes 1998) and '(post-)critical literacy'. But it is also to take account of the substantive claims and assertions of postmodern thinking – for instance, the significance of border crossings and boundary blurrings and mergings, and the new emphases on process and complexity, on flows and networks.

A key issue here, in this merging and mingling of previously disparate realms, is the loss of 'critical distance', which might also be understood and conceptualised as the supersession of the representation problem in modern(ist) curriculum (Kemmis and Fitzclarence 1986; Green 1997). Jameson's now classic account of postmodernism as a new cultural dominant, originally published in 1984, is pertinent here. He writes of the loss of 'depth analysis' and the new rhetoric of 'surfaces' as symptomatic of the postmodern, along with a new emphasis on and valorisation of commodification, the market and consumer culture (Jameson 1991). What is *is*, and is to be duly appreciated as such, in all its glittering immediacy and its immaculate conception. 'Critical distance', that 'time-honoured' formula, has effectively disappeared:

distance in general (and critical distance in particular) has very
precisely been abolished in the new space of postmodernism. We are
now submerged in its henceforth filled and suffused volumes to the
point where our new postmodern bodies are bereft of spatial co-
ordinates and practically (let alone theoretically) incapable of
distantiation.

(Jameson 1991: 48–9)

As with 'distance', so too with 'differentiation' – for some, the very mark
of the Modern. The effects of 'de-distancing' and of 'de-differentiation'
are therefore to be observed everywhere, including in the new knowledge
economy. The manner in which higher education is increasingly articulated with business and industry, the vocationalisation of the university and
its increasing subordination to economic and commercial agendas, and
also its accommodation to and with new modes of knowledge production,
might well be understood in these terms – that is, as a specific expression of
the postmodern.

Linked with this are new concerns with 'learning organisations' and
'the learning society', and on 'organisational learning' as a characteristically postmodern managerial response to changed organisational and
social realities. As Garrick and Rhodes (1998: 174) argue: 'If the postmodern is a reflection of rapid change to the assumptions that underlie
our view of organisational realities, then "organisational learning" has
emerged as a way of managing through this change.' Moreover: 'organisational learning is an approach to management which is attempting to reap
organisational and managerial benefits through workplace learning. It
attempts to do so by conflating the notions of learning and work' (Garrick
and Rhodes 1998: 173).

Analyses such as this suggest the need for a properly sceptical view of
the new rhetorics of 'learning' and 'research', not simply as a register of
changing organisational forms and dynamics, but also as expressive of
new forms of capitalism and social–governmental order. Hence:
'Organisational learning is a version of the progress myth suggesting that
learning can lead to business success and that business success is unquestionably a valuable social goal' (Garrick and Rhodes 1998: 175) – another
form, therefore, of what elsewhere has been described as the Dream of
Reason and Progress (Bigum and Green 1993), in which, above all else,
'technonomic' rationality and the meta-logic of performativity prevail as
the final marker and maker of social meaning (Lyotard 1984; Idhe 1990).
In this regard, what commentators propose as deconstruction's virtue – its
scepticism towards all knowledge-foundationalist claims, and its character
as 'an ethical practice that is concerned with "what happens to ethics" as

knowledge frameworks are increasingly challenged' (Garrick and Rhodes 1998: 177), and indeed its relentless concern with questioning and problematising what is all too often and too readily taken as the 'bottom line' (Johnson 1981; Green 1997) – becomes readily apparent as a crucial resource for doctoral research and professional practice. How are 'research' and 'learning' co-opted into the service of the organisation and the corporation? What is the relationship between the 'inside' and the 'outside'? What is gained and what is lost when learning and research become identified with the work of business and industry, within a (re)new(ed) *and* enduring postmodern capitalist social order?

There is a growing call in literature on postgraduate education for the development of high-level professional, communication and interpersonal, as well as technical, skills in graduates generally (Burgess *et al.* 1998). This is hardly surprising, given the closer harnessing of higher education to the economy. These moves, by and large, are intended to *supplement* the existing structures of doctoral education, rather than fundamentally shifting them. In the professional doctorate as it is emerging in Australia, on the other hand, there are both implicit and explicit moves to conceptualise and structure the programme quite differently. In general, these moves can be understood in terms of a (partial, at least) relocation of knowledge production, including its legitimation, from the university to the workplace. These moves, in tandem with changes in workplaces and their practices and modes of learning and work, go to produce different kinds of knowing and different kinds of expertise – different kinds of knowing subjects. Such moves are still in their infancy, but there are some conceptual developments in this direction that are worth noting here.

We have sought to situate these relations, however, in terms of the implications of these changed structures and relations of knowledge and authority between the university and 'outside', arguing that these changes call for the production of new and hybrid knowledges and new pedagogical practices that will produce new subjects. The research on professional doctorates with which we have been involved in the past three years asks such questions as: Who will be these new 'doctors'? What will be their roles in the organisations they work in and for, and also in social life more generally? What are the research, pedagogical and textual practices that will produce them? What implications are there for the university and the professions, *and* for organisations, populated by these differently trained and licensed professionals in these newly articulated relations of research and practice? Clearly, there are important and even urgent pedagogical, institutional, political, ethical, epistemological and methodological implications and challenges in the issues raised here.

134   *Alison Lee* et al.

Notes

1   Royal Melbourne Institute of Technology University. The name of this institu-
    tion speaks eloquently of the history of Australian higher education, in terms
    of its former colonial relationship to Britain and the Crown, to its initial posi-
    tioning in a higher education system which was 'other' than the university
    system, and to its subsequent repositioning and renaming within the unified
    national system of higher education in Australia in the 1990s.
2   It should be noted that we are basing our account on representations of these
    programmes in papers published in two recent collections on the professional
    doctorate in Australia (Maxwell and Shanahan 1996, 1998). It is highly likely
    that the programmes in questions have gone beyond these particular published
    accounts, in their own practice.

References

Bigum, Chris and Green, Bill (1993) 'Technologising literacy, or, interrupting the
    dream of reason' in Pam Gilbert and Allan Luke (eds) *Literacy in Contexts:
    Australian Perspectives and Issues*, Sydney: Allen and Unwin (pp. 4–28).
Burgess, Robert (1998) 'Editorial', *European Journal of Education* 33, 2: 141–4.
Burgess, Robert, Band, S. and Pole, C.J. (1998) 'Doctoral education and research
    training in Germany: towards a more structured and efficient approach?' *Euro-
    pean Journal of Education* 33, 2: 145–66.
Evans, Terry (1998) 'Are current innovations in professional doctorates all for the
    best?' in Tom Maxwell and Peter Shanahan (eds) *Professional Doctorates: Innovations
    in Teaching and Research*, Proceedings of 2nd National Conference on Professional
    Doctorates, Coffs Harbour, 8–10 July (pp. 3–10).
Foucault, Michel (1972) *The Archaeology of Knowledge*, translated by Alan Sheridan,
    London: Tavistock Publications.
Fuller, Steve (1995) 'Is there life for sociological theory after the sociology of scien-
    tific knowledge?', *Sociology* 29, 1: 159–66.
Garrick, John and Rhodes, Carl (1998) 'Deconstructive organisational learning: the
    possibilities for a postmodern epistemology of practice', *Studies in the Education of
    Adults* 30, 2: 172–83.
Gee, J.P., Hull, G. and Lankshear, C. (1996) *The New Work Order: Behind the Language
    of the New Capitalism*, Sydney: Allen and Unwin.
Gibbons, M., Limoges, C., Nowotny, H., Schwartzman, S., Scott, P. and Trow, M.
    (1994) *The New Production of Knowledge: The Dynamics of Science and Research in
    Contemporary Societies*, London: Sage.
Green, Bill (1997) 'Reading with an attitude; or, Deconstructing critical literacies'
    in Sandy Muspratt, Allan Luke and Peter Freebody (eds) *Constructing Critical
    Literacies: Teaching and Learning Textual Practice*, Cresskill, NJ: Hampton Press (pp.
    227–42).
Green, Bill and Lee, Alison (1998) 'Theorising postgraduate pedagogy' in Alison
    Lee and Bill Green (eds) *Postgraduate Studies / Postgraduate Pedagogy*, Sydney: Centre

for Language and Literacy and the University Graduate School, University of Technology, Sydney.

Gregory, Michael (1995) 'Implications of the introduction of the Doctor of Education degree in British universities: can the EdD reach parts the PhD cannot?', *Vocational Aspects of Education* 47, 2: 177–88.

Grichting, Wolfgang (1998) 'Professional doctorates in Australia', report of survey undertaken for the Australasian Deans and Directors of Graduate Studies Group, March.

Idhe, Don (1990) *Technology and the Lifeworld: From Garden to Earth*, Bloomington: Indiana University Press.

Jameson, Fredric (1991) *Postmodernism; or, The Cultural Logic of Late Capitalism*, Durham: Duke University Press.

Johnson, Barbara (1981) 'Translator's introduction' in Jacques Derrida *Dissemination*, translated by Barbara Johnson, Chicago: University of Chicago Press.

Jongeling, Sybe (1996) 'Professional doctorates in Australian universities', paper presented at the Council of Australian Deans and Directors of Graduate Studies meeting, Adelaide.

Kemmis, Michael and Fitzclarence, Lindsay (1986) *Curriculum Theorising: Beyond Reproduction Theory*, Waurn Ponds, Victoria: Deakin University Press.

Lee, Alison and Green, Bill (1997) 'Pedagogy and disciplinarity in the "new university" ', *UTS Review* 3, 1: 1–25.

Lee, Alison, Green, Bill and Brennan, Marie (1999) *The Rise of the Professional Doctorate: Changing Doctoral Education in Australia*, Rockhampton: Central Queensland University Press.

Long, S., Schapper, J. and Wild, T. (1996) 'Action learning in a professional doctorate for managers' in T.W. Maxwell and P.J. Shanahan (eds) *Which Way for Professional Doctorates? Contexts and Cases*, proceedings of 'Which way for professional doctorates?' conference, Coffs Harbour, 16, 17 and 18 October 1996.

Luke, Timothy (1998) 'Digital discourses, on-line classes, electronic documents: developing new university techno-cultures'. Electronic journal article: http://ultibase.rmit.edu.au/Articles/luke1.html

Lyotard, J.-F. (1984) *The Postmodern Condition: A Report on Knowledge*, Manchester: Manchester University Press.

Maxwell, Tom and Shanahan, Peter (eds) (1996) *Which Way for Professional Doctorates? Context and Cases.* Proceedings of 1st National Conference on Professional Doctorates, Coffs Harbour, 16–18 October, Armidale: Faculty of Education, Health and Professional Studies.

Maxwell, Tom and Shanahan, Peter (eds) (1998) *Professional Doctorates: Innovations in Teaching and Research*, proceedings of 2nd National Conference on Professional Doctorates, Coffs Harbour, 8–10 July, Armidale: Faculty of Education, Health and Professional Studies.

Morley, C and Priest, J. (1998) 'RMIT reflects on its Doctor of Business Administration program', in Tom Maxwell and Peter Shanahan (eds) *Professional Doctorates: Innovations in Teaching and Research*, Proceedings of 2nd National

136   *Alison Lee* et al.

Conference on Professional Doctorates, Coffs Harbour, 8–10 July, Armidale: Faculty of Education, Health and Professional Studies (pp. 23–36).

NBEET (National Board of Employment, Education and Training) (1989) *Australian Graduate Studies and Higher Degrees*, Report of Higher Education Council, Canberra: AGPS.

Noble, Keith Allan (1997) *Changing Doctoral Degrees: An International Perspective*, Buckingham: Society for Research in Higher Education and Open University Press.

OECD (Organisation for Economic Co-operation and Development) (1995) *Research Training: Present and Future*, Paris: OECD.

Parker, Stuart (1997) *Reflective Teaching in the Postmodern World: A Manifesto for Education in Postmodernity*, Buckingham: Open University Press.

Pearson, Margot and Ford, X. (1996) *Open and Flexible Research Degree Study and Research*, Evaluations and Investigations Program, Canberra: Department of Employment, Education, Training and Youth Affairs.

Reich, R.B. (1992) *The Work of Nations*, New York: Vintage Books.

Reid, Jo-Anne (1998) 'The Professional Doctorate: a professional practice?' in Alison Lee and Bill Green (eds) *Postgraduate Studies/Postgraduate Pedagogy*, Sydney: Centre for Language and Literacy and University Graduate School, University of Technology, Sydney (pp. 57–66).

Schön, Donald (1983) *The Reflective Practitioner*, New York: Basic Books.

Scott, Peter (1995) *The Meanings of Mass Higher Education*, Buckingham: Society for Research in Higher Education and Open University Press.

Scott, Peter (1997) 'The postmodern university?' in Anthony Smith and Frank Webster (eds) *The Postmodern University? Contested Visions of Higher Education in Society*, Buckingham: Society for Research in Higher Education and Open University Press (pp. 36–47).

Scott, Peter (ed.) (1998) *The Globalization of Higher Education*, Buckingham: Society for Research in Higher Education and Open University Press.

Stehr, Nico (1994) *Knowledge Societies*, London: Sage.

Trigwell, Keith, Shannon, Tony and Maurizi, Russell (1997) *Research–Coursework Doctoral Programs in Australian Universities*, Canberra: DEETYA.

West, Roderick (1998) *Learning for Life: A Review of Higher Education Financing and Policy*, Canberra: Australian Government Printing Service.

Wittrock, Bjorn (1993) 'The modern university: three transformations' in Sheldon Rothblatt and Bjorn Wittrock (eds) *The European and American University since 1800: Historical and Sociological Essays*, Cambridge: Cambridge University Press.

8 Research and engagement with trade unions

Bridging the solitudes

Carla Lipsig-Mummé

Canadian perspectives

In the 1980s it became clear, within the Canadian context, that the post-war world of work and employment was disintegrating. Both *the organisation of work* and *employment patterns* changed profoundly, but from the early 1980s through the early 1990s, it was not clear in which direction these changes were going. Was this to be the brave new knowledge-based economy, freeing workers to use their minds and rediscover their craft, bringing employers to understand how fundamentally their economic well-being was based on the skill and commitment of their employees and on their own willingness to invest in the constant betterment of those skills? Or was this a polarising work world, where some workers and some companies moved towards the liberation described above, while other companies sought market advantages by sending employees spiralling into precarious employment, deskilling, alienation and, in some instances, impoverishment? From the beginning of the 1980s there were indications that polarisation rather than generalised meliorism would characterise the new work order, but it was not until the 1990s that the concept of the 'jobless recovery' came to be widely accepted as a just description of the emerging shape of civil society.

These profound and disintegrative developments at the macro-social level foreclosed the assumptions of the 1960s and 1970s that social change would move towards greater social equality. The macro-social move right, weakening the power and social authority of trade unions across the developed world, also triggered profound and painful self-questioning within trade unions as to strategy, tactics, relation to the state, union democracy, militancy and eventually goals themselves (Hyman 1999). That institutional self-questioning, common to all the OECD countries but varying in intensity and language, led in many countries to defensiveness, confused thinking about partnership, radical changes in union structure and a weakening of union–party political links. But it also revealed – newly, in some countries like Canada – the weakness of union voice in public debates over societal choices, and the link between public weakness and the attenuation of member engagement and militancy. This recognition of the weakness of union voice in the world outside the labour movement has led, in Canada in the 1990s, to a union turn towards research. It has also led unions to look inward at the link between research, education and mobilisation. And it has led them to look outward for collaboration with activist academics, as co-producers of knowledge, educators, and as a new breed of trade unionist. In short, the turn right of the past decade has called upon committed academics to redefine their place and role in research as engagement. In posing a series of urgent questions about what we do, what we can do, how we work and what we should be doing, the new environment brings the question of the limits and possibilities of research by academics as action and engagement again take centre-stage.

This chapter is thus located within the chilly light of the emerging millennium, being at the intersection of experience, frustration and hope. It draws particularly on my experience as an academic union activist and blue-collar union organiser in the US, English Canada and Quebec, and on the experience of the Centre for Research on Work and Society at York University, one of English Canada's oldest and largest research centres in which trade unionists and academics define research jointly. (It also takes into account my long-term contact with the Australian labour movement and activist research institutes in Sydney and Melbourne.) Section 1 sketches the changes in the world of work and employment that have created new opportunities and pressure for academic–union research partnerships. Section 2 looks at forms of research partnerships between trade unions and university-based researchers. Section 3 looks at several partnership experiences in Quebec and English Canada. Section 4 indicates conclusions and the questions they raise.

1   New employment patterns and the emerging work order

Patterns of employment

From the matrix of the 1980s, three new patterns of employment emerged. First, employment feminised. The feminisation of employment is expressed through the convergence between male and female labour force participation rates and the increasing percentage of the work force that is female (Lipsig-Mummé and Laxer 1998: 5). Feminisation also refers to the fact that the traditional way in which women have entered the paid labour force – through part-time and other forms of precarious employment – has now been generalised to men. Half the part-time jobs created since 1981 are involuntary, and involuntary part-time work has multiplied five-fold since 1977 (Betcherman 1990). Further, the union membership in Canada is now almost half women: virtually all net growth in union membership between 1976 and 1992 has been from new women members (Lipsig-Mummé and Laxer 1998: 6). And finally, there is emerging a sad convergence in the way that older men and older women cope with premature and forced retirement: in their early sixties, their fifties and even their late forties, they return to the labour market and take what jobs they can get, the McJobs, often for a pittance, in small workplaces and the garage and basement service sector. Thus the prematurely 'elderly' are becoming a reserve army of the precariously employed, as women have traditionally been.

The second dimension of employment change is the privatisation of the service economy. The growth of the public sector in Canada from the 1950s through the 1980s pioneered secure employment and decent career paths (James *et al.* 1997: 115; White *et al.* 1998). Unionising rapidly, the public sector became the most important point of entry for women into the labour movement. But from the 1980s public employment plateaued, then began to decline and by 1997 was at below 25 per cent. Private services employment growth, however, has continued growing since World War II, to 52 per cent of all employment. This sector is the 'Jekyll-and-Hyde' of the Canadian economy. Unionisation is lower, wages more polarised, firm size smaller and precarious employment more rampant than in any other part of the economy. This is a chaotic, polarised world which mirrors the future.

The third dimension of the new world of employment is insecurity, and it takes many forms. The generation after World War II had been marked by the uneven deepening and broadening of worker security in Canada as elsewhere as a product of the welfare state. From the mid 1980s, however, the pendulum began to swing back. Unemployment – long-term, tenaciously high unemployment – took root and became a fact of life. It would be difficult to overestimate the impact of here-to-stay unemployment on social policy, managerial militancy, worker action, individual understanding of personal futures; difficult to underestimate how insecurity is becoming a fact of life for everyone, and security disappearing as a right and re-emerging as a privilege. Precarious employment, cloaked in the language of flexibility, autonomy and the need to heal the artificial split between family and work, comes to be not only the employment form of choice for employers in all sectors, but accepted as the natural form of employment by the young entering the labour market. Not only the weakly unionised private services, but the traditional bastions of trade unionism in manufacturing and the public sector now privilege precarious employment over secure and on-going jobs. Creative new forms of the employment relationship have emerged, and thought-to-be obsolete forms re-emerged, such as cyclical, on-commission, tips-only employment, and false self-employment (in which the worker is defined as a small business rather than the vulnerable employee she in reality is).

Taken together, the growth of employment in hard-to-unionise sectors, the privatisation of formerly public jobs, and the rise and spread of employment insecurity, have exploded the post-war labour market, while challenging unions to speak to and for the next working class. Research now becomes a crucial tool for union strategic repositioning.

Patterns of work

Where *work* is concerned, this new social order seems for us in Canada to be directed towards the undoing of the hard-won gains of a generation of strong unions and a functioning welfare state. In the Canadian context, we can identify two structuring agencies which have transformed not only patterns of employment, but patterns of work as well. The first, *the uneven but revolutionary introduction of new technologies*, is shared by every industrialised or industrialising country. By their very adoption, these new technologies create a whole new set of polarities, dividing industry from industry, company from company within each industry, and groups of workers into isolated individuals. Just as, in the 1920s, the choice of whether or not to adopt the assembly-line or not made the difference between success or stagnation for companies and industries, so today the new technologies – and the social mystique surrounding them – open the way to corporate experimentation with decomposing and recomposing the traditional division of labour established by the second industrial revolution. Is the hollowing out of office and factory and the contracting out of hospital services a step forward? A liberation from scientific management? For some, of course, it spells liberation and a return to craftsmanship lost well before Henry Ford. (The idyllic image of the stock analyst sitting on his deck with his computer on his lap, overlooking the Pacific Ocean, comes to mind.) For others – usually women – it spells isolated work, the intensification of work and precarious employment. (The teleworker inputting data in her family room, the industrial cleaner whose government employment has been privatised, and the homeworker sewing in her bedroom, come to mind here; Aguiar 1999.) In Canada, there is only a weak and fragmented union presence in these sectors to negotiate its impact.

In the new technological and social divisions of labour, contradictory developments have crystallised. In manufacturing and office work, production is becoming ever more spatially decentralised, moving from manufacturer to contractor, moving out of the office and the downtown core to the suburbs, the industrial park, the home office. Work therefore becomes more isolated. As workers leave the collectivity for home or contractor, they leave behind their work-tie to civil society, to their union, their workmates, their training courses, their job mobility. On the other hand, the work that stays *in* the factory or office is being reorganised into teams, recomposing the division of labour fragmented by the second industrial revolution, exporting worker conflict with management *to* the work groups themselves, importing competition and insecurity *into* worker-to-worker relationships. In the private services, experimentation with work teams, polarised and endlessly changing hours of work, inter-age group competition and new Taylorism have together created a most effective fragmentation and demoralisation of the enormous work force.

The second development – *the move towards continental integration* – is lived differently by different countries. For Canada, the Free Trade Agreement with the US, followed by the North American Free Trade Agreement (adding Mexico) and the imminent extension to other Latin American economies, all add an unexpected dimension. By opening Canada to a nearby cheap labour zone, wages competition on a continental scale intensifies the spiralling-down pressures on manufacturing, and some service industries in Canada, encouraging employers to experiment with the introduction of new technologies and the spatial reorganisation of the labour process domestically so as to compete with Mexico, undermine trade unions and employment security. They also call upon Canadian unions to make effective rather than protectionist links with US and Mexican labour, to put forth complex and compelling proposals for continental regulatory institutions. Again, the need for new research to buttress new thinking is evident.

In summation, the years from 1981 to the present were marked by a polarisation of workplace change in Canada: the good jobs became better still, at least in terms of their opportunities for individual growth and autonomy, while the bad jobs got worse indeed. The search for security has become central to workers of all ages, and the omnipresence of insecurity has become the ghost at the banquet for trade unions, community organisations, and public policy-makers.

2   Bridging the solitudes: forms of research collaboration

However dramatic the implosion of the post-war labour market, decline in union membership in Canada has been less dramatic and more recent than elsewhere. Union density hovered around 33–5 per cent from the mid-1970s to 1992, with the growth of labour force participation and union membership among women shoring up the decline in participation and the stagnation in union membership among men (Lipsig-Mummé and Laxer 1998: 3). But since 1992, women membership growth has stagnated, and overall union density has declined to 31 per cent.

While all unions are now discussing the need for new and effective strategies to organise the young, there is still no overall labour movement strategic planning on this and other pressing issues. Above all in Canada, the influence of labour is slight at the level of federal state determination of social and economic policy. Indeed, the combination of recent membership decline following long-term stability has triggered – or revealed – a split in the labour movement's understanding of the threat and possibility of the emergent, continental work order. Those unions which emphasise the menace of globalisation, state powerlessness and managerial militancy face off against those which emphasise the opportunities that continental economic integration offer for international worker solidarity and new forms of state-focused and supra-national power. For engaged academics, the new work environment opens up new uses for research and new ways of linking students to committed research. It also calls for academics and unions to develop new ways to collaborate around research, so that research is linked to member education and involvement on the one hand, and to the articulation of a progressive voice in public policy on the other.

Autonomist and collaborative research traditions

Among individual Canadian unions, two distinct approaches towards research have crystallised: *the autonomist* and *the collaborative*; this section explains these concepts.

While every national labour movement is composed of diverse traditions, by the late twentieth century it is possible in most countries to identify at least one dominant culture of trade unionism. In Canada, there are three cultures which partly overlap and partly compete. These are: the formerly Catholic, presently post-confessional syndicalism of the Quebec-only trade unions; social unionism; and labourism. Business unionism, dominant for a century in the US, now plays a minor and marginal role in Canada. Cultural and organisational competition occurs among competing peak councils, or *centrales* in Quebec. In English Canada, it is played out within the Canadian Labour Congress.

In English Canada, the new importance accorded research on work by unions was catalysed by the profound structural changes of the 1980s, but also coincided temporally with a growing nationalism within the Canadian labour movement. During the 1980s and 1990s, a number of Canadian-national unions were newly formed by Canadian workers disaffiliating from US unions which had operated in Canada for a century, in manufacturing, mining, electrical, chemical processing, electronics, papermaking, autos, communications and other sectors. These newly decolonised unions joined the Canadian-only public sector unions, to increase the size and importance of the Canadian national unions within the Canadian labour movement. (In 1962 about two in three Canadian unionists belonged to US-based unions, in 1992 only three in ten.) The Canadian-only unions, generally in the social unionism tradition, quickly developed a full range of services, including research. The remaining US-affiliated unions in Canada – in steel, food, clothing and textiles, construction, commerce, trade and other private services – can be identified with the labourist tradition, or, occasionally, with an older business union tradition that is marginal in Canada. They continue to obtain many of their member services from their US parent union. In general, both the services provided in Canada, including research, and the topics on which the unions took public positions, were correspondingly narrower in the Canadian branches of US unions than they were in either the Canadian-only unions or the Quebec centrales. In the Quebec labour movement, composed partly of US-based and Canadian-national unions and partly of Quebec-only centrales, recognition of the importance of research occurs as early as the 1940s in the centrales, but it grew in importance and radicalised in content with the growth of Quebec's independence movement and the leadership of unions within it during the 1960s and after (Lipsig-Mummé 1991). In other words, in both Quebec and English Canada, the nationalist construction of independent labour unions led to an increase in the use of research and the breadth of issues that research engaged. It also led to the development of new forms of union–university partnership.

Historically, we can identify four areas of union research, or areas in which unions need research to carry out their work: collective bargaining; social and economic policy; work organisation; and union structure and function. It is only in the current decade in the English-speaking unions that there has been a growing interest in moving beyond the 'core business' of collective bargaining to two of the other three areas of union concern: social and economic policy, and work organisation. While social and

Carla Lipsig-Mummé

economic policy was traditionally the domain of the national or provincial labour federations, a wide range of affiliated unions now devote resources to research on policy. This research is carried out both in-house and in partnership with external intellectuals. Work organisation is new to research in English Canada, although not in Quebec. In English Canada it remains principally the preserve of individual unions, with occasional work from the Canadian Labour Congress, and it is here that a growing number of collaborative projects between unions and academics is located. The fourth research topic – changing union structure and function – is delicate terrain. Unlike the UK and the US labour movements, where national, regional and sectoral union–university research collaboration on the modernisation needed in union structure and the locus of union power have been the subject of a number of projects, in English Canada unions have been traditionally reticent about inviting academics to help them with critical self-evaluation (Waddington and Whitston 1993: 25). Instead, academics have carried out their critique of union structures and functions – somewhat removed from the movement. Again, Quebec is the exception.

Autonomist research

The goal of autonomist research is to make the union more fully independent of all external agencies. *The autonomist tradition* traces its roots both to the wariness about intellectuals, particularly those in universities – characteristic of North American blue-collar unionism, and to the now-outmoded idea that research is not essential to a union's core business. In the autonomist mode the union may be very research-active, but it sets the research questions, and determines what results are to be publicised and which are unacceptable. The research may be carried out by staffers, because several unions in the autonomist tradition have sizeable research departments, or it may be contracted out to labour-friendly, external research institutes or individual academics. Sometimes, the autonomist unions seek to train rank-and-file members as researchers (Schenk and Anderson 1995: introduction). But whoever carries it out, control of the research from beginning to end remains with the union. The engaged intellectual becomes a brain for hire. In recent years, the autonomist unions in English Canada have also distanced themselves from their traditional political ally, the New Democratic Party, and thus from the kind of intellectual cross-pollination so valuable for effective intervention in the wider society.

Collaborative research

The collaborative approach begins with a different goal and is anchored in a different set of beliefs. Its goal is to deepen and broaden union influence and social authority. Its core assumptions: first, contemporary trade unions need extensive and varied links with engaged intellectuals not on staff, and closer and more institutionalised relationships with universities and independent research bodies, if they are to articulate convincing and influential alternative visions of the organisation of work and society. Second, working with 'external' organisations and academics cannot be effective if the research is simply contracted out, but must engage a real partnership at each stage of a research cycle. Third, drawing external intellectuals and research institutes into research work with and for a union will make the union organisation more permeable to outside influences, and this may have repercussions for union dynamics. Research results are not always predictable. But the collaborative approach does link research to member education, and does work at developing real partnerships with intellectuals outside the union's ranks. It is on the diverse forms of collaboration that the next sections of the chapter focus.

Representative vs affinity-based research partnerships

'Partnership' has become a distended and abused word, employed promiscuously. Where research on work is concerned, there are two different forms of partnership – *the representative* and *the affinity-based* – and each is linked to different ideas about power, democracy and inequality. Representative partnerships insist that all 'stakeholders' participate. Affinity-based partnerships link only those who share a basic worldview.

There are also two different macro-social contexts for research partnerships. Representative partnerships tend to flourish in corporatist societies, while affinity-based partnerships develop in societies where polarisation and class conflict are acknowledged at all levels. Even in the latter, however, in workplace research representative partnerships are the collaborative form of choice for governments and government-funded research.

Representative partnerships are distinguished by the requirement that all socially relevant institutional stakeholders must participate. For example, the Canadian Labour Force Development Board (CLFDB) – a consultative and not decisional body – was governed by a model of representative partnership before its demise in 1999. Business and labour and the equity groups participated. CLFDB chose to work by consensus rather than by formal voting. Research themes were decided by the Board, and carried out by CLFDB staff.

But even in a representative partnership, research can be a volatile political instrument. The business representatives withdrew from the CLFDB, causing its closure, following a research exposé by staff of the chaos besetting Canadian training provision in the wake of the federal government decision to decentralise training to the provinces (Critoph 1999). In this case, research questions, which were central to understanding where government policy was taking training, were explosive to the maintenance of the representative partnership.

Sometimes representative partnerships in corporatist societies develop a larger sense of their own importance than the state is willing to allow. Thus the Consultative Board of the Société québécoise de la main d'oeuvre (Quebec Manpower Commission) is in serious conflict with the Commission itself as to whether the 'labour market partners' make state policy or simply advise the Commission. The unions, the business community and the community sector are all agreed that they are decisional. At stake is the whole edifice of partnership in training in Quebec, which has been absolutely crucial not only to the creation of Canada's only integrated strategy of training but also to Quebec's larger macro-political objectives.

In other words, if the representative research partnership is to remain a place of consensus rather than contested terrain, there will be silences, compromises, and adjustments, that begin with the shaping of the research question and continue to the crystallisation of conclusions. Simply identifying the shared terrain may become an end rather than a means. But sometimes the very identification of research issues may become contested, if one or all of the 'stakeholders' is using the collaboration to further the struggle to take charge of defining social priorities.

Does this condemn all research partnerships to blandness or implosion? Not at all. *Affinity-based partnerships* are more familiar in a society which recognises that it is divided by divergent class and community interests, and in a state which has no more than a formal interest in consensus or inclusiveness. They draw together only those individuals and groups who share concerns and a worldview beyond the project in question. Affinity research partnerships tend to be small-scale, and develop through the will of the specific partners rather than through the requirement to be representative of all stakeholders. Research projects and their solutions are shaped to respond to the issues as the partners see them rather than as a compromise of vision. The partners collaborate at each point of what we have come to call a research cycle: from defining the research question, to choosing method and collecting data, through popular and academic dissemination, to turning the research into education for union membership and leadership. This is, in effect, where the research partnerships I have been involved with fit in, both in Quebec and with the Centre for Research on Work and Society in English Canada, and most recently with the Centre for Union Research and Education in Victoria. We do not assume that we are required to represent the entire spectrum of interests clustered around the subject studied, and we recognise that the inclusion of some interest groups would muddy the work. And, while we certainly have internal debates and discussions and sometimes struggles, we are able to identify a shared vision and define our problematics in terms of the issues as we see them. As honest researchers we know that every researcher is influenced by her/his own social location.

Working in a society in which there is no assumption of social consensus makes research more difficult. It almost always means working at arm's length from the state and its quasi-governmental bodies. Does being at arm's length mean that affinity-based research partnerships are doomed to marginality? Not necessarily. In the light of the disintegrative and polarising changes the world of work is undergoing, research has become newly important to trade union strategic repositioning. The next section discusses three Canadian experiences with union–university collaboration on research.

3   Research partnerships in Quebec and English Canada

Institutionalising partnerships

The research partnership between the Institute for Applied Labour Research (IRAT) and the Service à la Collectivité Programme in Quebec is an illustration of what can be achieved in partnering arrangements. It is not merely nostalgia to reflect on the late 1970s as being a time of creative nationalism, rapid modernisation, social radicalisation and challenging questioning of the role of both unions and the university in civil society in Quebec. They were also a time of relative openness to social and political models that had been tried out elsewhere, particularly in France or in what was then called 'the third world'. Out of that questioning, two union–university research initiatives crystallised. Both the Institute for Applied Labour Research (IRAT) and the Service to the Collectivity Programmes lasted for at least fifteen years. The former drew in all major unions and universities in Quebec, but was free-standing. The latter was university-specific, and only developed at the Université du Québec à Montréal and Laval University. Both were multi-project, and both required the unions and university administrations to create infrastructure and commit publicly and financially to the collaboration.

The logic behind both these projects was threefold. First, universities needed to redefine their social mission in order to serve the community more democratically than they had done in the past, and trade unions, as well as women's groups, housing co-ops and other community associations (*groupes populaires*) were important parts of the community. Second, academics and research students would benefit from research partnerships with community organisations of all sorts, and the flow-on nature of that benefit was just beginning to be explored. Third, in the increasingly complex and internationalised work world, unions were being forced to reconsider how much research they needed, on what topics, and who would carry it out. Because most unions had neither the expertise on staff to confront the new questions, nor the desire to transform the activist/professional ratio among their staffers, collaboration with unionised university researchers offered an interesting avenue of widening and deepening union influence. Issues of ergonomics, health and safety, women's health, organisation of work, ageing workers, pensions and benefits, and other topics were at the top of the list (Messing and Mergler 1992; Lipsig-Mummé 1988).

The Institute for Applied Labour Research (IRAT) was set up as an independent research centre funded by a consortium of the three principal union centrales and six Quebec universities. Its core funding came from the unions and the universities as well as the provincial Ministry of Higher Education. Its research funding came from a series of federal and provincial government and quasi-governmental sources, with occasional access to the principal government sources of funding for university-based research. IRAT was a free-standing research institute which employed a number of respected researchers to work on a big-picture research agenda defined by an executive on which sat all the (often warring) union centrales. IRAT's research programme was negotiated at executive level every two years, and projects were carried out by one or two staff researchers in some conjunction with union staff and, rarely, an academic. The staff researchers did not hold university appointments, which became a real obstacle to obtaining funding. Once completed, the research was published in book form or in academic journals, became the subject of a union–university conference or workshop, and returned to the unions who might hold member education courses and/or publish shorter and more popular versions in very large numbers to disseminate it to their members. Over the almost two decades until IRAT was discontinued, it set the intellectual agenda in Quebec on work reorganisation and policy issues concerning older workers, and contributed to the debate on the reform of collective bargaining legislation. It also understood that for some of its participating unions there were research no-go zones, and if it pursued these topics, backlash (in the form of union withdrawal or request to terminate ideologically troublesome staff researchers) could be paralysing.

The UQAM and Laval Universities' Service to the Collectivity programmes – popularly known as *le Protocole* – were also meant to develop research projects that would serve community organisations, but they were also geared to help academics develop their own (funded) research with union partners and train graduate students. It was with the Protocole that the idea of a *Research Cycle*, linking academic research to union needs, member education, collective bargaining and the training of the next generation of labour-friendly university knowledge workers, first crystallised.

UQAM created an office for the Protocole, with full-time co-ordinators. The university paid for the staffing and functioning of the Protocole office, as well as for certain of the start-up costs on the research.

The general pattern was this: a union identified a research need or was helped to crystallise that need by the co-ordinator or an activist academic. If no academic was in on the union's first contact with the Protocole, the co-ordinator put the union together with one or several potential academic collaborators. The university freed ('liberated', in French) the academic from some part of her teaching in order to carry out the research. Often, the academic associated a graduate student with the research, who then completed her master's or doctorate on its subject. Once the research was completed, the academic and the union submitted a text to an oversight committee for review and revision. The academic prepared the project for scholarly publication. The academic and the union then collaborated on developing education modules for the union on the basis of the research. They also developed other forms of dissemination through union publications. Over the twenty years since the Protocole has been in operation, it has completed approximately 150 projects, revolutionising union expertise in the areas of work re-organisation, training for health, safety and work re-organisation, ergonomics, women's health, health and safety, member education and other areas. It has also trained a generation of PhDs in biology, ergonomics and sociology on union-related research topics. We can discern a research cycle here which links the research to its implementation, to education of subjects and future researchers, to democratisation of union life through sharing knowledge and to dissemination to a wider public as well.

In general, Protocole projects were linked to unions' specific local or industrial needs, and were designed with that priority in mind.

At the beginning of the 1990s a combination of the IRAT and Protocole model was taken abroad, to Australia and to Ontario. In 1990, the Australian Council of Trade Unions and the then Australian Vice-

Chancellors' Committee signed the National Academic–Union Scheme (National Statement of Cooperation on Secondments Between Higher Education Institutions and Unions, 1990). Also in 1991 York University chartered the Centre for Research on Work and Society. But at the same time as the Quebec model was internationalising, IRAT began having serious funding problems, compounded by an increased enthusiasm on the part of each of the three union centrales for developing union-to-employer partnerships in particular sectors, at the expense of the union-to-academic partnerships that had characterised IRAT. It was closed in the early 1990s. The Protocole continues at UQAM, albeit with less funding for co-ordination and for the 'liberation' of academics from ordinary university duties during their research time with the union.

Anchoring partnerships in the university: the Centre for Research on Work and Society at York University

In the 1980s, a number of English Canadian unions created the Canadian Centre for Policy Alternatives to carry out social and economic policy research, at arm's length from the labour movement, capable of intervening effectively in public debates but representative of progressive labour's interests. Like IRAT it was free-standing rather than university-affiliated, drew unions and academics together, and received union contracts for research on particular topics. Also like IRAT, it was not able to tap into sources of research funding open to academics, or to train graduate students on its projects. Unlike IRAT, it did not have formal university involvement or receive university funding, and had much less formal union involvement. Also unlike IRAT, CCPA did not keep a staff of researchers, but turned to its member intellectuals to fulfil research contracts. Despite the problems which had constrained IRAT, CCPA's research agenda is ambitious. In its own conception, CCPA is a left-wing think tank.

In 1989 York University in Toronto began discussions with the Canadian Autoworkers to develop a research unit that would foster on-going collaboration on research. For unions such as the CAW – newly seceded from the US- based United Autoworkers – there was a need for substantial Canadian research projects that were one step removed from, but directly relevant to, the day-to-day industrial issues the union faced. Although the CAW was already in the forefront of Canadian unions looking at the larger questions of work restructuring, few other Canadian unions had researchers who had the time to do more than write speeches for the leadership or support collective bargaining. (One notable exception is the Canadian Union of Public Employees.)

For academics at York and the other universities who were drawn into the Centre for Research on Work and Society (CRWS), researching directly with the union movement offered both the possibility of directing their research towards visibly useful ends and a privileged space for training students. It also required openness and sensitivity in developing research problematics, and a willingness to redefine the meaning of academic autonomy. (For some English Canadian academics, researching with unions offered the tempting possibility of an easy way in to influencing the unions' larger social agenda. The English Canadian unions, still not too distant from their own historic anti-intellectualism, tend to be more than cynical towards these researchers, and in general keep them at arm's length.) It was assumed that CRWS research would be linked to rank-and-file education, to conferences and workshops, and to the training of university students. The publishing programme and the international links which later developed were not part of the original conception.

Quebec's experience with IRAT and with the Service à la collectivité programme were of great importance in planning CRWS. They indicated pitfalls and possibilities. First, it was desirable to institutionalise research collaboration by creating an on-going research centre rather than one-by-one, ad hoc research relationships. Second, CRWS should not be free-standing, but should be firmly anchored in a university. Third, CRWS was structured for recessionary times: it was assumed that there would not be a lot of money from the university or from the unions, and that the centre would have to rely on scholarly and government research funding. Fourth, both the IRAT and Protocole indicated that the widest possible union participation should be sought, even though the English Canadian labour movement was notorious for internecine struggles between social unionism and labourism during the 1990s. This broadening of CRWS' engagement from a small number of unions to the labour movement as a whole had a twofold significance. Becoming a research centre in which a number of unions with competing ideologies could develop useful research *and would be prepared to leave their factions at the door*, rather than a centre in which one union played a hegemonic role and drew in many academics, developed naturally out the unions' growing research needs and CRWS' willingness to deal evenhandedly with all unions. It signified a desire to create a 'safe house' for labour research at the same time as it provided the opportunity for competing unions to discover common territory in research. Next, this broadening out to work with many unions signified a move away from the autonomist mode of union engagement with academics, and offered the space to develop affinity-based research and real collaboration. Finally, the ideology of research activism CRWS worked with and refined was the Research Cycle.

Over the nine years since CRWS' chartering by York, it has both put the Research Cycle idea into practice, and discovered its limits. CRWS now has thirty-five Research Associates in nine countries, and about one hundred trade unionists, academics and community activists in Canada who worked on projects in 1998. It publishes two regular twice-yearly publications, *Training Matters* and the *CRWSnews* (circulation 2,200); a Working Paper Series; runs a Trade-Unionist-in-Residence programme and Trade Union Speakers' Series; and has held a number of international conferences, at which the speakers are drawn from the trade union and international academic communities. It directs a Work Internship for students with the labour movement, and is developing a specialist graduate degree.

Activist research is, of course, the core. At present it has approximately forty funded research projects throughout Canada. CRWS people are researching new union-organising strategies; young workers and precarious employment; education equity for excluded youth; the dilemma young workers pose to unions; competitive organising in the hotel sector; privatisation in the public sector; changes in education industry working conditions; unions as employers; cross-border organising; survivors of downsizing; contrasting ideas of partnership in training and manpower development in Quebec and English Canada; and apprenticeship.

Many of the funded projects are associated with the five-year grant on the Political Economy of the Training Industry ('Training Matters'), funded by the Social Science and Humanities Research Council of Canada. This network is a group of researchers (about thirty in all) from fourteen universities, five community colleges and about twenty organisations. Most major trade unions are members, as are some commercial trainers and businesses. It researches in seven provinces and the Yukon, and in English and French. It has German, Belgian, Australian, American and French associates. It has to date published thirty-two working papers, with a book forthcoming.

Two and a half years into this project, it demonstrates many of the benefits, most of the pitfalls and some of the unanswered questions of academic–union research partnership on an institutionalised, larger than project-by-project scale. One project in particular may serve as an example.

The Vancouver Island Highway project

In 1994, the British Columbia government, a New Democratic Party government, embarked on a project to build a highway for Vancouver Island. The project was to cost $1.2 billion. Unlike most highway construction projects, it was meant to be:

a laboratory for the idea that capital spending has the potential to generate major economic and social spinoffs if there is a conscious, deliberate and systematic effort to incorporate these objectives into the planning and implementation of major capital projects.

(Calvert 1996: 9)

In other words, to use public capital spending for provincial economic development, local job creation, employment equity and training. From the beginning, this narrowed down to local hiring (which would be drawn largely but not exclusively from the aboriginal communities the highway linked) and employment equity. The context, however, was not promising. Over the ten years preceding the project, the highway construction industry had become effectively non-union, with membership down to 20 per cent from an earlier 65 per cent. As unionisation rates declined, both training and apprenticeship suffered. The largely non-union industry was awash with unemployed white males, and both the private contractors competing for contracts and the construction unions would be looking to place their most senior unemployed (white male) people first.

The provincial government, however, had decided to make the Vancouver Island Highway a lever to get women, members of aboriginal communities, people with disabilities and visible minorities the training necessary to enter the construction trades. There is no employment equity legislation in British Columbia for the private sector, and this pro-active government meant to use the highway to prise open the construction industry. In order to make this happen, the government created a Crown Corporation which became the sole employer of all workers on the new highway. The Corporation was the sole employer and allocated all workers to the private contractors who had obtained contracts to build the highway. There was competitive tendering: private contractors competed on everything but labour supply. The contractors then reimbursed the Crown Corporation for the cost of labour it had supplied them. The Crown Corporation, in total control of labour supply, went pro-actively after local residents and members of the four equity groups (members of aboriginal communities, women, people with disabilities, and visible minorities). This reduced the pool of qualified workers. After commissioning a study of the available skills pools in the local communities within 100 kilometres of the highway, it was determined that there were not enough qualified people. Training programmes therefore had to be created from scratch by the Crown Corporation in order to obtain the local and equity trainees to which the project was committed. The unions helped with designing the courses and the community colleges with delivering them. By March of 1996, as the project entered its third year, there were

9,249 applicants for training, of whom 2,522 were from the four designated groups. By May 1996, 18 per cent of all workers on the highway were members of the equity groups, and the hours matched up as well. This was not easy to sell to the unions or the contractors. The private non-union contractors fought it through the courts, and lost. The unions were ambivalent. On the one hand, the government offered them union recognition and required trainees and workers to become union members upon obtaining work. On the other hand, unions were faced with outrage from their unemployed members from all over the province: they were out of work, with considerable seniority, and wanted to know why the unions thought they could give their jobs away. The no-strike, no-lockout agreement was not a source of contention, but the agreement on wages that were $2 below the standard rate for the province, was. In defence, both the unions and the Crown Corporation noted that the unions themselves had been widely negotiating under-standard wages for several years.

What role for research in this unusual, and to date quite effective, megapartnership? On the face of it, not much. The government official responsible for this project presented it for the first time to CRWS' Conference on the Service Sector Revolutions in November, 1995. When he was asked about the role of research, he began by saying that the minister responsible, now the premier, had been committed to the project from the beginning and didn't need research to back him up. But as he talked further, we discovered that research had had an important but modest role. As the government sought out the four traditional equity groups to make the idea of training for these unconventional occupations interesting to them, it found that it did not have the wherewithal to reach some of them on its own. It turned, instead, to research on the skill pools in the local communities, research that was painstaking, detailed and carefully respectful of the groups it was reaching out to. It also turned to the Women's Bureau of the government and Women in Trades and Technology, and research became community outreach became dialogue became an on-going community monitoring process of the highway project. As the training programmes were set up and started to function, an Employee Equity Plan was established. It had five dimensions: education and awareness; outreach; skills development; bridging programmes; and removal of barriers. Out of this plan, an Equity Integration Committee was established. Working within the Plan, the Committee not only selected the applicants to be given training and monitored progress on the five dimensions of the Plan, but it also created a sophisticated data base for monitoring the progress of equity trainees and employees. The major failure here was that people with disabilities did not participate in the Committee.

In 1997, an additional dimension was added to the role of research. The Training Matters Network funded a research project on the experience of women with training in the Vancouver Island Highway project (Cohen *et al.* 1998). Although the unions which had greeted the highway project with ambivalence initially responded similarly to this evaluative research project, they were drawn in by presentations of the research to examine the larger issues of women, apprenticeships and training in the trades, and are participating in a subsequent project on that subject. The original Training Matters Project, in turn, is being used to document best practices in training women for the trades. And it has been linked to three subsequent studies on retention of women in apprenticeships – in the national postal service, construction, and the national apprenticeship training survey (Little and Pajot, in press; Gibson and Trade Union Research Bureau, in press).

4 Conclusions and the questions they raise

The research cycle

Good and useful activist research creates a research cycle to bridge the solitudes in three directions: inward to the labour movement, outward to the university, and outward to the wider public. Within a union or the union movement, research is developed with the people it studies and will affect, and then the results are brought back to the rank-and-file who participated in shaping the project, through workshops, roundtables, and publications. It is also used to acquaint the wider union with the issues facing the group in question. It may also be used to shape collective bargaining demands or wider mobilisation. Thus, when Canada Post privatised 'admail' and terminated 10,500 workers, the union got involved with a study of that termination which analysed corporate strategy, the profile of the terminated workers and their fates six months later (White *et al.* 1998). The admail workers responded to the study of their experience with an astonishing 87 per cent response rate. The union printed 20,000 copies of the results in both summary and extended form. These were distributed not only to the admail workers but to union activists throughout the country, and then used as an orientation document to analyse the limits and possibilities of action.

Within universities, the research cycle contributes to the training of students and the creation of a labour-friendly, multi-disciplinary stream of teaching, graduate programmes and research. While most graduate students will not go on to work for unions, they will have developed their research skills by taking workers into consideration from the outset.

Working on a problematic they know to be of concrete use to a group of workers, they will finish their training with a clear and unromantic view of the obstacles facing worker defence and mobilisation.

In the wider public fora, the research cycle insists that useful and grounded research be not only transformed into education and mobilisation, but made to contribute to public education as well. This may be accomplished through ordinary publishing, but it more usually occurs through unconventional intrusion on the public attention. Thus in the admail study discussed above, the researchers ensured that there was newspaper and electronic media coverage of the study. In a 1993 study of garment homeworkers in Toronto, the researchers and the worker participants attended a government committee hearing wearing garments to which two price tags were attached: the store price of the garment and the amount the homeworker had been paid. There are many examples.

For activist research to fulfil its role, it needs to be both useful and embedded in a research cycle which links research and discovery to training, education and implementation. For research to realise its potential, it must not only awaken and mobilise, shake things up, but it must also sow the seeds of the next generation of discovery, education, mobilisation, social and political change, and, of course, further research.

References

Aguiar, L.L.M. (1999) 'Getting the dirt', PhD dissertation, Department of Sociology, York University.

Anisef, P., Ling, Z. and Sweet, R. (1999) *The Causes and Consequences of Attrition in Apprenticeships: An Analysis of the 1994–5 National Apprenticed Trades Survey*, Training Matters Working Paper, York: York University, Centre for Research on Work and Society.

Betcherman, G. (1990) 'Good jobs, bad jobs: employment in the service sector', statement by the Economic Council of Canada, Ottawa.

Calvert, J. (1996) 'Maximizing social and economic development spin-offs from public capital spending: the experience of the Vancouver Island Highway', unpublished paper.

Cohen, M., Braid, K. and Gibson, D. (1998) *The B.C. Island Highway Project: A Model for Access and Retention of Equity Groups in Skilled Trades and Semi-Skilled Blue Collar Jobs*, Training Matters Series, Working Paper, York: York University, Centre for Research on Work and Society.

Critoph, U. (1999) 'Monitoring labour market programs and policy', unpublished report, Canadian Labour Force Development Board.

Gibson, D. and Trade Union Research Bureau (in press) *Factors in the Long-Term Success of Women in Trade Employment and Training Programs: A Case Study of the BladeRunners Program*, Toronto: Trade Union Research Bureau.

Hyman, R. (1999) 'An emerging agenda for trade unions?' unpublished International Labour Organisation paper.

James, P., Veight, W. and Wright, S. (1997) *Work of the Future: Global Perspectives*, Sydney: Allen and Unwin.

Lipsig-Mummé, C. (1988) *A Trade Union–University Secondment Scheme*, Sydney: Evatt Foundation.

Lipsig-Mummé, C. (1991) 'Future conditional: wars of position in the Quebec labour movements', *Studies in Political Economy* 36 (Fall): 73–107.

Lipsig-Mummé, C. and Laxer, K. (1998) *Organising and Union Membership: A Canadian Profile*, Ottawa: Canadian Labour Congress.

Little, M. and Pajot, L. (in press) *Integrating Women Apprentices in Canada Post*, Training Matters Series, Working Paper, York: York University Centre for Research on Work and Society.

Messing, K. and Mergler, D. (1992) *Union–University Collaboration to Improve Women's Occupational Health in Quebec*, Montreal: Centre pour l'étude des interactions biologiques entre la santé et l'environnement, Université du Québec à Montréal.

Schenk, C. and Anderson, J. (1995) *Reshaping Work*, Toronto: Ontario Federation of Labour.

Waddington, J. and Whitston, C. (1993) 'Research as engagement: trade unions in the 1990s' in Keith Forrester and Colin Thorne (eds) *Trade Unions and Social Research*, Aldershot: Avebury (pp. 24–43).

White, J., Janzen, R. and Lipsig-Mummé, C. (1998) *When Public Jobs Go Private*, York: York University Centre for Research on Work and Society, Working Paper No. 18.

9 The negotiated management of meanings

Research for policy

John McIntyre and Rosie Wickert

In their introduction to this book, Garrick and Rhodes articulate two inter-related ways to think about the notion of 'research at work'. The first concerns the practices of 'doing' research at work. The second, which is the focus of this chapter, concerns the ways that research-based knowledge is employed in workplace situations. Although in this chapter our discussion is oriented to the 'workplace' of public policy production, we suggest that our analysis of the changing relationships between research and its utilisation has relevance to other work contexts as well.

This chapter, then, explores the question: when research goes to work for policy, what does this do to research and to policy? What kinds of relationships are constructed? The chapter first explores how we can understand policy as a context for research. Our sources of theory for this task include, first, Ball's policy cycle framework with its five contexts of action, and second, Yeatman's analysis of the state and policy processes, including her concepts of corporate managerialism, the new contractualism and the notion of co-production. We explore how policy co-production involves the negotiated management of research meanings

We ask how the work of research has been shaped by new kinds of policy work in the contemporary state. We critique older ideas of the way that research has been constructed by policy and policy by research, and offer an alternative view of research and policy relationships as co-production. We introduce the idea of policy knowledge, in part to point up how 'policy' has been conceived of as other than knowledge and in part to signal how contemporary policy is changing. We extend this by discussing two examples, referring to the stated and unstated problematics of a research brief.

We conclude by asking what scope there is, given these conditions, for research to influence policy, or for that matter for policy to influence research. We conclude that conservative efforts to control academic work are misplaced and that research-for-policy exemplifies how the academy is already engaged in the production of 'practical' knowledge formations.

Research and policy: a troubled relationship?

Relationships are often troubled because of issues of territory and how different parties understand the domain in which they relate. This observation can be applied to the relationship between research and policy where, traditionally, these are seen as independent domains. As we shall show, a linear, top-down notion of policy production informs traditional models, and this limits, conceptually, the contexts that policy provides for research activity.

In contrast, Ball offers a 'policy cycle' framework that presents as a set of interrelating and interactive loops, which, although they have a temporal dimension, are not simply linear. His notion differs, then, from the usual cycle construct which is caught within a conventional and linear feedback-loop planning model (see Davis *et al.* 1993). Ball categorises five identifiable contexts of action in the policy process. He argues that these contexts operate in a continuous policy cycle and that their operations enable policy to be recontextualised and rewritten throughout the processes of its existence: they have to be understood as interrelated in unpredictable ways. The five contexts that he identifies are the context of influence, the context of policy text production, the context of practice, the context of outcomes and the context of political strategy (Ball 1994). The importance of this model for our argument here is that it offers a framework for understanding how research activity gets to engage in policy in a number of different kinds of ways and for a range of purposes.

This model implies a more emergent and contingent relationship between policy and research and yet the academic discipline of policy science remains as oriented to the perfection of the relationship between policy and research as it has since its establishment, by Harold Lasswell, in the 1950s. Lasswell's dream was to unite the social sciences and the natural sciences in a 'policy sciences of democracy'; 'to comprehend and deliberately shape applications of scientific and professional knowledge to the manifold problems facing contemporary society' (Dunn and Holzner 1988: 5). Since then, and particularly since the mid-1970s, a distinct and growing field of study has developed around exploring the problematics of this dream – namely, how knowledge gets better utilised in policy-making (cf. Weiss 1977).

In spite of evidence that policy-makers appear to make relatively little direct use of research information in making policy decisions (MacRae 1991; Oh 1997), a major concern of policy analysts remains focused on how to 'perfect decision making ahead of time rather than practising politics contingently' (Schram 1995: 379). A substantial and on-going literature and, indeed, specific journals are dedicated to this activity. Papers regularly appear describing efforts to identify variables considered most likely to affect utilisation and impact (Oh 1997; Rich and Oh 1993). This suggests that the presumption that 'good, sound' research can feed directly into 'good, sound' decision-making remains strong, despite conflicting empirical evidence.

Concern about the value of perfecting policy research utilisation is not new. As far back as 1977, Rein and Schön commented that much of the contemporary doubt about the field of research utilisation rested upon a somewhat narrow view of what policy research can or should do. They noted then that the dominant conception of policy research was its use within a rationalist framework of decision-making and problem-solving, concentrated – to draw on Ball's terms – within the elite contexts of influence and of text production. Perhaps, as Watkins (1994) notes, it is also the limitations of conventional models of policy production that result in a lack of attention to other possibilities and to other relationships between policy-makers and researchers. Underlying the positivist approach of many who use research in policy are a set of assumptions about what policy is and how it gets to be made. Such rationalist, or 'executive' as Yeatman (1998) puts it, models of policy production carry with them presumptions about the objective nature of knowledge and how certain methodologies can produce this outcome.

Our own experiences of engagement in research, policy and especially the work of doing research for policy have been far more messy and undisciplined than much of the research utilisation literature suggests. Nonetheless, the influence of traditional models remains strong. Rather than dismiss, then, supposedly discredited or inadequate models of policy production, we need to understand them as part of the field, carrying with them their own constitutive effects. Drawing on our experience as researchers in policy contexts, we conclude this section by noting that the models of action with which contemporary policy researchers work need to take account of the following:

1   a rationalist model of policy analysis continues to dominate in research and policy discourses;
2   the process of policy development almost inevitably requires the production of policy research;
3   there is a complex set of relationships (working) between researchers and policy-makers despite a continued commitment to a rationalist

process, and despite the apparently limited direct utilisation of research findings and recommendations.

Some effects of the contemporary moment

More recent contributions to the knowledge utilisation and policy-making literature have begun to engage with the realities of the turbulent policy environment of current times. Stimulated, for example, by the work of Schön and Rein (1994) and Fischer (1995), the dream that 'solutions' can be found through a better understanding of how research can inform policy-related decisions has begun to give way to the challenges posed to policy-makers and researchers by seemingly intractable policy problems that appear susceptible neither to research nor to policy. Thus, whatever tacit agreement there might be about the 'public' stories of both research and the policy process, there are many other stories of policy practice.

The relatively ordered and predictable policy climate of the post-war years has, more recently, been thrown into upheaval by economic fluctuations, rapid technological change, looming ecological crises and major social and demographic developments. The realisation that some policy problems may, in fact, be intractable is a profoundly unsettling realisation for researchers and policy-makers committed to the set of certainties that are attached to rationalist modes of knowledge production and policy production.

The realisation that science does not only have the capacity to 'solve' problems, but, furthermore, has the capacity to 'create' disasters is shocking for many. The collapse of certainty, alongside a growing demand for evidence that 'something is being done' can be argued to be responsible, in part, for creating the space into which the regulating mechanisms of the market have been introduced as an arbiter – a supposedly reliable indicator of will. This regulating mechanism acts to commodify services, as well as goods; and research, or knowledge, is no less caught up in this than other services.

In other words, as there is no longer a monopoly on what is worthwhile knowledge, then many forms of knowledge are emerging as worthwhile and legitimate. Furthermore, the criteria for validity of what has value as worthwhile knowledge lie, in a market-oriented political economy, as much in the hands of its consumers as with its producers. Consider, for example the Research Director of Synergy Brand Values in the UK, who was cited as claiming, 'We don't want to prove whether our research is right or wrong. If the stuff doesn't work for our clients, that's the bottom line for us' (cited in Stronach and MacLure 1997: 16).

Similarly, Stronach and MacLure (ibid.: 88) suggest that what counts as a 'policy solution' is increasingly being driven by a desire to be seen to act by answering symbolically to 'a need to dramatise a political response' – rather than *solve* a problem. Furthermore in the postmodern moment, the politics of any one particular settlement are legitimately open for acknowledgement, discussion and challenge. We note here, then, a tension whereby the demands of modern government generate pressures on policy-makers to 'get it right', as well as to flexibly and pragmatically accommodate difference.

Though this point of view grows out of our interest in public policy, there are many reasons to think that it is also true of the ways that business policy is made, and indeed, the interactions between public and private sectors, particularly as economic reform impinges on both. Though the chapter may emphasise the 'reform' of the public sector management as a context which makes research indispensable to government, it is clearly also true that national projects such as privatisation, industrial relations or taxation reform generate complexities in the business policy environment that have to be managed. In this sense, uncertainty and changeability make 'perfect policy-making' difficult or impossible, so that both business and government emphasise the *management of policy* as never before. Research, we will suggest, has become increasingly important in managing policy in the sense that it can be deployed as a key means to manage the *meanings* in play in the policy environment.

What is policy?

Despite claims that things might be otherwise, most policies are 'ramshackle, compromise, hit and miss affairs' (Ball 1998: 126), made on the run. In the arena of public social policy, terms such as policy 'hysteria' (Stronach and Morris 1994); 'turbulence' and 'epidemic' (Levin 1998); 'waves' of reform (Stronach and MacLure 1997); 'rage' (Silver 1990); and 'volatility' (Colebatch 1993) are all suggestive of the intensity of the experience of 'policy' in this historical 'policy minded moment' (O'Regan 1992). This intensification of policy activity, albeit not necessarily coherent, is the policy context in and with which research now has to work. The prevalence of terms such as those listed above are suggestive that this period is somehow an aberration and that calm and order will once again descend on the policy environment. But as Stronach and MacLure so cogently argue, this change is neither temporary or dysfunctional – it is what is consistent with the challenges of postmodernity, wherein policy becomes part of the moving mosaic of the postmodern performance (Hargreaves 1996).

If policy is as contingent and provisional as the metaphors above suggest, researchers in both the public and business arenas need to engage with a notion of policy that accounts for these complexities, and which can accommodate differing relationships and practices and recognise opportunities for differing types of collaboration at differing moments. What is needed here is a conception of policy which not only recognises its multiple contexts of performance (Ball) but which also 'opens it up to the appropriate participation of all those involved in policy all the way through points of conception, operational formulation, implementation, delivery on the ground, consumption and evaluation' (Yeatman 1998: 43). Yeatman elaborates this notion in the following way:

> Policy then is reconceived as the policy process ... it is not just the democratisation of our social relationships which underlies this conception of policy and a policy process. It is also the dynamics of increased complexity and uncertainty in our lives. When attention is paid to these two dynamics it becomes clear that rationalistic and intellectualistic models of policy that are predicated on some idea of rational mastery engage those who follow them in a rather dangerous kind of fantasy. We cannot predict or plan our futures in ways which enable us to subject our lives to rational direction and control. Rather, we have to learn to live in ways which enable us to adapt to ongoing change, complexity and uncertainty.
>
> (Yeatman 1998: 31)

In other words, policy is a dynamic process that engages multiple participants in a range of contexts. Ball's work is useful in developing a model of these contexts and this helps us to develop our discussion about how policy-related researchers become involved in negotiating meanings in their work with decision-makers and others. What is also important is some elaboration of the types of policy–research relationships that might develop in various contexts and a broadening of the scope of criteria for judging their performance.

Although there is not the space to explore this question here, it is important to note that there is an emerging strand of policy analysis engaged in serious exploration of these questions. These writers emphasise that the relationship between research and policy is neither unidirectional nor unifunctional. They argue that judgements about utility need to relate to different kinds of validation which can take account of the multi-dimensionality of policy use and policy impact. Watkins (1994: 57) argues that 'the deterministic image of a linear directionality to research, dissemination and use that comes from the traditional research use field does not account for the complex kinds of problem posing, resolution and relationships of now'. The normal – discipline-derived – controls on research are not the only or perhaps even the appropriate criteria for judging policy research. There are matters of relevance, morality and lack of certainty, for example. As Ewan and Calvert explain in Chapter 4, this 'diffusion' of academic research is indicative of a crisis. For others, however, it is indicative of the quest for a 'constructive politics' (Luke 1995: 83) of research oriented to the provisionality and contingency of contemporary policy-making conditions. We see that the new negotiated management of meanings, including the 'research for policy' design process, is explicitly a matter of creatively responding to the factual uncertainties and normative ambiguities of ever-changing realities in relationships of *co-enquiry*.

In policy work at least, we must address new definitions of 'researchers', 'useful research' and 'research use'. It is more a matter of understanding when, why and how the outputs and processes of many different types of research activity intersect with the production and enactment of policy rather than determining which is the most appropriate approach for the contemporary policy moment, or of arguing the old quantitative/qualitative divide. We think it is more a matter of unsettling the categories that attempt to fix meanings, such as those of policy and research.

As discussed by Edwards and Usher in Chapter 3, 'postmodernity' has already unsettled the couplet between research and knowledge in the sense that academically produced knowledge has lost its exclusive claim to both the production and the elaboration of knowledge. What we are now seeing is not only a proliferation of 'knowledge-producers' but a recognition of the legitimacy of different kinds of 'knowledge' (Hargreaves 1996). So, is there such a thing as 'policy' knowledge? Webber (1991–2: 10) makes a distinction between policy analysis and policy knowledge. He defines policy 'analysis' as 'systematic policy information presented as an explanation of how a policy alternative works or will work if adopted'. Policy 'knowledge' he defines as 'the body of human knowledge available to assist policy makers in their understandings of the causes and consequences of the outputs of government and the subsequent social impact' (ibid.: 11). As Webber crucially points out, 'research' is inquiry or activity intended to identify knowledge, but, for the most part, 'policy information', 'research', 'analysis', and 'knowledge' are synonymous from the perspective of policy-makers.

If one accepts this kind of analysis, then it becomes clear that the question of a relationship is not so much a matter of that between research and policy as that between the researcher and the policy-maker, and the matter of success is connected with the congruence of the stories each adopts about what each is involved in and the purposes for which policy-related research is sought. It is in this context that we emphasise the contingency of the work of research and its contribution to policy, the work that research can do in the negotiation and management of meanings in the policy production process.

Research for policy

In the previous section we discussed how policy provides contexts for research work, exploring some understandings of policy drawn from the work of Ball and Yeatman. We suggested that models of research and policy relationships have defined the work of research as a domain independent of policy, one that hopes to have impact on the policy process. These traditional models, we suggested, position the researcher (that is, the academic researcher) as an agent acting from outside the policy process. Research is something that the researcher hopes will be 'utilised', and the researcher works in various ways, including advocacy, to achieve its dissemination.

We are arguing, however, that the contemporary moment is setting new conditions for research and policy relationships through 'policy intervention' by the state and projects of economic and public sector reform. The way 'policy processes' are now constituted changes the way research is put to work by policy and policy-makers.

In this section we will explore several features of Yeatman's analysis of the contemporary state – her theorisation of corporate managerialism and its 'new contractualism' and the thesis of policy activism in spaces of the changed state. We argue with Yeatman (1998) that public sector reform has set up new demands for research to work for policy production, creating a need and rationale for commissioned research which is governed by contractualism. These conditions redefine the domains of 'research' and 'policy' and their relationships, and generate new roles for agents in the policy process.

The corporatisation of the public sector has brought into being the phenomenon of commissioned research and the consultant researcher. If, from the point of view of the academy, research tended to be located outside the policy process, it is now brought into and managed as part of the process of policy production. Here, there are key questions about what capacity there is for researchers to influence the policy agenda that has, as it were, required their services. Are they mere agents of the new managers, or is there scope for 'policy activism' as it has been discussed in Yeatman's recent work (Yeatman 1998)? In what ways does *the work* of commissioned research give scope for shaping policy, when researchers are positioned by policy as authoritative sources of knowledge for policy?

To answer these questions thus requires some analysis of the nature of the working relationships that are predicated by the new conditions of policy production. What is the nature of the research contract and how is this realised? What discretion does the contract give the researcher over both research and policy outcomes? More significant, perhaps, how is there a 'play' of possibilities in the working out and the 'managing' of research that gives such scope? Yeatman's theorisation of the 'new contractualism' provides one basis for understanding how research and policy relationships are worked out and worked through in the contemporary state (Yeatman 1995; Sullivan and Yeatman 1997).

Corporate managerialism and research for policy

Yeatman's analysis of the 'shift' in the nature of the contemporary state has been influential in Australasian accounts of public policy (see Marginson 1993: 56–7; Taylor *et al.* 1997: 81–4; Considine 1994; Peters and Marshall 1996), though it is rarely explored in the kind of depth it was given in her original discussion (Yeatman 1991: 13–32). Her argument drew on the work of Melucci and Cerny to theorise the emergence of a leaner and more efficient state, which is pressed by intensifying global competition to create competitive conditions for private sector investment. To accomplish this steering role, the emerging state shrinks the public sector and makes it more managerial in character (Yeatman 1993).

Yeatman described numerous features of corporate managerialism. It is outcomes-focused rather than rule-bound; flattens authority structures but exercises management prerogatives; professionalises bureaucratic work but subjects it to management control; humanises public service employment through a 'people-and process' orientation but implements more stringent accountability practices; adopts meritocratic selection which admits cultural minorities but excludes the under-educated from its professionalised work; opens decision-making to value-led debate but subordinates values to technical/administrative concerns; and, in the absence of firm value commitments, produces technocratic managers indifferent to the social ends of their work (Yeatman 1991: 13–32).

Reference to Yeatman's idea often overlooks her important insight that the contemporary state, though certainly shrinking in terms of public sector employment, is also more 'dispersed' 'complex' and 'interventionist' in function. Yeatman suggests that it is the emergence of new social movements making claims on government that has differentiated and dispersed the state's activity so that it has become 'intertwined in complex ways with the agents of civil society' (1991: 35). The corporatisation of the public sector is thus to be understood as one feature of the 'complex interventionist state'.

This view of the state is important to understanding Yeatman's concept of corporate managerialism. Though it shrinks its direct activities, the reach of the new state is extended, as boundaries between its activities and those of other agencies are opened up. This cultural shift has made commissioned research an important resource for the new policy managers. The key point, perhaps, is that the new public sector manager thinks of policy differently – as something that is strategic and 'managed' so that it has 'outcomes', particularly where funding is diminishing. This implies that the bureaucrat is open to whatever knowledge bases provide 'timely and relevant' information that will 'move the policy agenda forward' (such phrases suggest something of the flavour of the new policy discourses). Where good information is lacking, targeted research may be seen as necessary. The new bureaucrats are professional managers who may have little accumulated experience of the portfolio, whereas the old public service bureaucrat was a 'portfolio advocate' (Yeatman 1993) with an expertise and a loyalty accumulated over a long career.

The point about the 'dispersed' activity of the contemporary state is well illustrated by the fate of research infrastructure in the old state education bureaucracies. Restructuring has virtually destroyed this research capacity, but it is not thereby the case that government is less interested in research for policy. The new public sector managerialism has, if anything, intensified the need for research for strategic policy, which can be resourced by drawing academics into the work. At the same time, the state has 'intervened' to orient universities to a more competitive environment and made them painfully aware of their status as public sector entities. Higher education management has been 'reformed' through a corporatising of authority structures, subjecting academic work to redefinition, accompanied by an intensification of research consultancy which then weaves the academy into the state's 'dispersed' activity. Academics network closer relationships with the restructured bureaucracies, which need their services as much as the academics need the external funding. This is the new political economy of policy research.

Thus the nature of the 'knowledge resource' for policy-making has shifted from a closed knowledge base captured within the portfolio to a relatively open system where relevant knowledge can be assembled or constructed around immediate policy requirements. By 'shifted', we mean that restructuring has in a deliberate way invalidated, or perhaps purged (if that is not too strong a term), the policy knowledges embodied in the old regime. Though some grieve the 'loss of corporate memory' restructuring brings, there is no 'loss' if that memory is regarded as an obstacle to public sector reform. Reform assumed that the problem with those older policy knowledges was their embodiment in the old bureaucrats, while the new regime claims to look beyond portfolio expertise to whatever knowledge might support policy formation. It can certainly be argued (thinking of old education bureaucracies) that much of their in-house research was captive to policy and to the pragmatics of portfolio advocacy.

In such an account it is important not to gloss over the difficulties of the adaptations demanded of those employed in policy work. The point here is that a changed bureaucratic culture does create new spaces and opportunities for research to shape policy, and at the same time it also creates pressures for people to learn new ways of thinking and *doing* research for policy. In this complex, and at times contradictory, state of affairs, it is worth noting that reform has brought about a huge increase in the amount of commissioned research. With this change, the nature of 'knowledge-for-policy' has changed, creating new policy knowledges and making space for new kinds of policy-action. This is, of course, true not only of the public sector, but also of many large organisations reinventing themselves as they demutualise, shed non-core businesses, become absorbed into global businesses or otherwise reinvent themselves for a more competitive business environment.

One consequence of these changes, we wish to argue, is a new influence of research on policy. The nature of the new policy regime is at first negotiated in character – it has to be worked out. Public sector reform is a political project of economic rationalism. One way its goals of *policy management* have been realised is through research commissions which set a context in which bureaucrat and consultant come to negotiate common understandings about the role of research in policy. They do so because of the very contractualism of the new regime, which is above all else performative. The point is that the research performances have to be negotiated.

For this reason, we argue that the changing nature of research-for-policy cannot be well understood by calling on typical dissemination models of research described in the literature (cf. Weiss 1977; Husen and Kogan 1984; Finch 1986; Anderson and Biddle 1991; Halpin and Troyna 1995). These usually presuppose a bureaucratic order relatively impermeable to the discourses of academic researchers, who then construct their problem with policy as one of the difficulty of achieving 'policy impact'. What happens, then, when the policy process constitutes itself as one open to research discourses and invites researchers to provide perspectives on policy problems?

These claims about research and policy envisage the public sector as the site of changing relationships, yet they apply no less to the private sector and the corporate structures – as Clegg has shown in Chapter 5 – that are furnishing models for public sector reform at every level. Indeed, as other chapters in this volume attest, there is nothing static about the contemporary workplace, and hence there are a host of questions about how workplace dynamics are predicating new relationships between business policy and management information. To the extent that the strategic character of corporate policy-making has intensified with increased global competition, and to the extent that the workplace is 'humanised' – with employees more self-regulating – there are new demands for research to answer to strategic corporate policy questions and help 'manage professional intellect' (Quinn *et al.* 1996: 71). It remains an open question as to just how far the so-called 'knowledge workers' of the new workplace are transforming 'management information' into strategic policy through their corporate research. It is most certainly the case that in both public and private organisations, changed managerial structures are predicating new relationships of research and policy.

Commissioned research and the research contract

Having examined how corporate managerialism sets particular conditions for policy research, it will be useful to explore in more detail how research practices are shaped by these conditions. Here we will want to generalise about the experience of the research commission and the production of the policy research texts. In doing so we acknowledge that we are talking about wide variations in the circumstances of state-commissioned research.[1] At the same time, the concept of a 'research commission' can extend to any circumstances where a researcher is given a brief, and what we say about it may equally apply to the market researcher who has to negotiate the policy significance of research with supervisors, as well as manage the process. It is the negotiation of significances that is interesting.

The new bureaucratic culture, like the corporate world on which it is modelled, requires a negotiation of research and policy relationships just as it assumes a well-managed research contract adapted to policy production, and this implies considerable scope for variability. Commissioned research can involve highly specified research contracts or commissions which prove to have considerable latitude, if not in their contractual 'deliverables' then in the substance and implications of what was reported.

One approach to understanding commissioned research is to focus on examples of such research around key policy arguments and highlight tensions between research and policy in particular constructions of policy. Here we write about two examples of such research in order to suggest how research and policy practices interact in the co-production of policy knowledge. Of particular interest is how the 'research process' is understood within a policy context by policy workers and how research meanings are managed through the policy process.

Policy research, in both process and product terms, is often regarded as problematic from the position of orthodox academic research in that it is seen as constrained rather than independent, interested rather than disinterested, narrow rather than broad in scope, atheoretical rather than sophisticated and, above all, worldly rather than esoteric. This suggests that the one is regarded by the other as conforming to other, different (and often inferior) norms of practice. At worst, policy research consultancy is perceived as expedient work that gives the policy-makers the answers they want. As we have already suggested, this seriously misunderstands the process, especially in assuming the closed information environment of classical bureaucracy rather than the performative workplace.

Clearly, the negotiated character of research commissions can be represented and interrogated in a range of ways, and we recognise that it is impossible to convey its high contextuality without being very descriptive. The point is to highlight the dynamics of the work, and in the following discussion we will give attention to two concerns:

- To the extent that there is a question or problem to be investigated, how is this understood by the parties to the process? What stated and unstated problematics are to be managed in pursuing the question, and to what extent is there a play of competing research questions?
- How important are questions of perspective and methodology, given that research can be discredited by alleging flaws in the researcher's glass? To what extent do policy-makers specify methodology, and to what extent is this discretionary? How do the parties understand and manage such issues?

The first example refers to a recent investigation conducted by one of us (Wickert) into the incidence of adult literacy in Australia. The circumstances of the research were the coincidence of the approach of International Literacy Year (ILY) alongside a potential withdrawal of state funds for any adult literacy programmes that were not aligned to vocational skills development. A further context for the research was the complex politics of literacy professionals and experts, many of whom were likely to contest any research findings and thus potentially weaken their impact on the policy process.

The research brief initially asked for some exploratory literature research to be undertaken with a view to developing an acceptable research framework. As the imperatives of ILY and budget cycles intensified, so did the desire for the actual survey work to be undertaken. How this was to happen and within what conceptual and methodological frames was not, therefore, contained in any research brief. Rather, these evolved through the on-going explorations of the researchers and their interactions with an advisory committee. This committee comprised bureaucrats, academic colleagues and advocates from relevant fields. What they were engaged in through their various meetings could perhaps be called 'policy conversations' (Schön and Rein 1994) within which learnings of various kinds occurred and through which agreements were made, tacitly and otherwise, that this research could be designed to enable it to perform in a number of kinds of ways on its policy environment.

The second example refers to an investigation of the vocational outcomes of general adult education courses for a state adult education bureau (McIntyre *et al.* 1995). The circumstances of the research are those of the Australian education policy context of education reform in the early 1990s and the changing nature of adult education provision. Adult education in this respect refers to short course, non-credit programmes provided by community-managed agencies. This provision in Australia and elsewhere historically has been marginal to the main business of publicly funded education and training.

At the time, education institutions at all levels were dealing with unprecedented 'policy turbulence' as the national government spearheaded a period of 'national training reform' whose main thrust was an expansion of vocational education and training. Again, part of that turbulence was the intensification of policy work that was entailed by the corporatisation of public sector activity, that was an accompanying feature of 'reform'. The community adult education agencies were confronted with the possibility that they might be excluded from a mooted 'national system' of education and training unless they could demonstrate their potential contribution to vocational education. Their exclusion would mean further marginalisation, while inclusion meant being recognised as legitimate vocational education and training providers, with access to new funding. A point was reached where research was becoming a necessity for policy. The imperative for the policy bureaucrats was to manage the threat the new regime posed to the sector by assembling credible evidence that adult education activity, as well as formal 'vocational training', produced vocational outcomes – for example, by contributing to individual skill formation or employability.

Oversimplifying what were complex circumstances, the first point to note about both these examples is that the policy environment provided enormous pressure for research to produce information strategically vital for the sector, in ways that are analogous to the press of the market-place on business policy. In what ways, then, did this pressure lead bureaucrats to dictate the problem and method of the research? And from the standpoint of contractualism (Yeatman 1995), what discretion was there for the researchers to design and mould the research to their own interests, including their academic interests? In short, how much 'play' was there in the terms of the project?

Without glossing over the complexity of the dynamics, it could be shown that at many points in a research commission there are issues to be resolved as to its scope, meaning, direction and implications. There is no question that the contractual framework means there are negotiable and non-negotiable features to the work, bearing particularly on the acceptability of the research text that is produced. The argument is, however, that the research is a negotiated accomplishment produced through an interplay of research and policy understandings. What is crucial in this *negotiability* is the extent to which the parties had understandings that were developed and modified through the research process, since neither bureaucrat nor researcher is in a state of perfect information, and both parties need to learn (as well as gain) from the process as they managed it, in different ways. Indeed, it is a hallmark of the new bureaucrat (and certainly the new consulting researcher) *that* their activity is open to 'learning' from the experience of policy production.

Thus to assume that research contracts always mean what they say is to ignore their intent to provide scope for work on a policy problematic that is not tractable to routine analysis. It is precisely the point that doing research, under the new conditions of public and private sector workplaces, can generate new thinking – policy assumes its imperfectibility. In turn, this opens up questions of the relative importance of the perspectives generated by research as distinct from the methodologies applied to predetermined questions. The real usefulness of research may be that it provides not only new information, but also a reconceptualisation of a problematic on the basis of new information. In short, the conceptual outcomes may be as significant as the empirical findings they organise.

Under such conditions, there is no simple research question to be 'answered' by routine methods, but rather a set of problematics to be explored more or less creatively, with a range of interests to be acknowledged, since such research works always with the background of its contexts – the presumed policy audiences. The research process itself can be understood as a context where policy problematics can be worked on.

In this way, what was interesting about the projects in question was the shift of understandings that occurred from one project to the next. The dilemma for the academic researcher is the extent to which their ideas and interest must bend to policy imperatives (such as determining literacy levels or vocational outcomes by simply 'counting' what is a complex, multi-dimensional cultural phenomenon) while yet yielding scope for producing respectable scholarly work. For the bureaucrat, the dilemma is that while the research text produced must be useable (be politically acceptable, readable, implementable or workable in a range of ways), there must be scope for the researcher to exercise their expertise on the problematic, to render it analysable and reportable in interesting ways. Yet the parties may, at the same time, have in common a dominant interest in producing a report that speaks to policy and 'makes a difference'. This is particularly so when the researcher takes a position as advocate for the professional field.

In this context, the question of the relevance of methodology or perspective arises. We are representing the research commission as permitting a degree of play or discretion in the nature of the research, though this can be more or less circumscribed. Clearly, bureaucrats (or their corporate counterparts) may determine the methodology or leave it open to proposal by researchers at the tender stage – at issue then will be the quality of their argument about what kind of research is needed for the problem. It has to be borne in mind that the researchers are bidding competitively for the contract. What kind of criteria then determine which researcher is commissioned? Clearly, these might include the adequacy of the methodology (and/or its creativity, cost-effectiveness and so on), given some understanding of the issues. However, the research commission heightens the *arguability of method* by bringing various criteria into play. Methodology is contingent on how the research is argued, to the point where it may be subordinated to the grasp of issues and the proposed conceptual approach. Thus, the decisive factors (in our experience) are the kind of research perspectives the research will make available, given some 'reading' of the policy issues – in short, just what research meanings are going to be brought into play.

This feature of the subordination of methodology to perspective is well illustrated by the vocational outcomes of the project we have just described. This specified the development of multiple perspectives on the problem of 'vocational outcomes' and did so for good policy reasons – to demonstrate the rich complexity of the achievement of the 'vocational' in adult and community education. In this way, the policy aims of the research demanded methodological flexibility of the researchers (and their record of prior research performances). Furthermore, the interests of the parties favoured a multi-dimensionality which could produce 'authoritative' research to serve both policy and academic purposes. Here, the bureaucrats were working with an understanding of the usefulness to policy of 'research of substance', though this understanding was entirely contingent on threats and opportunities presented in a turbulent policy context. In this case, the outcome of the process was the co-production of a research text that could 'perform' for the agency and position the sector to advantage. No doubt a single methodology, a single point of view on outcomes, would present an easy target for its enemies.

This account highlights the co-production of authoritative texts that do the work of representing policy realities, so that such texts have symbolic properties as well as providing a knowledge base. What is of interest is the convergence of policy and research understandings in the assumption that 'substantial' or 'authoritative' research could be achieved through multiple research perspectives (participant surveys, employer interviews, provider case studies). Through these multiple perspectives, the final report of the first project constructed a more complex, multi-dimensional account of the vocational contribution of the sector than might have been the case. Similarly, the final report of the second became a source of policy-related advice for a wide range of adult literacy activists and advocates, within and outside the original commissioning agency.

Conclusion

We began this chapter by treating as dubious the legitimacy claims of both research and policy that are presented in idealised accounts of their relationship. We argued that contemporary conditions have opened up new possibilities for engaging in doing research for policy, supported by our experiences as researchers engaged in policy research. We have suggested that the challenge is to represent the complexity of the negotiated relationships of research and policy, where the researcher is not a naive 'outsider' ignorant of the demands of the policy context, nor is the policy manager ignorant of the possibilities of research.

While we have represented 'the researcher' as an external consultant to a public sector organisation, we suggest that much of the argument applies to research consultancy in the private sector, or indeed internal organisational research. This is so, we have suggested, because time pressures and other exigencies of the contemporary workplace and the competitive business environment mean that research is enmeshed with policy – linear models of research-for-policy are likely to lack application to the realities of business policy formation. Though we have not explored the point here, conceptions of research drawn from behavioural science that entail such linear and exceedingly rational models of policy decision-making may be less applicable.

We have advanced a different view of research and policy as a co-production. Research contributes to the development of policy through the formation of reciprocal understandings by parties to the policy process, where each party grasps both their own and the other party's perspectives on the policy question as a basis for working together on it. This is the basis for what we have described as the management of negotiated meanings in research for policy, and this always assumes the changeability and imperfectibility of the policy process.

Notes

1 By 'state-commissioned research' we are referring to research projects that government agencies contract university researchers or private consultants to design and carry out. In the Australian context, the authors have conducted research of this kind for such national bodies as the Australian Language and Literacy Council and the Australian National Training Authority, and state authorities such as the Office of Training and Further Education (Victoria), the NSW Board of Adult and Community Education, the NSW Department of Education and Training, and the West Australian Department of Training. This is regarded as distinct from federal government university research funding, independently managed by the Australian Research Council.

References

Ahier, J. and Flude, M. (eds) (1983) *Contemporary Education Policy*, London: Croom Helm.

Anderson, D.S. and Biddle, B.J. (eds.) (1991) *Knowledge for Policy: Improving Education through Research*, London: Falmer Press.

Ball, S.J. (1990) *Politics and Policymaking in Education: Explorations in Policy Sociology*, London: Routledge.

Ball, S.J. (1994) *Education Reform: A Critical and Post-Structural Approach*, Philadelphia: Open University Press.

Ball, S.J. (1998) 'Big policies/small world: an introduction to international perspectives in education policy', *Comparative Education* 34, 2: 119–30.

Colebatch, H. (1993) 'Policy-making and volatility: what is the problem?' in A. Hede and S. Prosser (eds) *Policy-Making in Volatile Times*, Sydney: Hale and Iremonger (pp. 29–46).

Considine, M. (1994) *Public Policy: A Critical Approach*, Melbourne: Macmillan Education Australia.

Davis, G., Wanna, J., Warhurst, J. and Weller, P. (1993) *Public Policy in Australia*, Sydney: Allen and Unwin.

Dunn, W.N. and Holzner, B. (1988) 'Anatomy of an emergent field', *Knowledge in Society* 1: 3–26.

Finch, J. (1986) *Research and Policy. The Uses of Qualitative Methods in Social and Educational Research*, London: Falmer Press.

Fischer, F. (1995) *Evaluating Public Policy*, Chicago: Nelson Hall.

Halpin, D. and Troyna, B. (eds) (1995) *Researching Educational Policy*, London: Falmer Press.

Hargreaves, A. (1996). 'Transforming knowledge: blurring the boundaries between research, policy and practice', *Educational Evaluation and Policy Analysis* 18, 2: 105–22.

Husen, T. and Kogan, M. (eds) (1984). *Educational Research and Policy: How Do They Relate?* Oxford: Pergamon Press.

Lasswell, H. (1951) 'The policy orientation', in D. Lerner and H. Lasswell (eds) *The Policy Sciences*, Stanford: Stanford University Press.

Levin, B. (1998) 'An epidemic of education policy: (what) can we learn from each other?' *Comparative Education* 34, 2: 131–41.

Lingard, R., Knight, J. and Porter, P. (1993) (eds) *Schooling Reform in Hard Times*, London: Falmer Press.

Luke, A. (1995) 'Getting our hands dirty; provisional politics in postmodern conditions' in R. Smith and P. Wexler (eds) *After Post-Modernism: Education, Politics And Identity*, London: Falmer Press.

McIntyre, J., Foley, G., Morris, R. and Tennant, M. (1995) *ACE Works: The Vocational Outcomes of ACE Courses in NSW*, research report commissioned by the NSW Board of Adult and Community Education, Sydney: Board of Adult and Community Education.

MacRae Jr, D. (1991) 'Policy analysis and knowledge use', *Knowledge and Policy: The International Journal of Knowledge Transfer* 4, 3: 27–40.

Marginson, S. (1993) *Education and Public Policy in Australia*, Cambridge: Cambridge University Press.

Oh, C.H. (1997) 'Explaining the impact of policy information on policy-making', *Knowledge and Policy: The International Journal of Knowledge Transfer* 10, 3: 25–55.

O'Regan, T. (1992) 'Some reflections on the "policy moment"', *Meanjin* 51, 3: 517–32.

Peters, M. and Marshall, J. (1996) *Individualism and Community: Education and Social Policy in the Postmodern Condition*, London: Falmer Press.

Quinn, J.B., Anderson, P. and Finkelstein, S. (1996) 'Managing professional intellect: making the most of the best', *Harvard Business Review* March–April: 71–80.

Rein, M. and Schön, D. (1977) 'Problem setting in policy research' in C.H. Weiss (ed.) *Using Social Research in Public Policy Making*, Lexington, MA: Lexington Books/D.C. Heath (pp. 235–51).

Rich, R. and Oh, C. (1993) 'Utilisation of policy research' in S. Nagel (ed.) *Encyclopedia of Policy Studies*, 2nd edition, New York: Marcel Dekker (pp. 69–94).

Schön, D. and Rein, M. (1994) *Frame Reflection: Towards the Resolution of Intractable Policy Controversies*, New York: Basic Books.

Schram, Sanford F. (1995) 'Against policy analysis: critical reason and poststructural resistance', review essay, *Policy Sciences* 28, 3: 375–84.

Silver, H. (1990) *Education, Change and the Policy Process*, London: Falmer Press.

Stronach, I. and MacLure, M. (1997) *Educational Research Undone: The Postmodern Embrace*, Buckingham: Open University Press.

Stronach, I. and Morris, B. (1994) 'Polemical notes on educational evaluation in the age of "policy hysteria"', *Evaluation and Research in Education* 8, 1/2: 5–19.

Sullivan, B. and Yeatman, A. (eds) (1997) *The New Contractualism*, Melbourne: Macmillan.

Taylor, S., Rivzi, F., Lingard, R. and Henry, M. (1997) *Educational Policy and the Politics of Change*, London and New York: Routledge.

Watkins, J. (1994) 'A postmodern critical theory of research use', *Knowledge and Policy: The International Journal of Knowledge Transfer* 7, 4: 55–77.

Webber, D.J. (1991–2) 'The distribution and use of policy knowledge in the policy process', *Knowledge and Policy: The International Journal of Knowledge Transfer and Utilisation* 4, 4: 6–35.

Weiss, C. (ed.) (1977) *Utilising Social Research in Public Policy-Making*, Lexington, MA: D.C. Heath.

Yeatman, A. (1991) *Bureaucrats, Femocrats, Technocrats: Essays on the Contemporary Australian State*, Sydney: Allen and Unwin.

Yeatman, A. (1993) 'Corporate managerialism and the shift from the welfare to the competition state', *Discourse* 13, 2: 3–9.

Yeatman, A. (1994) *Postmodern Revisionings of the Political*, London and New York: Routledge.

Yeatman, A. (1995) 'Interpreting contemporary contractualism' in J. Boston (ed.) *The State Under Contract*, Wellington, NZ: Bridget Williams Books.

Yeatman, A. (1998) (ed.) *Activism and the Policy Process*, Sydney: Allen and Unwin.

10 Research partnerships at work

New identities for new times

Hermine Scheeres and Nicky Solomon

In this chapter we focus on collaborative research and, in particular, 'partnerships' between workplaces, government and the academy. We argue that these new partnering relationships constitute new modes of knowledge production. They involve new work practices which construct and produce new knowledge. New partnering relations are having a profound effect on researchers at work as they engage increasingly in entrepreneurial, multi-disciplinary (knowledge) work. For academic researchers, new identities are being forged in these new times.

We want to examine the construction of positions and possibilities for researchers working in this context. Our analysis draws on our experience as 'language' and 'culture' experts in two collaborative research projects located in enterprises embracing the new work order. Thus the two workplace sites, industry and the academy, are discussed so as to expose a range of self-regulating activities inherent in the research projects within them, and to draw attention to tensions and issues concerning the politics and prospects inherent in the new forms of research. Indeed, we see vital possibilities in the creation of new knowledge at work and in the quest for its validity and acceptance.

New work: new workplaces

While it is true that academic research workers have engaged with workplaces for many years, both as sites for research and as recruiting grounds or work placements for students, it is the new context of economic globalisation that is significant in the re-contextualisation of these practices. The discourses of global markets dominate the economic agendas of governments, and in turn these discourses are becoming integral to the stated purposes of universities and other enterprises. Economic restructuring and workplace reform are consequences of a growing global, competitive market-place. Workplaces of all kinds, including universities, are struggling with new ways *to be* at local sites which are linked materially and/or rhetorically to a global context. Linked in this way, the academy, like other workplaces, is a socio-politically constructed site where discourses such as 'quality assurance' are prevalent, and in which productivity is measured.

The new 'working together' of the academy and other workplaces has, at its heart, similar 'performative' accountabilities and political motivations. At the same time, their different histories, with respect to knowledge, practices and working identities, have constructed differences in goals and interests. The changing economic conditions for the academy, where funding sources are now often government bodies with their own agendas (as distinct from governments) and/or workplaces themselves, are bringing to the surface epistemological and professional questions and tensions. As these new contractual, collaborative arrangements are developed it is somewhat ironic that academics engaged in (re)locating their own knowledge, practices and identities are often playing out this struggle when researching the (re)location of knowledge, practices and identities in industries and other organisations.

The growing relationships between the academy and industry are particularly significant to academic researchers as they struggle with the increasing pressure to view the academy as an industry – as a commercial enterprise. Today, when talking about the workplace and contemporary work practices, academics are no longer talking about the 'other'. We are suggesting that the binary of the academy and the workplace is now almost unsustainable. The unease that academics may sometimes feel in the new collaborative, commercial research relationships touches a broader discomfort with changing work practices in which research outcomes are increasingly measured, as Ewan and Calvert describe in Chapter 4, in terms of having met economic objectives.

New spaces

As academic researchers take up their partnership roles, two clear positions are available to them: compliance and resistance. In making choices about participating in funded, collaborative projects, for example, academics may either construct their practices as (problematic or unproblematic) compliant with the interests and politics of the funding bodies, or as resistant through refusing to participate, or even subverting the project. However, we suggest that these positions set up a restricted, unhelpful choice between the subject positions of passive complier or active resister. It is a binary that leaves no useful space to examine other possible subject positions.

The discourse of compliance is one we have been struggling with in our own research work and reflections on that work. We argue that the compliance discourse is particularly problematic because it fails to take account of the complexities of the new times for work: a global context within which traditional boundaries are blurring. Ideas about what constitutes knowledge and workplace practice have been changing rapidly in sites as seemingly dissimilar as production lines in industry and university departments. Also importantly, discourses of compliance fail to give academics space for more active roles in their collaborative relationships with industry and government partners. Space for academic researchers to take up positions as 'active subjects' creates a third or hybrid space at work for them. This hybrid space is not static or fixed, but rather it is a negotiated space open to change and development. The notion of the academic as an active subject is very different from the position of 'active resister' in which action is taken in direct opposition to the alternative option of compliance. The boundaries of the compliance/resistance binary construct compliance as characterised by inactivity, imposition, force and/or coercion. On the other hand, resistance is characterised by working to undermine the new project partnerships. Thus, academics involved in research partnerships, where industry funds the project and sets the goals, either accommodate the agendas of the funding body or sabotage them in some way. We believe that the accommodation is not a simple, one-way coercion. In a similar way, resistance can be understood as a more complex activity than an attempt to bring about failure. In this chapter we explore the academic's position as an active subject within a contested, hybrid space. We argue it is the active, self-regulating subject that is central to the struggles within the space in which the partnerships between government, university and industry are being played out. We take the view that self-regulation is not about compliance, but about the varied self-regulatory practices that accompany multiple subject positions.

Governmentality

In Foucault's conception of governmentality 'the state is viewed as an ensemble of institutions, procedures, tactics, calculations, knowledges and technologies, which together comprise the particular direction that government has taken; the residue or outcome of governing' (Johnson 1993: 140). We suggest that collaborative research arrangements constitute one of the multiplicity of outcomes of governing and, as one strand in an assemblage that aligns the academy, industry and government, they are an important social technology in contemporary governmentality. We see this formation and our participation in it as not a consequence of government *per se*, but rather a consequence of governmentality.

The reorganisation of academic work practices (as in all contemporary work practices) requires self-regulation to work effectively: that is, self-regulation by both the academy and its employees. Here we see a manifestation and intersection of technologies of power and technologies of the self where power shapes knowledge of the self and where technologies shape human conduct. This, we argue, is how governmentality works at the micro-level, where diverse forces and mechanisms shape the conduct of organisations (including the academy) and its employees. Importantly, then, in terms of our argument, self-regulation is an aspect of governing because it creates active subjects who create possibilities for resistance.

Foucault's ideas (in Miller and Rose 1993: 81) on 'governmentality' assist in exploring the discursive practices that are both cause and effect of the pressure to research collaboratively. In this case, our interest is in the political (and thus economic) rationality that foregrounds the interrelationship of work, education and the economy and the range of mechanisms that make this happen. These mechanisms operate in a number of discursive ways, including the construction of the combined Australian government portfolio of Education, Employment and Training; the emergence of a lifelong learning discourse; the call to realise the productive potential of the population; and the naming of employees as knowledge workers.

The discursive practices draw attention to the central role of language in government. Miller and Rose (1993: 81) use the term 'intellectual technology' to capture the significance of language:

> not language as a neutral or innocent medium that transmits information, but language as a technology for producing social realities, for creating domains of thought and action. Language provides a mechanism for rendering reality amenable to certain kinds of action.

In other words, language renders aspects of existence amenable to inscription and calculation and thus amenable to intervention and regulation. Language is therefore part of the complex process of negotiation involved in bringing persons, organisations and objectives into alignment (ibid.). We suggest that the push for collaborative research arrangements is to align the academy, industry and government to construct new language(s), new products and new processes. The rhetoric surrounding the push is that nations can become 'clever' by working together to achieve the productive potential of the population.

The economic policy context

In Australia, national training and workplace reforms were two of the key areas of policy direction that have brought together the academy, industry and government. Government funding was provided to jointly develop industry competency standards and competency-based training as well as a number of national frameworks to guide its implementation. Competency standards and competency-based training are part of the discursive practices that construct the worker as 'competent' and construct work as a set of practices that can be broken down into itemised parts that are described succinctly. Language professionals have a place here because their expertise can be used to make explicit the new language practices that are integral to contemporary work. In the contemporary workplace, competence not only refers to technical but also to linguistic and cultural competence (du Gay 1996). The ability to work productively in the 'textualised' workplace, the ability of individuals to align their own goals with those of the organisation, to learn, to do symbolic work, all require the worker to be linguistically competent. Increasingly the possession of such abilities can also mean, for employees at various levels of an organisation, the need to undertake research work.

Knowledge production and researcher identity

Researchers can be understood as a part of a human 'technology' – playing out the relationship of work, the economy and education through the relationship of power and the self. We, as workers, are ourselves being constructed (and construct ourselves) as particular kinds of subjects even as we take part in the construction of new knowledge at work. We bring our expertise to the task of inscribing language competence into the new texts (such as capability frameworks or competency-based standards) through which people's work, and indeed people themselves, are measured, calculated and valued.

The hybrid space being constructed and negotiated has so far been discussed in relation to struggles around the possibilities of new and multiple subject positions. We would also argue that the practices constituting the new research relationships are producing new knowledge in new ways. Gibbons *et al.* (1994) outline two co-existing modes of knowledge production: culturally concentrated knowledge and socially distributed knowledge. The characteristics of culturally concentrated knowledge include homogeneity and accountability to discipline-based notion of knowledge and methodologically 'sound' research practice; whereas socially distributed knowledge is characterised by heterogeneity and social accountability as the knowledge serves a number of social, economic and political interests. It is not so much that these two modes are in opposition to one another, or that one is 'newer' than the other (more binaries). Rather, the new work order is breaking down the boundaries around work/education/training/knowledge/skills – and bringing the 'different' conceptualisations of knowledge (and its sites and practices) into contact and sometimes contestation. Substituting a discourse of 'opening up' for the discourse of 'breaking down' locates this third space within a potential context for change – a context of possibilities.

We agree with the argument that the 'self' is culturally and historically malleable. We want to (re)present our work as collaborative researchers not simply as functional responses to, or legitimations of, already existing economic interests or needs but rather, as du Gay (1996: 53) puts it, as 'agents who actively make up a reality, and create new ways … to be at work'.

The projects

As academics involved in collaborative research our focus is on the various subject positions adopted during the research process. We take the view that the collaborative relationships are a mode of knowledge production resulting in knowledge differing from that produced by academics when doing research in a more 'isolated' way or subject to different accountabilities. Furthermore, we suggest that this mode of knowledge production also produces new kinds of academics. We are looking here at the discursive construction of the contemporary academic working within a context of collaborative activities and processes. This examination involves tracking the discursive unfolding of two collaborative projects. In this section we will examine the language and activities of the research to identify the different ways academics self-regulate, that is, position themselves through this unfolding process.

Our analysis begins with the typical textual products of commissioned, collaborative work – the submission (the tender document) and the final report (the text that signals the closure of the research project). In the submissions we will explore how we as academics positioned ourselves as experts and actively aligned this expertise to the needs and desires of the funding bodies. In the final reports we will look at how we (re)positioned ourselves in one case and how we were (re)positioned in the other. Our expertise is constructed differently in the two projects, as in the first project the final report was written by academics, while in the second project the final report was written by the government funding body.

Importantly, though, we suggest that the submission and the final report are just two of many textual practices within the research process. While these are public texts they represent one layer of the research processes and products. Therefore, we will present further textual practices that we argue are also sites of knowledge production as well as exemplars of the self-regulating activities of academics. These additional textual practices occur within the parameters defining the particular project itself, and also reach beyond it. The internal ones include various activities with other participants in the project: for example, the training sessions with the employees in Project 1 and the negotiations within the project teams in Project 2. Textual practices also occur within the academy, rather than within the project parameters, and these include our teaching practices as well as our conference papers and other forms of academic writing. While each of these textual practices tells a particular story, through our reflexive process we will tell a different story – a reflexive tale (Lather 1991) that has drawn us, the researchers, back into an examination of the texts. It is through this examination of a combination of these textual practices that different kinds of subject positions are revealed – complex subject positions that highlight the struggles and ambiguities of the active academic, a position that challenges a simplistic reading of our work as either compliant or resistant.

All the textual practices are located within the same contextual and cultural space – a space that foregrounds the relationship between work, education and the economy. However, through our analysis of the various textual practices we hope to illustrate that there are differences in the way this relationship is understood and enacted by academics. Indeed, while in the submission and final report the relationship between work, education and the economy is a naturalised one, in the other identified textual practices this relationship is problematised.

The two research projects have similarities and differences. They both occur in the context of a particular combination of government reforms and examine language practices in the contemporary workplace and the development of techniques and technologies that help to construct linguistically 'competent' workers. However, the brief of each of the projects is different in specific ways. Different sets of partners involved, each had specific and different goals and different collaborative activities.

Project 1, entitled *Effective Communication in the Restructured Workplace* (see Joyce *et al.* 1995, hereafter referred to as Project 1) was commissioned by the National Food Industry Training Council and involved tripartite committees at the industry level; managers, trainers and employees at three food industry enterprises, and academics working in the fields of language and literacy education and research. In this project, an academic research team was contracted to investigate the changing nature of work and the ensuing work practices in three food industry enterprises, particularly in relation to the language and literacy competencies needed for effective communication in these 'new' workplaces. This was followed by the development of training manuals and the delivery of the initial training programmes.

Project 2, entitled *Literacy at Work: Incorporating English Language and Literacy Competencies into Industry/Enterprise Standards* (see NBEET 1996, hereafter referred to as Project 2) was commissioned by the Australian Language and Literacy Council (ALLC) and involved government- and industry-level committees, representatives from the Warehousing and Distribution Industry Training Council, and managers, trainers and employees at ten warehousing and distribution sites. As indicated by its title, the aim of this research project was to develop a model for incorporating language into competency standards. This model would then inform the development of competency standards, which in turn would guide curriculum design, training and competency assessment. The research site (and pilot study) as directed by the commissioning body was the Warehousing and Distribution industry. The commissioning body, the Australian Language and Literacy Council (ALLC) was part of the National Board of Employment, Education and Training (NBEET), a Board set up as the principal independent advisory body to the Minister for Employment, Education and Training.

The context of the projects

Bringing together the workplace with language and literacy education was not a new idea. Both the Adult Migrant English Service (AMES) and Technical and Further Education (TAFE) had been involved in offering valuable courses in the workplace for many years. These were, in the main, courses in English language for non-English speaking background employees and basic literacy courses which focused on individual needs and development.

However, we would argue that there was a significant change in the early 1990s – a change from an individually focused and essentially humanistic view of language and literacy needs to an industry-based and economically focused view. As discussed elsewhere in this chapter, there had been a growing awareness during the 1980s/1990s by governments and industry of the importance of language and literacy (and numeracy) at work. This awareness developed into a direct and (often) causal link being made between economic productivity and a linguistically or communicatively competent workforce.

In 1991 the Australian Language and Literacy Policy (ALLP) was released, in which language and literacy are described as 'central to the education, training and skill formation necessary to produce a more dynamic and internationally competitive Australian economy' (DEET 1991: xiv). The ALLP recommended the setting up of the ALLC as part of NBEET. This combined portfolio exemplifies the way structures and processes are established to support the desired alignment of the economy, education and work. The ALLC has played an important role in setting agendas in language and literacy during the 1990s. Project 2 analysed in this chapter was one of a range of their commissioned research projects. A large number of government reports and projects released and funded over the next few years focused on language, literacy and work. It is interesting, and not unexpected, to note that the same kinds of close and causal links have been made between unemployment and language and literacy competence. We are not in agreement with the arguments naturalising these links and causal relationships; rather, we present this as the socio-political context in which these projects became possible. (See Black 1998; Gee *et al.* 1996; Hull 1995; Gowen, 1992; Luke 1992 for arguments interrogating these naturalised discourses.)

In 1996, with a change of government, the Boards and Councils were disestablished even though the new government supported the work, economy and education alignment. This dismantling is an example of the complexity (and transitory nature) of the technologies of government and the fluidity of the networks that enable governing.

The projects were located within a broad programme of training reforms manifested in numerous collaborative projects between government, industry and educational institutions carried out over recent years. These projects have included competency standard development for each industry (at national and state levels); national key generic competency projects; the development of a National Framework for English Language, Literacy and Numeracy Competence; and the development of a strategic framework for the integration of language, literacy and numeracy into vocational education and training programmes.

Project 1 is an example of how many industries are recognising that industry – and even enterprise – specific research and development work needs to be done to carry out the reforms successfully. Here, the focus was on collaboration with three individual enterprises in the food industry: the identification of language competencies and the development of strategies and training to acquire them. Project 2 arose from earlier work which found that no industry standards developed to date had included a comprehensive model for the incorporation of English language and literacy competencies. Thus, this project had a wider brief in that it identified a gap in industry standards generally, and sought to address it. The following quote from the foreword of the final report of Project 2 provides a succinct rationale for both the projects: 'English language and literacy is of fundamental importance for both individual and organisational development. Increasingly individuals need English language and literacy skills to do their job' (NBEET 1996: v).

The project texts: the submissions

The purpose of the submissions was to persuade the funding bodies that we had the necessary expertise to 'win' the projects. As language professionals, we needed to argue that our expertise gave us a role and status that legitimatised our involvement in the projects. In the submissions, therefore, we needed to argue our case that we were experts and that this expertise gave us an authority based on the belief that we had specialist knowledge and 'truths' that were invaluable to the desired outcomes.

It would have been inappropriate to present ourselves only as language academics. One of the tensions that 'language and literacy academics' have to work with is what is considered to be the narrowness of their field – both as language and literacy experts and as academics. Such professional categories carry a certain weighting, but in themselves are unlikely to carry the full set of entitlements that these kinds of projects require. A continuing perception of the academy as an ivory tower (removed from 'real' life and 'real' work) meant that we were required to make explicit the 'breadth' of our experiences and knowledge claims (Potter 1996).

This was done in several ways. We wanted to disclose our knowledge, skills and experience related to these particular projects and we believed an important part of positioning ourselves in the submissions was the representation of our past experience as entitling. In both projects, we described our involvement with relevant research projects which foregrounded experience in working with partners; working with industry; working in the design and development of language and literacy competency standards, and industry competency standards; and in understanding the changing nature of work. Reference was also made to projects and reports where we had had no involvement, but which demonstrated our awareness of relevant policies and other work in the area.

In the submission for Project 1 we begin almost immediately by framing our expertise within the current political and economic agendas: 'As effective communication is essential for the restructuring process to be effective [the communication training] will result in increased enterprise level productivity' (Project 1).

This message is further reinforced by the title of one of the subsections, 'How the proposed project would increase worker productivity' (Project 1).

Here we both accept the (government's) prevailing economic arguments regarding the centrality of communication skills to workplace improvement, and we also construct ourselves as researchers and practitioners who are able to develop communication practices to the extent that they will have a major impact on productivity. Thus we begin to textualise our expertise in language and training, and integrate it with the technologies of government shaping microeconomic reform. We bring together Fairclough's domains of practice–research, design and training of discoursal practices of workplaces (1996: 71) when we state even more specifically:

> These modules will assist industry to understand the oral communication competencies needed for effective participation in both training and the consultative processes, and provide them with training strategies for making these processes more efficient. In addition, the industry trainers will be given the skills to diagnose the oral communication needs of the employees in their respective industries.
>
> (Project 1)

This factualising of our expertise is juxtaposed in the submission with statements assuring the readers/judges of our knowledge about the changing work practices and the range of national training reforms and restructuring policies that were 'directing' workplace reform. For instance: 'One of the significant aspects of industry and organisational change is the increase in consultative and participatory processes at all levels of the workplace' (Project 1).

In Project 2, this kind of knowledge was foregrounded by devoting the first two pages of the 'issues' section of the submission to a brief historical description of the complex set of global and national activities within which the technologies of government were located.

In Project 1, an outline of the desired major outcomes from the project follows. Under four bullet points we promise: a detailed description and specification of oral competencies; a detailed description of training strategies to achieve these competencies; a set of four modules; and the delivery of 'train the trainer' programmes across the three workplaces. These are the tangible products of our research work – what we will deliver. The outcomes locate us as having language and literacy expertise; educative expertise and training materials development expertise – knowledge and skills which are both specifically field-of-practice based and broadly to do with education and training, all (expressed) within a context of cultural change which is also part of our knowledge repertoire.

Once we have constructed our expertise in this way, we go on to establish our academic credentials as researchers. The description of the research methodology outlines the ethnographic studies of the sites that we would carry out as well as linguistic analysis of the collected spoken and written texts. The methodology provides a linear, procedural description of tasks commensurate with valid, qualitative research practices.

The methodology can be read as reinforcement of our academic expertise and credibility. It can also be read as a rational, positivist process leading towards producing the desired outcome: that is, a description of communication skills needed for productive and efficient work and the kind of training that would lead to these outcomes. The methodology lists a chronological procedure that presents a kind of production-line set of activities – a genre familiar to the other partners in this project. At one and the same time, our text works to legitimise our involvement in the project and position ourselves as academics who 'do' academic research and as academics who understand and comply with a notion of success which: outlines a problem; finds where it is and what it looks like; proposes solutions and implements them.

The last section of the submission in Project 1 summarises the programmes for workplace reform, including language and literacy activities, of the three research sites. The four pages in this section demonstrate that the researchers had developed considerable knowledge about the contexts in which they would be working. We had, in fact, had a number of meetings with the industry involved before the tender was written, and the existing relationship was built into the submission. The textualisation of this information works to present the commitment to the reform process by the organisations, our acceptance of it by implication, and a commitment to our working relationship by both partners. This last commitment is reinforced by statements expressing mutual support and a promise of (in kind) financial contribution by the enterprises.

We also wanted to foreground our language expertise – not as linguist theorists but in terms of knowledge of the issues in the application of language expertise in the context of competency standard development. Some examples from the submission of Project 2 that suggest this are:

- incorrect perception that there is a 'basic' level of language which can or should be acquired before an employee can participate in mainstream training;
- because of the direct relationship between the standard and competency-based training, it is highly likely that both current

and future language and literacy demands of work will be ignored in training unless they are visible in the standards;
• the level of specificity or generality of the language used in competency standards depends to some extent on whether they are being developed at a national, state or enterprise level.

(Project 2)

In Project 2, we positioned ourselves as academics with a broad of repertoire of expertise – expertise that unproblematically aligned with the work, education and economy rationality. We actively argued our case and this case was subjected to the scrutiny of the commissioning body. Interestingly, our argument was both successful and unsuccessful. We were informed that our submission was accepted, but on the condition that we work together with another 'specialist' group who had also submitted a tender. This group comprised two vocational educators working as private consultants located in another state of Australia. These consultants had expertise in developing industry standards, but no expertise in language and literacy. The reasons for this decision are open to speculation. Perhaps our argument – that we had the required breadth of experience – was not a persuasive one, or perhaps as it was a 'national' project, members of the project team needed to represent more than one state. Whatever the reasons, we agreed.

For academics, this new work of submission-writing is one more step away from independent action and professional autonomy and from any notion of defined boundaries between the technical and political (Johnson 1993: 150). The discursive construction of our expertise in collaborative submissions for research funding produces hybrid discourses which see us as academic and political agents working in changing times.

The project texts: the final reports

The next significant texts in these projects are the final reports. They have a very different function from the submission texts, as their purpose is to present the outcomes of each project, including the way we met the objectives of the project, its rationale and its achievements.

Project 1's report was written by us (the academic researchers) and states how, and in what ways, we succeeded. The report reveals that we 'found' a deficit of language skills in the workforce (a consequence of the fact that most operator-level employees were from a non-English-speaking background in combination with the introduction of new work practices that required more communication skills); we identified what was needed; we then developed and delivered training (implicit in this is the expectation that increased worker productivity follows). In terms of the performativity principle, we performed well 'the best possible input/output equation' (Lyotard 1979).

The report focuses on the processes and products of the project. It is structured to emphasise the match between the aims of the project and the outcomes. Our expertise is (re)presented in several ways: as efficient workplace researchers who can follow complex processes effectively; as language and literacy educators who are able to identify and target communication 'problems' and practices; and as successful producers of textual products – training and training manuals – which can in turn be used to keep producing new knowledge workers long after we have signed off on our contractual obligations.

Thus, the report text is constructed to demonstrate that we were successful in finding out what kinds of communicative practices were needed and that we were able to reconstitute them as aims and outcomes in the training manuals. To prove the validity of these findings, details of interviews, shadowing and other processes are outlined, and examples of questionnaires and language collection proformas are attached to the final report as appendices. In order to claim further success for our pilot training of the draft modules, we include a lengthy series of comments from participants, extracted from their evaluations.

The report does reveal some of the complexities of the introduction and implementation of new management and work practices. In outlining the findings we raise a number of issues, calling them 'general tendencies'. Some examples of the tendencies that we are identified are:

- Meetings still *tend* to be hierarchically based if higher level management is present.
- Managers and supervisors still *tend* to dominate as they follow old and established patterns of communication.
- Men *tend* to take most turns at talk, often do not acknowledge the contribution of other members and often do not allow other members to have their full say.
- Non-English-speaking-background employees, especially women, *tend* to be disadvantaged in larger workplace meetings.

(Project 1)

These 'tendencies' are significant in the way they foreground the continuation of the hierarchical power relations in the organisations. There is a lack of analysis of these in the report and an assumption that managerial problems raised by the employees have been/will be addressed (successfully) within the body of the training manuals, and that the training programmes will be a site for raising and addressing them. An example of how this did occur will be discussed in the next section. However, in the report itself we do locate the 'tendencies' in ways that disturb a straightforward account of success. The very *writing* of the report and the decisions regarding what is included or omitted, is a significant example of the struggle for new academic space and identity. Our desire to conclude the project as contracted cannot be constructed as simply giving the industry and government body a success story.

The last section of Project 1's report looks forward to the final production of the manuals as a package: 'The final package of materials will consist of ...' and 'the four training manual listed above ... will each contain ...', emphasising the commodification of the new knowledge(s) (see Gee *et al.* 1996; du Gay 1996) and the new modes of knowledge production. Once our products are completed, efficiency and effectiveness will be on-going and guaranteed as the path towards mass consumption (which packages and 'train the trainer' programmes construct) is assured. In contrast to Project 1, the final published report of Project 2 was written by the commissioning body, the ALLC, and then published by the Australian Government Publishing Service. Our interest in academic identity in this text is in how we, as academics, were constructed by others.

Our 'expertise' had a very different representation in this text from the construction of expertise in the submission. It was in the interests of the commissioning body to persuade the readers (be they industry bodies, enterprise personnel, educators) that the outcomes of the project – a model for integrating language and literacy into competency standards – were valuable and useable. While in the submission our language expertise was a critical component, 'expertise' in the final report had quite different characteristics. The final report is organised around its particular applicability and acceptability by those who are to use it. The diversity of interests in the research and the wider set of criteria used to judge its usefulness led to a more composite multi-dimensional 'product', and this 'product' has quite distinctively different textual features.

Typically, knowledge presented in government reports is often distanced from the people involved in its production. This drawing away from the identity of the agent could be understood also as an approach that involves constructing consensus and corroboration by presenting a description as shared across different producers, rather than being unique to any single one. No single stake or claim is possible with collaborative projects. Anonymity is part of the discursive experience in the co-production of knowledge, and this is evident in the final report of Project 2: for example, the only reference to the names of the project consultants who carried out the research and wrote the draft report is on the publication page in a boxed section entitled 'Acknowledgments'. Even then the names are not connected to their institutional location. The word 'consultants' or 'project team' is the only other reference to the researchers. The model itself is defined completely as an agent-free process. There is no sense of who might be responsible or accountable.

The 'experts' may have disappeared, but their expertise in an infused and diffused way is evident in the text. In Fairclough's term (1996) this kind of knowledge would be an aspect of the technologisation of the discourse. While our names or the naming of the expertise has been essentially deleted, the language practices related to language and literacy competence have become embedded in the text.

Further textual practices

As stated earlier in this chapter, the submission and the report represent two public texts; it could be argued that although these texts differ from one project to another, their social functions remain fairly constant. We have analysed our examples of these texts as textual practices rather than texts, arguing that the construction of the texts is significant in the discursive, self-regulating construction of academics. In this section we will present further textual practices beyond the focus on the public texts. We will first explore aspects of the training manuals and training sessions from Project 1, and then analyse some of the collaborative processes from Project 2. We then look at the textual practices that have unfolded as part of our conventional academic practices.

Training manuals and training: Project 1

The training manuals complied (both in content and design) with the expectations of those who commissioned the report. Both manuals, *Teamwork: A Training Program* and *Spoken and Written Communication in Workplace Training: A Training Program*, present lists of competencies as outcomes of the training and lists of topics and activities leading to these outcomes. The genre of training manuals provides boundaries around knowledge and the mode of knowledge production. In so doing, the politics and power relationships of workplaces, which in many ways influence the effectiveness of communication more than discrete spoken or written language skills, are rendered invisible. Thus, the product, the training manuals, can be seen as a technology for regulating employees and restructuring them as particular kinds of subjects, as well as being an example of our own self-regulation.

The prescriptive boundaries established through the contents of training manuals reveal an additional significant factor. The research process involved investigation of the social and language practices at local specific sites, yet the local knowledge about these practices was not integrated into the manuals. This absence perhaps can be explained in terms of Foucault's notion of disciplinary power exercised through the panoptic gaze (1977). The prescriptive contents of the training manuals became part of the surveillance where workers regulate their practices 'automatically' according to 'anonymous' corporate power relations. The panoptic gaze is embodied in discursive practices which involve both the use of language (for example in relation to 'teamwork', 'empowerment' and 'self-direction') and particular kinds of activities which both shape and are shaped by training. This therefore becomes part of the technology involving the internalising of control and the imposition of 'self-discipline'.

However, training sessions or courses are textual practices that are, we would argue, closely linked to training manuals; they provide the 'doing' of the written manuals. Here the 'trialling' of the training manuals was part of the project, even though it remained largely 'invisible' to the industry and government body partners. Training sessions are a site where workers and their subjectivities, histories and sociocultural locations come to the fore. It was here that some of the tensions and differences in agendas became most apparent, and where the researcher–trainers and industry worker–trainees negotiated a hybrid space for different subject positions to emerge. In our dual roles as researchers and trainers in this context we had a number of overlapping interests: we were interested in pursuing consciousness-raising about the government/industry ideologies with the workers, and we were interested in exploring with the workers the changing workplace as a postmodern site. Significantly, though, at the same time we wanted to complete the training days with 'success' stories to tell: that is, that communication skills and strategies had been recognised, understood and learnt.

Collaboration within the project team: Project 2

We were working within two sets of collaborative arrangements. At the macro level, the project team was managed through the Project Steering Committee comprising representatives from the ALLC, other government departments and from the warehousing and distribution industry. At the micro level, this collaboration was within the project team itself, where we had to negotiate every step of the research process with vocational educators who were non-academics. This section will discuss the latter level, which was an extraordinary site of contestation.

An examination of this site reveals a number of different and complex kinds of subject positions constructed through the many layers of negotiation around the research design and methodology. Numerous tensions and conflicts surfaced around a number of critical issues. Some examples of the more specific ones were:

- How to talk and write about 'language competence'. The two positions that were contested and negotiated were whether to use everyday common-sense language to talk about language competence or to use technical language about language, just as one would for all other kinds of specialist areas of competence (fields of knowledge).
- The structure of the language competency standards. Again, there were two positions: either work within the conventional competency formatting or disturb these conventions. This tension spread to discussions on how to frame the 'development' of language competence – from a linear progression moving from simple to complex competence (again, each of these concepts had numerous perspectives) to descriptions that focused on the range of purposes of the communication and the relationships between the language users.
- What counts as language competence. Here the positions moved between the balance of the descriptions around language for instrumental and procedural purposes and language in interpersonal communication.

There was more general debate around the role of the project team. There were different views on whether or not we could disturb industry and government expectations regarding the final product. It was argued that we won the project because of our proven technical expertise and that we should not stray from this. We as academics, however, argued strongly in favour of challenge and change. We suggested that the project itself was political and that we should acknowledge this. The safe boundaries of neutrality were questioned as we argued for a recognition of the political location of the project. And this debate itself generated another debate – a debate around the role of each member of the team.

In this site, the level of negotiation between members of the project highlights the difficulty of understanding the academic position as a compliant one. Through our dialogues, all members of the team had to address the debates that emerged through the alignment of work, education and the economy. We all opened up the boundaries around technical and political expertise, around common-sense and theoretical understandings of language, around theory and practice, and around the significance of the project. We were neither simply compliant nor simply resistant, but the space within which we were working collaboratively forced us to present our academic selves at the same time as presenting our negotiating selves. While the boundaries between the academy and others were opening up, these same boundaries helped us to position ourselves, but not in any fixed state.

The issues and tensions within the project team were a microcosm of those that arose within the Project Steering Committee. Appropriately named, the purpose of this committee was to 'steer' the project process and outcomes. Despite our internal differences, the project team presented a united front as we were steered into various directions that challenged all our views. At times the push was towards presenting a simplistic model for industry, while at other times we were asked to develop a model that bore no relationship to the model described in the project brief. Not surprisingly, the steering committee meetings themselves helped the two other members of the project team to understand our job as a political one. In these meetings, the identity of our small team was constructed and affirmed. The pressure to conform to a particular agenda was a challenge that wasn't left to the academics, but one that was taken on by the team as a unit.

Again, our subject positions within this set of discursive practices could not be understood as compliant ones. As academics, throughout the negotiations we were positioned and repositioned and we positioned and repositioned ourselves as we were subjected to and actively subjected others to the questions that arose through the collaborative process.

University curricula

The final reports presented particular narratives of the research findings. But these were only one set of narratives. During the research processes we interviewed employees at all levels of the workplaces about the changing language and work practices in the context of restructuring, introduction of total quality management (TQM); competency-based training (CBT) and sophisticated technologies. We also taped and transcribed many team meetings and training sessions; we read and took notes from piles of documents and shadowed a number of trainers and workers. Our field notes tell quite different stories to the project text stories. While the complexities and details of these stories may have been 'lost' in the final reports, these stories have been and can be located and relocated and incorporated into our teaching practices within the academy.

The stories have a different location and we as academics have different audiences in our 'classrooms'. In developing curricula for courses that we teach and in our teaching practices we are engaged in what may be described as traditional academic practices. However, our collaborative research work can be seen as producing both new knowledge and new modes of knowledge production which are explored further in our work with our students. It is here, too, that there is potential for the insights from the training sessions, and collaborative practices with the project team discussed above can be given more space than that possible within the parameters of the research projects themselves. The transcripts of meetings, our field notes, our own narratives of the politics and tensions in doing collaborative research provided challenging sites of critical reflection for both the teachers and learners.

Conference presentations and papers and other writings are further illustrations of textual practices where the politics, processes, data and findings from research projects are employed to discuss and theorise emerging language and cultural practices in contemporary workplaces. These again link the collaborative work to traditional academic practices. Examining project work more reflexively creates a space for theorising the new academic and the new academy. The latter opens up discussion of new modes of knowledge production and the new knowledges created by them, and, not surprisingly, the practices of self-regulating academics.

Conclusion

In this world of getting our hands dirty (Luke 1995) we are being drawn into the economics of the global workplace – within our own universities and within the sites we research. Discursively we are separately and together constructing partnerships and alliances, which are reconstructing both our identities as academics and the face of academia. There is a symbiosis of professionalisation and state formation as governments throughout all OECD countries pursue policies that 'politicise established areas of expertise' (Johnson 1993: 151). Hybridity – a third space – symbolises our dislocation and relocation, new ways of working and the new textual practices. If there ever was a notion of a neutral researcher, there is no pretence or location for this person now, just as there is no place for a production-line worker 'who works from the neck down' (Gee *et al.* 1996: 26).

In terms of our analysis, all these textual practices are located within this third space – within a set of social and political conditions that contribute to the forging of partnerships between government, industry and the academy and the intersection of a number of discursive practices. All the texts are part of the technologies that construct the linguistically and culturally competent worker in industry as well as in universities. However, the textual practices analysed in this chapter are producing new knowledge through new modes of knowledge production, and our interest here has been in exploring new positions for academic researchers: in particular, how the knowledge and practices of academics change discursively through the bringing together of various institutions and people with such different histories and professional knowledge. Seeing ourselves as active self-regulating subjects recognises the complexities of changing workplaces and opens up possibilities for new ways to be in the academy.

References

Black, S. (1998) *Teamwork, Discourse and Literacy: A Case Study of Workers' Resistance to the Introduction of New Workplace Practices*, Research Report 4, Sydney: Centre for Language and Literacy, University of Technology.

Department of Employment, Education and Training (DEET) (1991) *Australia's Language: The Australian Language and Literacy Policy*, Canberra: Australian Government Printing Service.

du Gay, P. (1996) *Consumption and Identity at Work*, London: Sage.

Fairclough, N. (1996) 'Technologisation of discourse' in C.R. Caldas-Coulthard and M. Coulthard (eds) *Texts and Practices: Readings in Critical Discourse Analysis*, London: Routledge.

Foucault, M. (1977) *Discipline and Punish: The Birth of the Prison*, New York: Vintage.

Game, A. (1991) *Undoing the Social*, Milton Keynes: Oxford University Press.

Gee, J., Hull, G. and Lankshear, C. (1996) *New Work Order: Behind the Language of the New Capitalism*, Sydney: Allen and Unwin.

Gibbons, M., Limoges, C., Nowotny, H., Schwartzman, S., Scott, P. and Trow, M. (1994) *The New Production of Knowledge: The Dynamics of Science and Research in Contemporary Societies*, London: Sage.

Gilbert, G.N. and Mulkay, M. (1984) *Opening Pandora's Box: A Sociological Analysis of Scientists' Discourse*, Cambridge: Cambridge University Press.

Gowen, C. (1992) *The Politics of Workplace Literacy*, New York: Teachers College Press.

Hull, G. (1995) 'Controlling literacy: the place of skills in "high performance" work', *Critical Forum* 3, 2/3: 3–26.

Johnson, T. (1993) 'Expertise and the state' in M. Gane and T. Johnson (eds) *Foucault's New Domains*, Routledge: London.

Joyce, H., Nesbitt, C., Scheeres, H., Slade, D. and Solomon, N. (1995) *Effective Communication in the Restructured Workplace*, Victoria: National Food Industry Training Council.

Lather, P. (1991) *Getting Smart: Feminist Research and Pedagogy With/In the Postmodern*, Routledge: London.

Lee, A. (1996) 'Working together? Academic literacies, co-production and professional partnerships', plenary address to 1st National Conference on Tertiary Literacy: Research and Practice, Victoria University of Technology, Melbourne, March 14–16.

Luke, A. (1992) 'Literacy and work in new times', *Open Letter* 3, 1: 3–15.

Luke, A. (1995) 'Getting our hands dirty: provisional politics in postmodern conditions' in R. Smith and P. Wexler (eds) *After Post-Modernism: Education Politics and Identity*, London: Falmer Press.

Luke, T.W. (1996) 'The politics of cyberschooling at the virtual university' paper presented at the International Conference on the Virtual University, University of Melbourne, Australia.

Lyotard, J.-F. (1979) *The Postmodern Condition: A Report on Knowledge*, Manchester: Manchester University Press.

Miller, P. and Rose, N. (1993) 'Governing economic life' in M. Gane and T. Johnson (eds) *Foucault's New Domains*, London: Routledge.

National Board of Employment, Education and Training (NBEET) (1996) *Literacy at Work: Incorporating English Language and Literacy Competencies into Industry / Enterprise Standards*, Canberra: Australian Language and Literacy Council, Australian Government Printing Service.

Potter, J. (1996) *Representing Reality, Discourse, Rhetoric and Social Construction*, London: Sage.

Scheurich, J.J. (1997) *Research Method in the Postmodern*, London: Falmer Press.

Usher, R. (1997) 'Telling a story about research and research as story-telling: postmodern approaches to social research' in G. McKenzie, J. Powell and R. Usher (eds) *Understanding Social Research: Perspectives on Methodology and Practice*, London: Falmer Press.

Part III

Changing practices of research at work

11 The construction of 'working knowledge' and (mis)interpretive research

John Garrick

Research at work is most frequently conducted with practical outcomes in mind. It seeks to gather data from subjects (e.g. employees or customers) who are presumed to 'know about', have 'experience of' or are 'located' in a way that informs a particular work context, circumstance or change. Invariably this research will interpret the language and experiences of those subjects to enhance understandings of the work dynamics under scrutiny. Interpretive research presupposes a great deal about its research subjects. They are expected to reflect on their experiences and offer practical, rational insights into *being at work*. This chapter examines critically these underlying assumptions in workplace contexts, arguing that the methods of interpretive research are frequently used to legitimise practical knowledge *of work* and, at the same time, inscribe new political rationalities. The processes of legitimising know-how and the political inscriptions embedded in these processes are central to the construction of working knowledge.

Throughout this chapter (and indeed the book as a whole) a central issue is that we, as researchers, generally operate from within certain philosophical and practical assumptions. These are often unsurfaced and yet structure how we think, what we think research is (and does), what researchers are (and do) and what we think the outcomes of research are. As Schutz (1953: 292) put it in his influential analysis of interpreting human action:

> all our knowledge of the world, in common-sense as well as scientific thinking, involves constructs, i.e., a set of abstractions, generalizations, formalizations, idealizations specific to the respective level of thought organization. Strictly speaking, there are no such things as facts, pure and simple. All facts are from the outset … always interpreted facts.

For many years, as Barnett points out in Chapter 2, scientific realism has been *the* ruling research paradigm. But in social conditions of postmodernity, the construction of this paradigm is now facing 'real' doubt. With historical conditions opening space for new kinds of questions, new approaches to research and better (or worse) interpretations of people's needs, interpretive research has become a powerful shaper of knowledge. As distinct from scientific realism, interpretive research is about *lived experience*, in this instance, in the world of work. Yet the philosophical assumptions that underpin interpretive research are seldom critically scrutinised in organisation development, management or higher education literature. As Scheurich (1997: 6) aptly puts it:

> despite all the new positions that have emerged and the old ones that have re-emerged within social science research, we are still holding onto some primary assumptions, including a relatively autonomous individual subjectivity that thinks, does, turns the wheel of life.

In workplaces, individual subjectivity is generally governed by a range of interwoven, historicised and culturally bound forces – not to mention localised politics, power games and the dominant discourses that shape what one actually does at work. Indeed, professional identities are adopted and developed in relation to such workplace influences. The types of primary assumptions that Scheurich touches on above are thus deeply problematic, particularly when one adopts a *non-subject* centred view – for instance, a critical social theory or post-structural approach. For the remainder of this chapter I shall surface the assumptions of interpretive research and make explicit some of the important ways in which interpretive knowledge claims are made, giving illustrations from particular work-settings.

The assumptions of interpretive research

First, I should briefly clarify what I mean by the term 'interpretive research'. Concerned with social interactions, interpretive research assumes that all human actions are meaningful. The interpretive production of meaning occurs principally through interviewing and observation whereby a researcher gets an interviewee (subject) to tell his or her 'story' about their 'own' experience. It is qualitative in nature and rests heavily on cultural beliefs about the authenticity of the individual's subjective experience and that it is superior to more 'clinical', objective accounts. Contrary to this, in this chapter I will argue that authenticity and individual 'agency' ought to be subject to greater levels of doubt than is often the case at work.

Nonetheless, some useful 'knowledge' can be gleaned from interpretive data: for instance, interview transcripts can reveal the discourses which frame practitioners' stories. Experience can thus be 'read' as text; what of the story is 'true' depends upon whose truth is being told. The point is not simply that language is indeterminate, or that 'truth' is subjective, or even that interpretive stories represent an intersection between discourses and lived realities. What becomes important about interpretive research at work is that the story-teller is *speaking the tensions* of their working life. Their stories are discursively constructed at one level, but they are also living them at another. This is precisely where some of the post-structuralist ideas of Michel Foucault are valuable for re-viewing interpretive research, because these ideas demonstrate how influential discourses surrounding and shaping interpretive research practices constitute particular forms of subjectivity and are associated with the exercise of power. From a post-structural perspective, interpretive research is a set of practices that are organised within and constituted by discourses and enacted through power relations.

The individual agency of interpretive researchers is subject to the same 'postmodern doubt' as the individual authenticity of the subjects of their research. The subjectivity of both the interviewer and the interviewee is indeterminate and cannot be simplistically reduced. In workplaces, research discourses (including interpretive ones) are frequently used to 'legitimise' certain types of localised knowledge – for instance, in evaluations of internal management development or training programmes, where questions are asked of participants that can be interpreted in many ways.

From the standpoint of scientific realism, such interpretive research can be viewed as having little or no practical value – because it does not (and cannot) attain the prized research outcome of 'generalisability'. But this standpoint underestimates both the interpretive method's probing nature and the contextual complexities that surround experience. For example, personal stories and examples of experience bring to light a variety of issues from day-to-day work (workplace realities). It is an understanding of lived experience derived from participants themselves that is important to interpretive studies. This carries its own theoretical schemata based on assumptions about the subject-person, the life-world and the validity of making sense of lived experience through participants' stories. This is, in part, why interpretive research has been influential over the past decade or so in shaping understandings of organisational 'realities'. This influence has gathered pace particularly since the take-up in the social sciences of Thomas Kuhn's (1970) influential ideas on the structure of scientific revolutions. At the risk of oversimplifying one of Kuhn's key insights, an important reason has been that 'social' realism (sometimes referred to as positivism) has historically failed to adequately represent the social world. This failure can be partially attributed to the scientific assumptions on which social realism is based (see Table 11.1).

Table 11.1 Assumptions of research approaches

Main assumptions	Scientific realism / Positivism	Interpretive science	Critical social theory
Ontological (the nature of phenomena)	The social world is like the natural world with a cause–effect form; the world is objective and reality is independent of 'knowers'; there exists the possibility of discovering the truth.	The world is made up of tangible and intangible multifaceted realities; interacting events and actions are explainable in terms of multiple interacting factors; extreme difficulty in obtaining objectivity; all human actions are meaningful.	The social order represents powerful interests (oppressing the powerless); economic and political structures and systems shape individual. consciousness; understandings of the world are dialectical, with ideologies underlying social / cultural constructions.
Epistemological (the nature of knowledge)	Facts can be established with scientific rigour and appropriate methods; provable reality makes a distinction between facts and values.	Causes and effects are mutually interdependent; inquiry is always value-laden; context influences the framing and conduct of research.	Knowledge is socially constructed; 'truths' are manifestations of class structures and facts representative of systems of power.
Methodological (research approaches)	Positivistic, quantifiable, statistically based surveys and questionnaires test and control groups; stable / scientific conditions required	Ethnographic life-history method, story-telling, symbolic interaction, hermeneutic	Participatory, collective responses, some forms of action research
Ethical	Social good linked to the pursuit of truth; justice tied to tangible evidence and the pursuit of scientific knowledge the only reliable way of moving towards truth	Ethics and justice associated with the liberal value of respect for 'the person', freedom of the individual, individual agency and autonomy	Institutionalised power and systems of oppression are interconnected and ought to be contested; social progress linked to collective action
Underlying human interests	Technical improvement; to predict, control and make generalisations from established facts; universal laws	To develop an understanding of individual cases rather than universal or predictive laws	To free people from the conditions that fundamentally constrain them; emancipate; empowerment

Usher (1996: 12) identifies several often neglected assumptions of social realism including:

- The world is 'objective' and independent of knowers. The world consists of events or phenomena which are lawful and orderly, and through systematic observation and correct scientific methods it is possible to discover this lawfulness and to explain, predict and control events and phenomena.
- There is a clear distinction or separation between subjects and objects, the 'subjective' knower and the 'objective' world. There is a clear distinction between facts and values. The researcher is concerned with 'facts' and the subjective (the researcher's own concerns and values) must not interfere with the discovery of 'objective' truth.
- The social world is very much like the natural world. Thus there is order and reason in the social world with social life patterned and with a cause–effect form; things do not just happen randomly and arbitrarily.

Adoption of these types of assumptions leads to research that emphasises determinacy (that there is a certain truth that can be known), rationality (the more objective and less subjective, the better) and prediction (that research is the making of knowledge claims in the form of generalisations) (Usher 1996: 13). Such conventional scientific inquiry can liken the social world to a 'natural order' – by seeking to identify *patterns* of behaviour through the adoption of 'correct' methodologies. This approach to inquiry into workplace experience, for instance, can be highly problematic when it fails to adequately make sense of lived experience (see Lather 1991).

It is precisely the attempt to make sense of lived experience that has led interpretive researchers away from the assumptions of positivist/empiricist research. Interpretivist knowledge claims, as I have mentioned, rest upon assumptions that make use of participants' stories – their language, descriptions and metaphors – to highlight what is important to them as the subjects of the investigation. Interpretive research uses personal experience as its starting point. This starting point cannot be viewed unproblematically, as an individual's subjective experiences of work are immersed in and shaped by discourses of market economics, organisational imperatives and industrial issues, and so on. The individual's 'own' story is situated – it is historically and contextually framed – making any interpretation of lived experience at work less a matter of individual authenticity and more a matter for deconstruction of the text of the story-teller (see Garrick and Rhodes 1998).

Interpreting lived experience at work

Here I wish to briefly examine the assumptions that accompany interpretive research. Thus far, the argument is that the research methods of science, particularly positivism, have not adequately addressed the problems and issues of lived experience. As a consequence of this failure, interpretive perspectives have been increasingly used to probe everyday work experiences. Managers, human resources and organisational developers, staff developers or workplace trainers and trainees are frequently asked to talk about their job, its challenges and the dilemmas they have sometimes to face. Such interviews can construct 'working knowledge' by generating rich descriptions of the workplace and providing substantial insights – enabling the tracing of etymological sources, identification of main themes about lived experience in the workplace and key metaphors of working life. For instance, the interpretive model stresses the liberal value of respect for *the person*. A central tenet of this model is the belief that individuals are not merely passive vehicles in social, political and historical affairs but have certain inner capabilities which can allow for individual judgements, perceptions and decision-making – *autonomy*. Possession of such capabilities, it is assumed, can contribute to, influence or even change events – *agency*. Such a belief is based on five further assumptions commonly shared by interpretive theorists, such as Candy (1991: 432), including:

- The aim of inquiry is to develop an understanding of individual cases, rather than universal laws or (predictive) generalisations.
- Causes and effects are mutually interdependent and any event or action is explainable in terms of multiple interacting factors, events and processes.
- The social world is not objective – there is an extreme difficulty in attaining complete objectivity, especially in observing human subjects who may confuse or make sense of events based in their individual systems of meaning.
- The world is made up of tangible and intangible multifaceted realities best studied *as a whole* rather than being fragmented into dependent and independent variables. This recognises the significance of the context in which experience occurs.
- The recognition that inquiry is always value-laden and that such values inevitably influence the framing, focusing and conduct of research.

Table 11.1 categorises these assumptions and contrasts them with other research methodologies. It must be remembered, however, that the neat separation of research paradigms is an artefact. In conducting research at work, these different categories inform each other and often merge. They are not necessarily mutually exclusive. Further, the interpretive research assumptions I refer to are not as innocent as they might first appear. For example, the researcher (or 'observer') engages in the interpretive research process in an active way. He or she might simply be in the room, ask questions or elicit particular responses. The point is that *engagement cannot be separated* from the microprocesses of daily work practices – including the exercise of local power relations. The research act is immersed in them.

Interpretive research at work

Although arguments about the uses of interpretive theory need not be binary and oppositional, various standpoints are worth briefly contrasting. Interpretive theorists are by no means unified, but as Giroux points out, they do share (as do postmodern theorists) 'a rejection of the belief that human behaviour is governed by general [transcendent] laws' (1983: 7). The interpretive argument is that an individual's experience is best understood from the standpoint of the social world *of that individual*.

An interpretive approach seeks a mediated description often through 'story-telling' and the recording of a person's experience in symbolic (told or written) form. Candy, a leading proponent of interpretive theory, argues that 'human interactions are not governed by inviolable laws so much as by agreed rules which are consequently validated by people' (1991: 431). In this sense they are often symbolic. A methodological consideration for research is thus to capture symbolic meanings through personal accounts and metaphors that describe lived experience. Blumer (1962) asserted, in what has become interpretive theory's cliché, that this involves doing research *with* people rather than *on* people, although in contemporary organisations this comes across as a spurious claim.

Ball makes the claim that interpretive research also has the advantage of holding a useful conception of 'organisation': that is, 'the product of multiple social interactions' (1991: 167). In this conception, organisational 'realities' lie in the things that people do, say, feel and think, rather than the kind of abstract system that is somehow greater than the sum of its parts. Indeed, systems theory has been influential, used to promote ideas about 'the learning organisation'. For interpretive research that is conducted in workplaces, this means the ontological status of the organisa- tion is, in addition to participants' stories, very important to 'understanding' lived experience.

In most work-based research, the selection of interpretive approaches is usually intended to generate immediate descriptions of employees' personal experience of work. Interpretive approaches seek to explain how people attribute meaning to their circumstances and how they develop and use rules that govern their behaviour. Such approaches are popular after an organisational restructure or change process – to gauge how particular employees are feeling about their new work situation. By contrast, more critical approaches might be based on underlying motivations to change the structural conditions that shape one's experience – for example, as Lipsig-Mummé points out in Chapter 8, where there is an 'emancipatory' intent underpinning research such as that conducted for trade unions, or equal employment and affirmative action programmes. The implications of such different intentions of research raise the thorny issue of doubts about precisely what (and whose) interests are being served by workplace research.

Categories of doubt

At least three serious categories of doubt can be raised about the interpretive paradigm. First are the concerns of scientific realists about the subjective nature of interpretive studies (including their inability to make generalisations based on 'hard', 'factual' evidence). Second are concerns that come from critical social theory, that interpretive accounts simply do not go far enough to explain workplace complexities including exploitative structures, historical, social, economic and environmental forces that influence individual experience. Third are problems associated with the subject-person in the so-called 'crisis of modernity'. As I have argued, a postmodern view does not place human subjectivity at the centre of meaning construction.

Other categories of doubt about interpretive research can be identified, but for the remainder of this chapter I am going to focus on the third category – about the subject-person and the meanings (and validity of findings) derived from *the individual*, and the increased tensions between *the individual* and the demands now being placed on them at *work* and in *society* more generally. It is often these tensions that constitute the central problems for research (and meaning-making) at work.

Drawing variously on the theoretical insights of Foucault (1988), Derrida (1994) and Lyotard (1984), 'the subject' cannot be assumed to be autonomous and self-directing. A more 'realistic' interpretation of 'experience' is that it is discursively constructed. The subject is a new subject for new times, times that decentre 'the self' and construct multiple subjectivities. For instance, Derrida (1994: 32) points to the contradictions in human relations and problematises foundational knowledge, claiming there is no knowable social reality beyond the signs of language, image and discourse. It is these that shape (are?) 'actuality'.

The notions of decentred subject and multiple subjectivities have major implications for research at work. For instance, should methodologies assume an *already de-centred subject* as a commencement point for research? Can employees be assumed to reflect rationally upon their everyday experience and comprehend their 'own' experience 'objectively'? If we assume that interpretations of the meanings of an individual's experience do not go far enough in the construction of 'legitimate' knowledge, then what is to be done? Clearly, as human beings we do not live in worlds entirely of our own devising. We are subject to influences and pressures that shape our attitudes, perceptions and behaviour. Research of lived experience may be distorted by factors such as ideology, the politics of experience, language usage and power, and conditions of postmodernity. So, what is to be done to avoid mis-interpretive research? The following section gives a few practical illustrations of interpretive research in workplace contexts, highlighting some of its paradoxes.

The paradoxes of using interpretive research at work

As I have argued, interpretive research rests on assumptions about the 'authenticity' of the individual's subjective experience. The theory is that human actions are meaningful and interpretive methods reflect concerns about lived experience. An interpretive perspective is therefore used to probe the everyday experience of subjects with the aim of identifying *what is important to them*. Research in workplaces often seeks to capture 'what is important' to employees, customers and consultants – *from their own perspectives*. Interpretive data is sought to inform on staff satisfaction, organisational culture, organisational climate, experience of professional roles, customer satisfaction, critical incidents, industrial relations and, consequently, a range of influences on work organisation and management.

The following excerpts come from several interviews I conducted with various human resources managers and consultants (Garrick 1998: 73) to examine their informal learning in the workplace. They are provided to illustrate some of the paradoxes of interpretive interviewing.

Jodie, an HR practitioner in a major legal institution, told her story to illustrate her 'own' interpretations of events in the organisation:

> Our collective experiences are valued within our own unit. The training unit functions as a team, and teamwork is being promoted

throughout the corporation. It is a part of the new corporate language associated with becoming a learning organisation, in efforts to be more efficient and competitive. The idea is that teamwork will make work more rewarding.

Christine, HRD manager of a national financial institution, refers to her experiences of working in teams in a corporate banking environment. In telling of her job requirements to promote teamwork, she also highlights her *own need* to feel comfortable with team members:

> Other people's perceptions and ideas help to redefine your own ideas and also identify constraints and considerations. Getting other ideas helps you to step back and think about where you are going. This has been one of the most important impacts on my learning at work – involvement with small groups with a project team approach.

Trust is being promoted in each of these corporations through new organisational structures based on teams and corporate 'families'. The team to which one belongs is promoted as family-like and the HRD practitioners tell of the importance of trusting your team members. The notion of corporate-team is a convenient cultural formation. It is now a common corporate script for obtaining the desired sensibilities in employees. The above excerpts are thus expressions of personal perceptions and reflections of corporate scripts. 'One's own' story is tied to organisational discourses in several ways. This issue was addressed directly by Simon, a national HRD manager of a multi-national commerce and financial management consultancy, in the following way:

> Doing your job is not enough in this organisation. You have to be seen to be doing a good job. You don't have to be too overt about it, but you have to make sure that you are recognised for what you doing, and trusting people is important. When you delegate, you have to trust people. I think if I respect and trust my staff, work hard and am honest with them, we can feel as though we are doing something worthwhile. I now believe that being honest both to yourself and others is fundamental to one's learning – it is one of the things which is most important.

Belonging to a team or network is also stressed by Simon, who links 'belonging' to:

Knowing who holds power whether it be formal or informal ... Knowing about the interplay of personalities, networks and informal channels of communications. Working the network matters. I now make sure that my staff are involved in the outplace [networks external to the corporation] as well as on a range of internal committees. This helps with developing a collective team approach as well as giving the individuals on the team a profile and network of their own. I don't want people to interpret this as an attempt to manipulate the system. It comes back to honesty. You have to be honest about who you are and what you are doing.

Simon's descriptions – 'being honest about who you are and what you are doing' – illustrate very complex processes related to 'knowing oneself' when immersed in power relations and workplace imperatives. Drawing on Foucault (1980), Usher *et al.* point out that being a subject and being subjected: 'is not just a matter of language per se but of discursive practices. Practitioners find themselves at the very centre of these ambiguities and forced to act within them' (1997: 83).

The idea of 'knowing oneself' is related to what Foucault (1988) calls 'technologies of the self'. In particular, as the above interpretive excerpts illustrate, people are not so much regulated through objectifying power/knowledge discourses, but regulate themselves through subjectifying discourses that emphasise the need to talk about – and know – oneself. Where the 'autonomous self' becomes the centre of attention (e.g. through interpretive research), it can be argued that a form of 'confession' is occurring. In Simon's case, his confessional practice helped with 'developing a collective team approach as well as giving the individuals on the team a profile and network of their own'.

Postmodern arguments against using interpretive approaches centre on their philosophical alignment with a humanistic discourse which Usher (1992: 203) argues 'fails to adequately problematise autonomy'. The very notion of individuals reaching their 'own' understanding about phenomena like self-direction or informal learning, for instance, is problematic. Such understanding is 'structured historically in the traditions, prejudices and institutional practices that come down to us' (Taylor 1993: 59).

The postmodern challenge to interpretive research

The postmodern emphasis on plurality presents a direct challenge to interpretive narratives on subjective experience. Postmodern and post-structural writers emphasise the power-laden and political nature of discourse (Foucault 1980; Usher and Edwards 1994). For these writers, a discourse implies a political apparatus, a community and the power to assign legitimacy. Discourses set conditions of 'what kind of talk occurs, and which talkers speak' (Anyon 1994: 120). It is not merely a matter of *what* doesn't get said and *who* doesn't get to have a say, but also a matter of what discourses can excise or make taboo.

Two apparent paradoxes inherent in interpretive approaches are posed as a result of the political nature of discourse. The first is that one cannot place subjective accounts of learning at the centre of research, as such accounts are 'inscribed' through the circulating discourses. The second is that the postmodern insight into the power/knowledge linkage means that interpretive accounts can inadvertently marginalise the voices they are supposedly highlighting. They do this by telling someone's story back with additional perspectives, additional 'authority'. In other words, the researcher becomes a coloniser of the subjects through re-telling *their* stories. To an extent I have just done this in the previous pages. In doing interpretive research it is extremely difficult to avoid this issue, illustrating that interpretive research is, by definition, always a re-interpretation.

In seeking understandings of socially complex phenomena, interpretive accounts do rest heavily on making sense to the actors whose behaviour is being studied. As Carr and Kemmis (1983: 91) put it 'they must pass the test of participant confirmation'. Implicitly, this approach brings an ethical stance which involves participants in decision-making about the data-gathering and its subsequent uses. Interpretive accounts will therefore often state that they do not seek to reinterpret the actions and experiences of the 'actors', but give a deeper, more exhaustive account or systematic representation of events, highlighting the viewpoints of those involved. Despite this goal, as I have argued, interpretive studies are philosophically re-interpretive. They re-tell already interpreted experience.

Using the stories of others clearly raises important political and philosophical questions: Whose side is the researcher really on? What is the researcher's agenda? What purposes and interests will the researcher's outcomes ultimately serve? What types of knowledge are being constructed? In interpretive research at work, analysis of the functioning of the organisation (or site) depends on the way the actors define, interpret and handle their daily situations. As the above research excerpts show, the interpretive requirement for individuals to reflect 'rationally' on their working experience is clearly problematic. None of this means, however, that an interpretive approach is so flawed as to be useless. On the contrary. A key issue is how interpretive understandings are used, and whether they are used coherently. As Lather (1991: 8) puts it: 'the generation and legitimation of knowledge about the social world is stronger when not reliant upon a one-best-way approach'. A postmodern approach neither rejects systematic empirical observation and experiment nor embraces the alternative interpretive approaches, as these are still implicitly operating within the terms and discourse of the positivist/empiricist tradition (Usher 1996: 26). A postmodern approach seeks to subvert the 'objective–subjective' dichotomy and radically challenges the dominant epistemological assumptions of conventional work-based research. This includes the need for researchers to become reflexive and question how their research is contextually framed.

Although interpretive research usefully rejects the certainties of positivism, and its methods have become more attractive with the decline in grand theory (and the emergence of postmodernism), its underlying assumptions should be subjected to stronger critiques than have been prevalent in qualitative research literature. It seems to me that qualitative research practices can be enhanced if researchers can translate meaning between and across the different discourses that are found in and around one's research practices. The need to account for the status of the researcher (and their context) presupposes an inseparability of 'the knower' and 'the known'. It is impossible to separate subjects and objects. To an extent, this means being open to post-structural ideas about non-subject centred research. This, in turn, opens up the potential of deconstruction in the construction of working knowledge!

References

Anyon, J. (1994) 'The retreat of Marxism and socialist feminism: postmodern and poststructural theories in education', *Curriculum Inquiry* 24, 1: 115–33.
Ball, S.J. (1991) 'Power, conflict, micro-politics and all that!' in G. Walford (ed.) *Doing Educational Research*, London: Routledge (pp. 166–92).
Blumer, H. (1962) 'Society as symbolic interaction' in H. Rose (ed.) *Human Behaviour and Social Processes: An Interactionist Approach*, London: Routledge and Kegan Paul.
Candy, P.C. (1991) *Self Direction for Lifelong Learning: A Comprehensive Guide to Theory and Practice*, San Francisco: Jossey Bass.
Carr, W. and Kemmis, S. (1983) *Becoming Critical: Knowing Through Action Research*, Geelong: Deakin University Press.
Derrida, J. (1994) 'The deconstruction of actuality', *Radical Philosophy* 68 (Autumn): 28–41.
Foucault, M. (1980) 'Truth and power' in M. Foucault, *Power/Knowledge: Selected Interviews And Other Writing*, Brighton: Harvester Press (pp. 114–33).
Foucault, M. (1988) 'Technologies of the self' in L.H. Martin, H. Gutman and P.H. Hutton (eds) *Technologies of the Self: A Seminar with Michel Foucault*, London: Tavistock (pp. 16–49).

Garrick, J. (1998) *Informal Learning in the Workplace: Unmasking Human Resource Development*, London and New York: Routledge.

Garrick, J. and Rhodes, C. (1998) 'Deconstructive organisational learning: the possibilities for a postmodern epistemology of practice', *Studies in the Continuing Education of Adults* 30, 2: 172–83.

Giroux, H.A. (1983) *Theory and Resistance in Education: A Pedagogy for the Opposition*, London: Heinemann.

Kuhn, T.S. (1970) 'Revolutions as changes of world view' in T.S. Kuhn *The Structure of Scientific Revolutions* (2nd edition), Chicago: University of Chicago Press (pp. 111–35).

Lather, P. (1991) *Feminist Research in Education: Within/Against*, Geelong: Deakin University Press.

Lyotard, J.F. (1984) *The Postmodern Condition: A Report on Knowledge*, Manchester: Manchester University Press.

Scheurich, J.J. (1997) *Research Method in the Postmodern*, Washington: Falmer Press.

Schutz, A. (1953) 'Commonsense and scientific interpretation of human action', *Philosophy and Phenomenological Research Quarterly* 14, 1 (September). Reprinted in R. Zaner and R. Idhe (eds) (1973) *Phenomenology and Existentialism*, New York: Capricorn Books (pp. 291–316).

Taylor, G. (1993) 'A theory of practice: hermeneutical understanding', *Higher Education Research and Development* 12, 1: 59–72.

Usher, R.S. (1992) 'Experience in adult education: A post-modern critique', *Journal of Philosophy of Education* 26, 2: 201–14.

Usher, R.S. (1996) 'A critique of the neglected assumptions of educational research' in D. Scott and R.S. Usher (eds) *Understanding Educational Research*, London: Routledge.

Usher, R.S. and Edwards, R. (1994) *Postmodernism and Education: Different Voices, Different Worlds*, London: Routledge.

Usher, R.S., Bryant, I. and Johnston, R.A. (1997) *Adult Education and the Postmodern Challenge: Learning Beyond the Limits*, London: Routledge.

12 'Doing' knowledge at work

Dialogue, monologue and power in organisational learning

Carl Rhodes

Contemporary times have seen knowledge become an increasingly important theme in the way organisations are understood. In particular, discussions surrounding post-industrialism have highlighted the centrality of knowledge to economic and social life on an increasingly global scale. In addressing this knowledge theme, this chapter examines how communication in general, and dialogue in particular, is a way of 'doing' knowledge in organisations. Dialogue, as a process where people mobilise language by talking, listening and constructing meaning on the basis of their interaction with others, is vital to working knowledge. It is through dialogue that people use language to make sense of their organisations and their place in them. The implications this has for research are twofold. First, researchers interested in communication at work themselves employ dialogue and study the dialogue of others in order to develop understandings of organisations. Second, dialogue is in itself a form of informal research that people use in learning about and making sense of the organisations in which they work. Dialogue is then employed both through formal and informal research to inquire into organisations and human interaction, and therefore a theorisation of dialogue is central to the practice of research. The approach taken here sees language as being 'primarily concerned with the performance of actions and acts of various kinds' (Harré and Gillett 1994: 27) and hence dialogue is such a form of action. From this perspective, the question asked in this chapter is: 'how can we understand how knowledge is "done" in dialogue?' In particular, this question is asked in the context of how dialogue has been understood in theories and research on organisational learning.

Research and writing on organisational learning has demonstrated a keen focus on dialogue as a process of communication that can lead to shared meaning, team development and conflict resolution. It has been suggested that such communication is required to facilitate the learning that organisations require in order to account for escalating rates of change and the growth of technological complexity (Schein 1995) and that the contemporary focus on learning has emerged as one of the 'answers' to the uncertainties of contemporary organisational life (Garrick and Rhodes 1998). In terms of organisational learning, dialogue is seen as a capacity for conversation that leads to the discovery of new points of view and the articulation of intuition and tacit knowledge (Hosley *et al.* 1994). Dialogue is thus presented as a prescription for communicatory behaviour that leads to the creation of knowledge as groups of people form common meanings and generate ideas that are beyond the capabilities of individuals. This focus on the importance of dialogue is evident in the fact that 'dialogue projects' are defined as one of the four major areas of research at the Organizational Learning Centre connected with the Sloan School of Management at MIT, a bastion of mainstream research into organisational learning. These projects espouse a focus on enhancing the nature of 'conversation' in diverse working teams (Fulmer 1995).

While research into organisational learning has focused on dialogue as a process of communication and inquiry that leads to shared knowledge, little attention has been placed on dialogue as a way of understanding knowledge in terms of social and power relationships in organisations. Indeed, dialogue in general seems to be 'placed within a unitarist framework of relationships; a utopia to be ushered in through the pursuit of shared goals in a climate of collaborative high trust and a rational approach to the resolution of differences' (Coopey 1995: 199).

This prevalent view of dialogue has important consequences for how organisational learning might be used to research workplace interactions as the concept of dialogue – as a process of co-ordination of meaning – 'backgrounds' social and discursive differences and tensions that can operate unreconciled in organisations. The purpose of this chapter, then, is to contrast the orthodox view of dialogue as a communication process with that of dialogue as a social process, where different understandings and knowledges struggle in an arena of power relationships. In doing so, the chapter starts by reviewing the approach to dialogue expounded in mainstream organisational learning literature. The limits to this conceptualisation are then discussed in terms of its narrow theorisation of interpersonal relationships and its noticeable avoidance of issues of social power. To address these issues, an alternative view of dialogue is proposed through a reading of the work of the literary theorist Mikhail Bakhtin. This reading is then used to suggest a new approach to dialogue: one that accounts for social and power relationships in organisational life and in the ways that organisational knowledge is constructed. Finally, the implications for organisational learning research are discussed in terms of a new understanding of dialogue that accounts for a co-existence of 'common meaning' *and* diverse and interrelated experience, but where difference is not regarded as an anomaly in need of reconciliation.

Dialogue and organisational learning

One of the most influential theorisations of dialogue used to inform organisational learning has been that of David Bohm. In the popular organisational learning book *The Fifth Discipline*, Senge (1990) draws on Bohm's theory of dialogue to inform his understanding of and prescriptions for team learning. This theory suggests that there are two primary modes of discourse – discussion and dialogue – and while both are important to learning, dialogue is 'all but lost in the modern world' (ibid.: 239). For Senge, discussion is conceptualised through the metaphor of a ping-pong game, where topics are debated from independent perspectives and where the objective of each participant is to 'win' by having their views accepted by the other participants. Senge criticises this mode of communication because its emphasis on winning is not compatible with 'coherence and truth'. In contrast to discussion, Senge suggests that the practice of dialogue consists of a free flow of meaning between people, where the group accesses a pool of common understanding such that the whole organises the parts. What is promised is that dialogue can enable people to go beyond their individual understanding by exploring issues from different perspectives, suspending assumptions and communicating freely. In this conceptualisation of dialogue, thinking is viewed as participatory such that, when people can separate themselves from their thought and see that thought is produced collectively through shared language and culturally accepted assumptions. Dialogue therefore enables people to 'participate in [a] common pool of meaning' (Senge 1990: 242). Senge quotes Bohm's three conditions for dialogue as being the suspension of assumptions, all participants regarding each other as colleagues, and the presence of a facilitator who 'holds the context' for the dialogue. Adhering to these conditions is designed to diminish resistance to the 'free flow of meaning'. Calvert *et al.* (1994) explain further that Bohm's concept of dialogue encourages people to interact with one another such that they view each other as inquiring colleagues who explore possibilities rather than advocate their own points of view. This is proposed as a way to overcome conflict, break down communication barriers and generate organisational knowledge.

For Senge, dialogue, as he describes it, is of value in terms of its usefulness for 'team learning'. He suggests that effective teams need to master both discussion and dialogue, but that it is dialogue that can lead to 'deep trust' and 'rich understanding'. Dialogue for Senge is a 'team discipline' used to create learning, reflection and inquiry that can articulate a unique team vision (Senge 1990). Similarly, Bonnen and Fry (1991) see dialogue as a way to explore, mediate and cope with the tension between dominant and new organisational logics such that change and learning can be facilitated. Dialogue, in this sense, is a way that organisations can cope with the increased rate and size of change that they face in the contemporary world. This approach views organisations as a *negotiated reality*, with a certain degree of shared meaning where the quality of dialogue will be the key to ensuring confidence in communication so that learning occurs by confronting existing organisational realities.

At the heart of the linkage that organisational learning researchers often make between dialogue and learning is the focus on dialogue as a *process of communication*. Schein (1995) suggests that organisational learning and effectiveness depends on the ability to develop common language and shared 'mental models' (Senge's term). Dialogue is perceived to be at the 'root' of this communication and the basis for all effective group actions. As a communication process, dialogue is intended to focus on understanding our thinking processes through the natural flow of conversation. This conversation and the common meaning that results from it is said to lead to an organisational culture that facilitates 'effective' organisational change and learning (Schein 1993).

Burgoyne (1995) concurs by suggesting that dialogue is a core process of collective meaning-making in organisational learning. Similarly to Senge's distinction between dialogue and discussion, Burgoyne defines dialogue as the creation of a flow of joint meaning which is in opposition to debate, which attempts persuasion and victory over alternative points of view. He adds that learning can be further facilitated through a process of meta-dialogue that involves a discussion of the basis on which shared understanding can be achieved and an exploration of the ways in which the beliefs being discussed in dialogue can be seen as true or useful.

Isaacs (1993: 24) defines dialogue as a 'sustained collective enquiry into the processes, assumptions and certainties that compose everyday experience'. In this way, dialogue is a mode of inquiry and collective learning that leads to collaborative thought. For Isaacs, the central purpose of dialogue is to establish a field of 'genuine' meaning and inquiry for working and creating things together. This is said to be achieved through the way it changes the patterns that led people to disagree to begin with, by people learning to 'think together'. In this view dialogue is central to organisational learning as it promotes collective thinking and communication and involves learning about the context and nature of how people make sense of their worlds.

The limits to dialogue

The approaches to learning described above present possibilities for collectively beneficial interpersonal relationships, organisational communication and resultant organisational action where dialogue is conceived as a preferred mode of communication that leads to shared knowledge. Such an approach foregrounds communication as having the potential to inform the choices and actions of organisational members. Simultaneously, however, it backgrounds the social context within which dialogue is present. This focus on dialogue as a way of gaining consensus ignores any understanding of why differences existed in the first place. By relying on dialogue as theorised within a frame of interpersonal behaviour, the interaction of people is conceived as a mode of communication between independent selves who share and add to each other's individual and collective identity. What results is a prescription for the communication behaviour of organisational members that veers away from a more critical understanding of communication by assuming the value of coherence, consistency and continuity through attempts to construct an aggregate coherent story which encompasses all others (Keenoy *et al.* 1997). This consensus does 'violence' to the heterogeneity of language and becomes a tool for a form of authority that demands adherence to a particular set of rules (Lyotard 1984). Particularly, what this lacks is any considered understanding of the operation of power in organisational relationships.

Proponents of dialogue suggest that the people involved should suspend their assumptions and treat each other as equally as possible. This approach ignores the social relationships that construct people's sense of identity and assumes that social and power differences can be assumed away in the idealised context of organisational dialogue. What is missing is a discussion of how different ways of understanding organisations include or exclude the plurality of 'voices' that make up the organisation where communication suppresses some ways of thinking as it sheds light on others. Also missing is a discussion of how communication acts become central to knowledge production where 'selves' are produced discursively 'in dialogue and other forms of joint action with real and imagined others' (Harré 1998: 68). What I am proposing in this chapter is that research in organisational learning can benefit from a view of dialogue that addresses issues of difference without trying to 'talk them away' through concepts of common meaning and shared mental models. This proposition questions the approach which sees learning as being of value only if it can be expressed in the terms of dominant organisational logics: logics that conflate the education of adults with their work practices and suggest that learning is only valid if it is framed in the particular language of organisational performance (Garrick and Rhodes 1998).

For many organisational learning theorists, dialogue is seen as a communication process that is defined in opposition to debate or discussion. This key difference defines communication in terms of the intention of the participants and the outcomes of the conversation. In this sense, dialogue is a communication event that corresponds to certain conditions. What I am suggesting here is an approach which theorises it in relation to monologue instead of theorising dialogue in opposition to debate or discussion. In this way, dialogue is not just a communication event but an inter-subjective practice used to frame our relationship with others. This approach to dialogue offers the possibility not of a romanticised hope for equality in organisational relationships, but rather of an understanding of how communication practice relates organisational power through the way that people understand themselves in the context of other people. A monological approach, on the other hand, sees people's stories as emerging 'fully cooked' (Eisenberg and Phillips 1991) from a particular speaker instead of seeing communication as being co-constructed by all participants and emergent from social activity (also see the discussion on '(mis)interpretive' research by Garrick in Chapter 11).

As will be discussed, a reflection on a dialogic perspective sees difference as the basis of communication and suggests that this difference presents opportunities for knowledge rather than being a problem that needs to be resolved. This in turn poses questions about who is involved in the dialogue and what social discourses play a part in organisational knowledge.

Dialogue, monologue and power

To address the issues of power and communication highlighted in the previous section, what now follows is an approach to understanding dialogue based on a reading of the work of Mikhail Bakhtin. This approach uses dialogue as the 'subject' of research at work as well as a means of understanding organisations; this responds to scholars who are calling for more discursive approaches to the study of organisations (Boje 1995) where organisations are understood as stories, discourses and texts manifested in simultaneously occurring dialogues (Hazen 1993). The particular perspective of power to be examined relates to how people include or exclude the views of others in terms of how organisational learning is understood. Learning is then a process of inquiry and involves a questioning of homogenising and totalising accounts of the organisation through participation and dialogue involving diverse and potentially unreconcilable 'voices', so as to avoid rigidly defined 'consensus' externally imposed on people's experience (Rhodes 1997). In this context, power is exercised as a singular version of organisational reality is imposed as the 'real reality', and learning is a questioning of that power. As Hazen (1993: 16) puts it: 'when people in groups organise or are organised to work together to accomplish a complex task, there are at least as many voices as there are people. However, some are louder, more articulate, or more powerful than others.' Dialogue and the possibility of learning exists in the intersection of these different voices and research at work can focus on examining this interaction instead of demanding the resolution of difference.

To study organisational learning in this way, literary theory can provide directions and opportunities through a critical understanding of the interpretation of organisational 'texts'; particularly, in this chapter, the work of Russian literary critic Mikhail Bakhtin will be used to inform an understanding of organisational dialogue. Writing from the 1920s through to the 1970s, one of Bakhtin's greatest contributions has been the development of his concept of the dialogic novel. His writing, however, is useful beyond the study of literary texts; indeed people have responded to Bakhtin not just as a literary critic, but also as a social thinker and as a philosopher of language (Holquist 1986). The breadth of applicability of his work allows his ideas to be used to inform an understanding of research and knowledge in the context of institutional and organisational life. Bakhtin's work is of particular relevance to the study of organisational learning because he directly addresses the concept of dialogue so that an opportunity is offered to study power and dialogue in a way not available to more conventional approaches. It is an approach which opposes the perception of language as being an isolated, finished and monologic process. Instead it favours a dialogic understanding of knowledge as contested, active, creative *and social*.

Bakhtin (1986) examines dialogue through the broad sense of the concept of 'text' as being a coherent complex of signs; the text is the primary given of all thought in social inquiry and it is the only 'reality' through which knowledge can emerge. In this way, social inquiry represents a complex interrelation between the text being interpreted and the context in which it is evaluated. This notion is specific to social inquiry (as opposed to the physical sciences) in the sense that it is not involved in the study of inanimate, voiceless or natural phenomena, but in the study of people – people who express themselves and create their own texts. In terms of dialogue, organisational knowledge is enacted as people 'read' and 'write' the texts of organisations through their everyday interactions with each other. What Bakhtin offers is an understanding that recognises the practice of 'authorship' (i.e. the creation of social texts) and the author's relationship to that which is being interpreted. This approach sees reality as a 'living text' that is simultaneously written and read, where readers of this text create their own meaning and in effect add their own authoring to the text. Each person is then the reader and author of their own reality; however, for any situation multiple 'authentic' readings are possible as each 'author-reader' can produce understandings shaped by their own horizon and by the interests being served (Morgan 1997a). Reading organisation is then active rather than passive; it is simultaneously a practice of authoring where interpretation is a creative process rather than being a mirror of a pre-given reality (Morgan 1997b). In this way, people, as the authors of social texts, enter into those texts that they create and are indispensable to them. Bakhtin's work allows for an understanding of knowledge as conversation and dialogue, such that the texts employed and mobilised by different people can intersect in a dialogic relationship and participate in the knowledge that is produced. As explained by Stam (1988) the construction of any self involves interacting with the discourse of others through dialogue. As each member of an organisation is the author of their organisational reality, the issue relates to the way in which other perspectives are incorporated into the practice of authorship.

Bakhtin addresses this process through the concepts of dialogue and monologue. Bakhtin (1986) notes that an understanding of the physical world is monological in that one person contemplates and expounds a 'thing' – this 'thing' is voiceless and therefore there is only one subject. When one person tries to understand their relationship with other people, however, both have voices and therefore the understanding can only be dialogic. He goes on to comment that it is possible for consciousness to attempt to monologise by making the words of others anonymous and assimilated, such that the dialogue is transformed into one continuous text and it is only the authoritative word that evades anonymity. The challenge presented by Bakhtin is to hear the different voices and to write the dialogic relations among them. As noted by Morris (1984) the notion of discourse as dialogic, and developed from text to text, accounts for the interplay of power and social hierarchy as determining the interaction between self and other. In terms of organisational learning, using language is not a matter of free choice but rather the adoption of an authoritative verbal consciousness, where the discourse and voice of one individual is borne of the authoritative and persuasive discourse of others (Bakhtin 1981).

In reaction to this potential authorial monologisation is a situation where the reader-author does not retain the final word, but is conceptu-alised as an organiser and participant in the dialogue (Bakhtin 1984), where 'truth' is seen as a conversation rather than a set of propositions (Morson and Emerson 1994). Individuals participating in organisations then organise their understanding based on their interaction with others. Dialogue enters this understanding to the extent that people are mindful of the role of others in their knowledge of themselves and their organisations. As explained by Swingewood (1986), Bakhtin's contribution here is the distinguishing of monological and dialogic traditions. This distinction sees the monological tradition as being based on a single-voiced utterance where one person manipulates the voices of others so that they express the interpreted authorial intention, whereas the dialogic tradition is based on a multi-voiced utterance, where different and opposing 'voices' dominate. Such a tradition lacks a unifying discourse and instead uses a plurality of centres that are separate from any authoritative discourse. Dialogue and organisational learning then create a plurality of views that exist simultaneously rather than monologising into shared 'mental models'. People can be seen as subjectively conscious in their representation of 'self' and 'organisation' and not confined by the single authorial consciousness that predominates in monological forms. As Waugh (1992) explains, Bakhtin's dialogism sees knowledge of the world, self and other not as a self-sufficient concept, but as a result of a relational process based on provisional and continuous authorship. Reality is an experience of exchange that calls for a response from the individuals situated in it.

This distinction between dialogic and monological forms of discourse offers a key insight into the process of organisational learning. Accepting that knowledge is produced dialogically brings into question the power relationships implicit in practices of understanding organisations. Particularly it draws attention to how monological forms, where one person speaks for others without acknowledging them, create a hierarchical relationship of the author over the people being spoken about where the authority of the author is positioned so that his/her subjectivity is made out to be super-ordinate to that of other people. The practice of interpretation can be used in this way to suggest that the self-interpretations of organisational members are regarded as unimportant and that the only interpretations worth noting are the meta-interpretations of the person whose voice has the opportunity to be heard. This is a knowledge practice that regards one person as capable of understanding others such that their self-understanding is relegated as not worthy of mention. As Bakhtin (1986) suggests, what is brought into question is how people address the dialogic nature of their practice and whether they attempt to present final arguments from their own point of view or accept the dialogic overtones of their statements. Dialogic relations are always present even in profoundly monological statements; the question is to what extent is this dialogue explicit. In these terms organisational learning becomes an understanding based on difference rather than sameness.

For Bakhtin, dialogue extends into an understanding of the social as being constituted through the interaction of a plurality of social texts operating within and between individuals (Stam 1988). What is created is a dialogic intersubjectivity where each subjectivity operates outside of the particular body of any individual as a multitude of subjectivities are adopted by individuals in an attempt to represent their 'selves'. The resultant social discourses are intertextual, where the possibility of meaning is a result of negotiation, conflict, compromise, collaboration and tensions between different texts (San Juan Jr 1995). Organisational learning can then work in an intertextual form and create a site for the dialogic relationship between alternating representations of social and organisational realities, rather than trying to write the final word.

Dialogue, sameness and difference

Comparing the consensus and shared meaning based conceptualisation of dialogue in organisational learning with the dialogism of Bakhtin leaves us with a conflict between an understanding of dialogue based on the prescription of sameness with one based on the acceptance of difference. Through one frame, we see dialogue as creating the possibility for common understanding and co-ordinated action; in the second frame we see dialogue as being a state of difference where multiple interpretations co-exist and compete in a discursive arena. In an attempt to come to terms with this apparent dichotomy, this section explores further the work of Bakhtin to offer the opportunity to see dialogic consensus and plurality as existing within the same social 'space'. Understanding dialogue this way is intended to provide conceptual opportunities that can account for co-ordination and conflict within the study of organisational learning.

Bakhtin's understanding of the dialogic relationships of communication is extended to social understanding through the concept of 'heteroglossia', meaning literally 'different speech-ness'. This notion of heteroglossia opposes the view that a single unified language operates in any society and focuses instead on how language is multiplanar and breaks down into different discourses. Heteroglossia relates to the difference between the various discursive strata within any language, such that any individual utterance is conceived of as a struggle between convergent and divergent meanings (Clark and Holquist 1984). Through heteroglossia, a range of competing dialogically related speech practices operate at any particular point in time, these speech practices representing different points of view on the world and different ways of understanding experience (Stam 1988).

Bakhtin sees the creative interaction of contradictory and differing voices as being opposed to a passive and receptive understanding (Morris 1984). In language, which is the arena of this interaction, there apply centripetal forces which aim at centralisation and the production of shared meaning used by dominant social groups (such as researchers of organisational learning, management consultants and managers themselves) to impose their own monological and unitary perceptions of truth. Such power works to establish stabilisation on its own terms and thus the exclusion of other possible realities (Gergen 1995). Working against this is a centrifugal force which is what Bakhtin calls 'heteroglossia'. This asserts that centripetal power can only exist against the possibility of alternatives (Gergen 1995). It is the existence of these alternatives that marks heteroglossia – a breaking up of a unified image of the world into a multiplicity of linguistically created worlds (McHale 1987).

Through this concept of heteroglossia all monological truth claims are relativised against other views of the world in a way that counters the dominance of single languages and absolute forms of thought. In this way, authoritative and persuasive social voices become ironically or parodically relativised against other voices within heteroglossia. The centrifugal force of heteroglossia opposes the centralising imposition of the monological world through multi-vocal discourse. As Gagnon (1992: 231) puts it, 'heteroglossia is accompanied by polysemy, the proliferation of socially uncontrolled meanings for these voices'. Heteroglossia highlights how Bakhtin's concept of dialogism differs from the binary oppositions of dialectics in the way that it conceives of plurality as a both/and instead of an either/or operation through the centrifugal forces that try to keep things separate, and the centripetal forces that strive to keep them unified (Clark and Holquist 1984).

Through this concept of heteroglossia, Bakhtin (1981) describes language as being stratified into multiple social discourses, each of which represents different ways of seeing the world. This multiplicity is the site of a struggle between different social languages where 'truth' exists only in dialogic relations between social discourses and where meaning is produced in an unending process, a process where 'centrality is displaced by heterogeneity and an adhocing through the complexities of an ever shifting sea of meaning and action' (Gergen 1992: 223). Language is used to represent worldviews and perform subject positions rather than to mirror abstract conceptualisations. For Bakhtin words are appropriated by individuals not from a neutral or impersonal language but from the language of other people. In this sense Bakhtin sees language not as being the 'private property' of individuals but as being an inter-subjective process. Other people's discourse strives to control our representational relationship with the world; it performs as an authoritative discourse. The voice of one person is borne out of the discourse of others. In heteroglossia, however, each person operates through many languages. As described by Morson and Emerson (1994), the insight from Bakhtin is how a language is composed of innumerable languages that are based on different experiences and have their own way of understanding and evaluating the world. Individuals participate in a number of these languages, each of which claims a privileged view of the world. The languages of heteroglossia compete with one another as the many 'languages of truth' participate in dialogue with each other and with the experiences they attempt to represent.

Heteroglossia draws attention to the way that language operates discursively through and between individuals. The centripetal forces of language operate to create singular and shared meaning through operations of power; the centrifugal force of heteroglossia works to create diversities of meaning through the different language practices and discourses used by different people. The languages used by all people involved in an organisation are themselves derived socially and operate together through heteroglossia to provide a multi-layered text where both the voices of individuals and the multiple discourses that inform them reside inextricably together. It is here that 'knowledge work' is played out, and where research at work might point its attention.

Implications for organisational learning and knowledge

The notion of dialogue draws our attention to how people construct their knowledge of the organisations they are a part of. It suggests that this construction is based on the interaction of different people and the subjectivities they draw on in defining themselves and the collectives to which they belong. To research organisational change, adaptation and learning is then to study how organisational change is interpreted and created through practices of dynamic discursive interpretations of organisational life. A Bakhtinian approach to dialogue provides a way of understanding the process through which these discursive understandings are constructed. Particularly, what is highlighted is the partiality of all organisational knowledge. As people researching or working in organisations, we construct understandings of our experience based on our interaction with the language of others. As we read and write these understandings, we can only ever engage in an understanding that accounts for the perspectives, the contexts and the temporalities that we have access to. As others similarly construct their own images, some of which we interact with and some of which we do not, organisational knowledge is understood through a plurality of potentially conflicting practices of constructing understanding. What has been argued is that an over-reliance on conceptions of dialogue as a process of constructing shared meaning operates through discursive power where a monologous representation of organisation is posited as a preferred 'reading'; this preference closes off possibilities for simultaneous alternative readings and imposes a false finality on the dynamic process of understanding. The very achievement of shared meaning marks the end of dialogue as all voices are supposedly reduced into a single, shared monologue. The maintenance of dialogue requires heteroglossia: without difference and the conflict of ideas knowledge becomes the domination of one voice in the dialogue over all others and research becomes an attempt to represent such a monologue. 'Shared meaning' can hide dialogue, marking the dominance of a single discursive position and rejecting more democratic approaches to knowledge and learning – where, as Edwards and Usher argue in Chapter 3, knowledge is seen as being plural and contested. The understanding of dialogue put forward here sees it as a 'doing' of knowledge through a multiplicitous process of reading/authorship, and suggests that organisational learning, as well as being plural, is possibly contradictory. From this position, claims of 'truth' in learning are seen to hide a discursively powerful monologisation under the rhetorical rubric of common meaning. What has been suggested as an alternative is an understanding of organisations where sameness and difference struggle to co-exist and where difference need not be eradicated through the construction of 'shared mental models'. Studying and researching organisational learning can contribute to the practice of organising without having to rely on narrow perspectives that valorise sameness by ignoring the hegemony of monologisation. Instead, social interaction, as an arena for learning, can embrace discursive diversity as an opportunity for the existence of different and co-existing knowledges across people, sites and contexts. This is an organisational learning where difference is not a problem, but rather where learning operates in a site of unreconciled discursive and heteroglossic diversity.

In summary, my objective in this chapter has been to question dominant views of communication and organisational knowledge by offering a critique of theorisations of dialogue in organisational learning. To do this I have used insights from the work of Mikhail Bakhtin to inform possible alternatives and augmentation. Particularly relevant to this discussion has been an understanding of the discursive power embedded in competing conceptualisations of dialogue. In examining this 'competition', my objective has not been to resolve issues of power, but rather to theorise organisational learning in a way that is cautionary of the practices of communication and interpretation that seek to impose particular views of an organisation. Richer understandings of dialogue can lead to approaches to research in work contexts that account for diversity rather than trying to resolve it or stamp it out with false consensus. As dialogue performs knowledge, it is through interaction and difference that knowledge continues to be created.

References

Bakhtin, M.M. (1981) *The Dialogic Imagination: Four Essays*, translated by C. Emerson and M. Holquist, edited by M. Holquist, Austin: University of Texas Press.

Bakhtin, M.M. (1984) *Problems of Dostoyevsky's Poetics*, translated by C. Emerson, Minneapolis: University of Minnesota Press.

Bakhtin, M.M. (1986) *Speech Genres and Other Late Essays*, translated by V.W. McGee, edited by C. Emerson and M. Holquist, Austin: University of Texas Press.

Boje, D.M. (1995) 'Stories of the storytelling organization: a postmodern analysis of Disney as "Tamara-Land"', *Academy of Management Journal* 38, 4: 997–1035.

Bonnen, R. and Fry, R. (1991) 'Organizational innovation and learning: four patterns of dialog between the dominant logic and the new logic', *International Studies of Management and Organization* 21, 4: 37–51.

Burgoyne, J.G. (1995) 'Learning from experience: from individual discovery to meta-dialogue via the evolution of transition myths', *Personnel Review* 24, 6: 61–72.

Calvert, G., Mobley, S. and Marshall, L. (1994) 'Grasping the learning organization', *Training and Development* 48, 6: 38–43.

Clark, K. and Holquist, M. (1984) *Mikhail Bakhtin*, Cambridge, Mass.: Harvard University Press.

Coopey, J. (1995) 'The learning organization, power politics and ideology', *Management Learning* 26, 2: 193–213.

Eisenberg, E.M. and Phillips, S.R. (1991) 'Miscommunication in organizations' in N. Coupland and J.M. Wiemann (eds) *Miscommunication and Problematic Talk*, Newbury Park: Sage (pp. 244–58).

Fulmer, R.M. (1995) 'Building organizations that learn: the MIT Center for Organizational Learning', *Journal of Management Development* 14, 5: 9–14.

Gagnon, J.H. (1992) 'The self, its voices and their discord' in C. Ellis and M.G. Flaherty (eds) *Investigating Subjectivity: Research on Lived Experience*, Newbury Park: Sage (pp. 221–43).

Garrick, J. and Rhodes, C. (1998) 'Deconstructive organisational learning: the possibilities for a postmodern epistemology of practice', *Studies in the Continuing Education of Adults* 30, 2: 172–83.

Gergen, K.J. (1992) 'Organization theory in the postmodern era' in M. Reed and M. Hughes (eds) *Rethinking Organizations: New Dimensions in Organization Theory and Analysis*, London: Sage (pp. 207–26).

Dialogue and knowledge at work   231

Gergen, K.J. (1995) 'Relational theory and the discourses of power' in D.-M. Hosking, H.P. Dachler and K.J. Gergen (eds) *Management and Organization: Relational Alternatives to Individualism*, Aldershot: Avebury (pp. 29–50).

Harré, R. (1998) *The Singular Self*, London: Sage.

Harré, R. and Gillet, G. (1994) *The Discursive Mind*, London: Sage.

Hazen, M.A. (1993) 'Towards polyphonic organization', *Journal of Organizational Change Management* 6, 5: 15–26.

Holquist, H. (1986) 'Introduction' in M.M. Bakhtin, *Speech Genres and Other Late Essays*, translated by V.W. McGee, edited by C. Emerson and M. Holquist, Austin: University of Texas Press (pp. ix–xxiii).

Hosley, S.M., Law, A.T.W., Levy, F.K. and Tan, D.S.K. (1994) 'The quest for the competitive learning organization', *Management Decision* 32, 6: 5–15.

Isaacs, W.N. (1993) 'Taking flight: dialogue, collective thinking and organizational learning', *Organizational Dynamics* 22, 2: 24–39.

Keenoy, T., Oswick, C. and Grant, D. (1997) 'Organizational discourses: text and context', *Organization* 4, 2: 147–57.

Lyotard, J.F. (1984) *The Postmodern Condition: A Report on Knowledge*, translated by G. Bennington and B. Massumi, Manchester: Manchester University Press.

McHale, B. (1987) *Postmodernist Fiction*, London: Routledge.

Morgan, G. (1997a) *Imaginization: New Mindsets for Seeing, Organizing and Managing*, San Francisco: Berret-Koehler.

Morgan, G. (1997b) *Images of Organization*, 2nd edition, Thousand Oaks: Sage.

Morris, P. (1984) 'Introduction' in P. Morris (ed.) *The Bakhtin Reader*, London: Edward Arnold (pp. 1–24).

Morson, S. and Emerson, C. (1994) 'Bakhtin, M.M.' in M. Groden and M. Kreiswirth (eds) *The Johns Hopkins Guide to Literary Theory and Criticism*, Baltimore: Johns Hopkins University Press (pp. 63–8).

Rhodes, C. (1997) 'The legitimation of learning in organizational change', *Journal of Organizational Change Management* 10, 1: 10–20.

San Juan Jr, E. (1995) *Hegemony and Strategies of Transgression*, New York: State University of New York Press.

Schein, E.H. (1993) 'On dialogue, culture and organizational learning', *Organizational Dynamics* 22, 2: 40–51.

Schein, E.H. (1995) 'Dialogue and learning', *Executive Excellence* 12, 4: 3–4.

Senge, P. (1990) *The Fifth Discipline: The Art and Practice of the Learning Organization*, New York: Doubleday.

Stam, R. (1988) 'Mikhail Bakhtin and left cultural critique' in E.A. Kaplan (ed.) *Postmodernism and Its Discontents: Theories, Practices*, London: Verso (pp. 116–45).

Swingewood, A. (1986) *Sociological Poetics and Aesthetic Theory*, London: Macmillan.

Waugh, P. (1992) *Practising Postmodernism/Reading Modernism*, London: Edward Arnold.

13 An adventure in 'postmodern' action research

Performativity, professionalism and power

Jill Sanguinetti

Participatory action research

In this chapter I tell the story of a 'postmodern' participatory action research project which I undertook between 1995 and 1997 among a group of teachers who were experiencing a stressful period of institutional change.[1] That the focus is on teachers is quite incidental as the story is applicable to many contemporary professionals who face work contexts of ambiguity, rapid change and restructuring. I had three main aims in undertaking this project. The first was to support the teachers by facilitating a series of discussion meetings about the issues affecting them at work. The second was to gather research data about how teachers were engaging discursively in the field of adult literacy and basic education in 'difficult times'. The third was to explore a 'postmodern' version of action research based on Foucauldian notions of power and discourse.

Action research is now well established as a means of educational, professional and organisational development (Zuber-Skerritt 1996: 3). It is commonly defined as a form of collaborative, reflective enquiry carried out by practitioners on their own practice, in order to find ways of improving that practice (Kemmis and McTaggart 1988; Zuber-Skerritt 1996). This definition reflects the two different, but related, purposes of action research: learning from reflection on practice and taking action to improve practice. The metaphor of the action research 'cycle' refers to on-going processes of planning, action, observation and reflection. The 'steps' in the action research cycle structure the approach to action for change and the research method.

The documentation of the processes and outcomes of projects, in which groups of people engage in cycles of action and reflection in a deliberate and planned way, is the basis of the research data. The knowledge produced from such projects emerges at the interface of institutional practice and struggles over change. Such working knowledge may primarily be of local interest, or it may contain broader significance.

A number of authors have grappled with the theoretical challenge that post-structural and postmodern ideas pose to traditional notions of action research (McTaggart 1994; Hall 1996; Kemmis 1996; Jennings and Graham 1996; Usher *et al.* 1997). My objective was to explore the implications of post-structuralist theory for the *practice* of participatory action research. My hunch was that Foucault's theory of discourse could facilitate more effective reflexivity about ourselves as workers, the institutional environments in which we work, and the broader social and political context. I considered that discourse theory would be a useful resource in exploring, and coming to terms with, our institutional and professional realities. This case-study was an explicit attempt to facilitate more complex and historically informed understandings, among all of the participants (including myself), of the discourses which construct our working environments and which constitute us personally, professionally and politically.

I came to the project both as an adult literacy teacher sharing many of the concerns and passions of the other participants, and as a university researcher who had an academic investment in the research. As facilitator, I had more power than the others to make judgements about what was significant and to shape the process and outcomes. I continually shifted between the positions of participant, academic theorist and facilitator as I strove to keep pace with, to document and sometimes to lead the changing energies and preoccupations of the group. I felt I was on a risky, stimulating and illuminating journey in uncharted methodological territory.

Context

Adult literacy teaching (like many professional practices throughout OECD countries) has been profoundly affected by the rise of neo-liberalism in government. Since the early 1990s, neo-liberal policies have radically changed the ways 'adult literacy' is constructed and teachers' work is organised. Teachers have had to adapt to formally accredited, competency-based frameworks and pressures to measure and account for 'outcomes'. Other changes have intensified the effects of the new requirements: the establishment of the competitive training market with pressure on providers to compete with each other for tenders; the downward pressure on pay and conditions; the increasingly fragmented and casualised nature of available work; and the bureaucratisation of technical and further education (TAFE) institutes as these reform themselves in the model of lean, mean, competitive business enterprises.

The implementation of competency-based assessment has reconstructed adult literacy teaching along neo-Taylorist lines, positioning
teachers as the 'deliverers' of pre-defined sets of skills and competencies.
For example, the competency-based Certificate of General Education for
Adults (the CGEA), developed in Australia (in the state of Victoria), is an
enormously complicated framework of streams (subjects), domains (genres)
and levels of competence. Modules at each intersection are defined as
'elements', which are associated with one or more 'competency' or
'competence statement'. Each competence statement has an associated set
of performance criteria, defined ranges of application and defined conditions. The progress of students is tracked and assessed by their
performance of tasks, each of which has been constructed in order to
display a particular competency in conformity with the given range and
conditions. Competency-based assessment in adult literacy and English as
a second language (ESL) has been found by teachers to have certain benefits, but to have pedagogical effects that are deeply problematic
(Sanguinetti 1995).

These changes have been described and interpreted in terms of 'performativity' (Lyotard 1984; Yeatman 1994; Lankshear, forthcoming).
Performativity, according to these authors, is the meta-discourse of the
globalising state. It arises in the world of transnational capital and *makes
sense* of the idea of technologising the functions of the state with a view to
minimising public expenditure and streamlining the provision of services
to the private sector. In Lyotard's words:

> the goal is no longer truth, but performativity – that is, the best
> possible input/output equation. The State and/or company must
> abandon the idealist and humanist narratives of legitimation in order
> to justify the new goal: in the discourse of today's financial backers of
> research, the only credible goal is power. Scientists, technicians and
> instruments are purchased not to find truth, but to augment power.
>
> (Lyotard 1984: 46)

As government policies and public institutions reconstruct themselves to
reflect and implement the meta-discourse of performativity, the worldview
of globalising capitalism increasingly penetrates all aspects of work and
society. Old certainties and securities are disintegrating and the demands
of work (for those who have it) are intensifying (Hargreaves 1994). Workers
are facing new sets of dilemmas about how to resist unpopular measures,
how to practise ethically and how to survive these pressures to perform in a
context of industrial insecurity and deep social and spiritual uncertainty.

I wanted to explore how the teachers were accommodating, surviving and resisting the various changes that flow from, and are required by, the meta-discourse of performativity. I began with the view that an orientation to the 'politics of discourse' (Yeatman 1990) might help us/them think more reflexively and therefore more strategically in that context. I saw action research as a process of collaborative learning which would provide a structure and a 'space' for examining the contending discourses of practice which structure the work of adult literacy teachers and constitute their personal and professional subjectivities.

Reflection and reflexivity in action research

The action research 'cycle' is built around processes of group reflection. According to Kemmis and McTaggart (1988: 86), group reflection is: 'the basis of the initial reconnaissance stage, in preparation for planning and action'. Further reflection – analysing, interpreting, synthesising, explaining and drawing conclusions – takes place subsequently as the basis for further planning and action.

Recently, a number of authors have written about reflection in action research in the quite different sense of 'reflexivity', or 'reflexive critique' (Schratz and Walker 1995; Hall 1996; Winter 1996; Usher *et al.* 1997). These authors discuss reflexivity as a kind of ethical/epistemological obligation on the part of the researcher, who should explore and disclose his or her own biases and investments in research projects. In Hall's words, it is about 'the obligation to "own up" to our personal contributions in the process of our knowledge construction' (Hall 1996: 47; see also McTaggart 1994: 2). More deeply, it is about 'living with recursiveness', the presence of the knower in the field which is to be known: the recognition that knowledges are always partial and incommensurable and that the subjectivity and purposes of the knower are inevitably embedded in the language through which the knowledge is constructed (Legge 1999).

Reflexivity also implies having an awareness of the ways in which personal preconceptions and passions feed into the development and outcomes of projects. The action researcher needs to develop a reflexive awareness of the power dimensions of her relationship with participants and the dynamics of power structuring her relationship with funding and auspicing bodies (Sanguinetti 1998: 48).

In this action research project, I set out to explore discursive positioning, subjectivity and power so as to facilitate greater reflexivity on the part of all participants, including myself. It was an attempt to test the extent to which action research could be used as a 'space' for collaborative reflection on the discourses that constitute professional subjectivity in particular institutional contexts.

A postmodern approach to action research

My intention in developing a postmodern version of action research was informed by the Foucauldian framing of power as 'capillary': dispersed throughout society and operating through language and discourse (Foucault 1980: 96). It was informed also by the insights of feminist post-structuralist research methodologists (Stanley and Wise 1983; Fine 1994 and 1995; Weiner 1994; Lather 1991 and 1997). In recent years, the notion of action research as an 'emancipatory' undertaking has been significantly challenged from post-structuralist theorists (Ellsworth 1989; Gore 1991; Usher *et al.* 1997). Ellsworth, for example, suggests that the emancipatory meta-narrative rests on a 'phallogocentric' paradigm of rational knowledge and abstract logic. It relies on the notion of the ideal rational person who will act rationally once they understand the cause or context of their oppression (1989: 306). It does not problematise our own implication in the structures we are trying to change (ibid.: 310).

The postmodern critique of action research is now being addressed by leading action research theorists. Kemmis (1996), for example, has written about the 'challenges of postmodernisms' to action research and the need, in the light of those challenges, for action research to be reconstructed. For him, those challenges centre around 'the death of the subject' as autonomous rational agent; 'the death of history' (that the Enlightenment notion of progress or the possibility of emancipation is no longer sustainable); and 'the death of metaphysics' (that science and rationality merely construct the illusion of an independent reality as a mask for human purposes of controlling the human and natural world) (Kemmis and McTaggart, 1988: 2). Authors such as Sanger (1996) and Jennings and Graham (1996) also apply postmodernist theory in order to build a more sophisticated understanding of the possibilities of action research.

Theories of discourse linking language and texts to particular institutional structures and structures of global power suggest an important shift in the way in which power can be theorised in action research. Knowledge, meaning, political and social values, and notions of 'self' are all constituted in discourse. Discourses reflect social and political contestations and we (who are the subjects of discourse) live out this contestation constantly, in the everyday language we use, the choices we make and the politics we enact. It follows that, if power is enmeshed in discourse, then 'action' can be theorised as action in the realm of discourse. To act, in this sense, is to follow a deliberate strategy of 'language politics' or the 'politics of discourse': speaking in ways which challenge dominant discourses and produce alternative meanings. In Yeatman's terms, 'discourse is the power to create reality by naming it and giving it meaning' (Yeatman 1990: 155).

Foucault's concept of power as productive and dispersed throughout society widens the scope of action research from an emancipatory meta-narrative of 'them' and 'us' to a deliberate investigation of discourses which construct our understandings of ourselves and our social situations. This becomes a focus on 'the practices, techniques and procedures by which power operates ... it involves the tracking of knowledge production (webs of power) and its power effects' (Jennings and Graham 1996: 174).

The post-structuralist notion of the discursively constituted, fragmented, 'in process' subject can be applied in action research in place of the modernist notion of the unitary rational self (Jennings and Graham 1996: 170). Action research participants are no longer regarded as rational, purposive beings who will automatically proceed to planning and action once they have been enlightened as to the cause of their problems through processes of collective reflection. Instead, and more realistically, they are conceived as complex, multiply positioned, and shaped by a multitude of historical, psychological and social forces. Their 'actions' are constrained by a dynamic and contradictory field of subconscious or conscious beliefs, apprehensions and ways of being – the discourses which constitute their sense of who they are and how they might act.

Reconceptualising the 'subject' of action research in this way requires a shift in focus beyond 'action' to 'reflection', in the sense of reflexive, critical praxis. This implies three levels of self-reflection and acknowledgement: reflection about our own discursive formation in relation to the problem at hand; reflection about how we might be implicated in the structures and practices we are trying to change; and reflection about our investments in the research project itself, our role in the dynamics of power structuring projects.

The case-study that I present in the following section was an attempt to develop and carry out such a postmodern version of participatory action research. I analysed the transcriptions of the teachers' discussions with a view to identifying and describing the discourses 'at play' within those texts. I progressively fed back my analyses and interpretations to the participants. I was hoping thereby to contribute to a more politically and historically informed level of self-reflective (reflexive) practice within the action research process. By introducing the notion of discourse and presenting the research collaborators with analyses of their own discursive practices, I hoped that we might reflect on and make connections between their representations of institutional and classroom experiences, and the broader social and historical context. Developing cycles of reflexive praxis in this way might correspond to a postmodern model of participatory action research that focused on strengthening the reflexive and theoretical skills of the participants and the possibility of more strategic action in the longer term.

Mapping discourses of professional and pedagogical practice: a case-study

The project was undertaken with a group of teachers of adult literacy and ESL in a teaching department in a large Melbourne TAFE college. The teachers, all of whom were previously known to me as colleagues, agreed to participate in a series of meetings in which they would reflect on and address issues of concern to them in the changing policy environment. I would share with them the transcripts of the discussions and my theoretical interpretations of their issues. My interpretations were to be based on the theory of discourse as developed by Foucault (1980, 1981), contemporary discourse theorists (Fairclough 1992; Lemke 1995) and leading feminist post-structuralists (Weedon 1987; Fraser 1989; Lather 1991; Davies 1994). I planned that together we would build our understandings of the structural and institutional changes taking place and how the teachers were teaching (their pedagogical practices) in the context of those changes. The teachers were keen to take part in the project. They were intrigued by my preoccupation with discourse and saw the project as an opportunity for working through the issues that were a cause of a good deal of stress at work.

There were six teachers in the group, not including me. Most were part-time teachers on short-term or sessional contracts. We had seven meetings between 1995 and late 1998, although not all participants attended all the meetings. I took notes and taped and transcribed most of the meetings, made analyses of discourses which I defined as 'present' in the discussions, and fed my analyses progressively back to the group.

Several themes featured during the discussions and in this chapter I am focusing on two of the most central of these. The first was the theme of institutional change: how the teachers were representing those changes and engaging discursively in that process. The second theme was about how teachers were teaching in the context of that change: how they were 'living the contradictions' (Seddon 1994) in the course of their classroom practice, and the forms of pedagogy which were emerging in that context. In this paper I report on part of the first theme: the teachers' representations of themselves as professionals, faced with the down-grading of their professionalism and loss of jobs through the introduction of marketisation into the field of adult literacy and basic education.

The case-study I am reporting here is one part of a larger research undertaking among adult literacy teachers (Sanguinetti 1999), which involved two separate action research projects and the use of discourse mapping as a method of analysing the teachers' writing and transcripts of interviews.

Discourse mapping

I had developed a method of analysing transcripts by 'mapping' the discourses that are prominent in structuring them. I adapted this mapping method to the particular texts being produced and to my interpretive purposes – to understand more about how teachers engage as professionals in rapid-change contexts.

1   I read and re-read the texts to familiarise myself with the way the teachers were representing the institutional environment, their practices, pedagogical understandings and individual struggles to survive and to teach well.

2   I iterated between the texts and my previous study of policy trends, movements and contestations within the teaching profession, the changing structures of institutional management and the pedagogical theories and traditions constructing the field of adult literacy.

3   I looked for traces, anywhere in the texts (in the themes, value statements, anecdotes, metaphors, arguments and lexical items), of the schools of thought and traditions (the discourses) of teachers' professionalism and pedagogical practice.

4   I developed a web chart in which the main traces are named as discourses and their interrelationships (interdiscursivities) with other traces could be depicted. The rules I used for determining whether or not a pattern of speaking could be termed a 'discourse' were that it must:

   •   recur across the texts (but not necessarily be in each text);
   •   be identifiably associated with a particular institutional sector, tradition, theory and set of practices; and
   •   reflect a set of power relations and a worldview.

5   After representing the discursive elements which I found to be present on the web chart, I collapsed these elements into two main discourses for the purposes of the analysis.

6   I then marked up each text in terms of the main orders of discourse. These were 'teacher professionalism' and 'performativity'.

7   Finally, I used the web chart as a reference point for studying the interdiscursivities as these appeared in the detail of the texts, and used this as a guide for my theoretical commentary on the teachers' discursive practices. Figure 13.1 illustrates this 'web'.

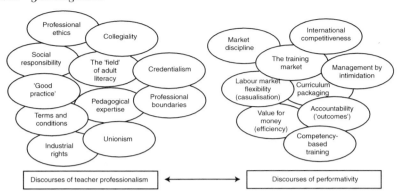

Figure 13.1   Discourses of teacher professionalism and discourses of performativity

Teachers' perceptions of institutional change

I shall describe and discuss the content of a discussion in which the participants chewed over the increasingly coercive style of institutional management, the effects of competency-based assessment and the overall impact of the marketisation of their field of practice. I will then summarise the findings of my discourse mapping exercise and my further interpretation of the discourse map.

During this discussion, the teachers gave a scathing and sometimes emotional account of the varying and interrelated impacts of competency-based assessment, marketisation and the down-grading of their industrial conditions (including the loss of tenure) and professional standing. They talked about the managerial attempts to contrive 'collegial' relationships, the loss of control over allocation of students to programmes, the insecurity caused by competitive tendering – especially the breaking down of professional networks – the with-holding of information about tenders by management, the rigidities of the competency-based assessment requirements in the Certificate of General Education for Adults (the CGEA) and new imperatives to 'prove' their capabilities by regularly having to report on 'measurable' outcomes. At bottom, they saw themselves as expendable in the push to centralise managerial power and to reduce unit costs so that their college could better compete against other providers.

The experiences of this group of teachers are similar to those of teachers in other Australian institutions of TAFE (Hattam 1995; Seddon 1998). With the leverage provided by short-term contracts and lack of permanent tenure, unpopular changes could be implemented with minimum resistance.

These teachers felt that their professional identity and autonomy was under attack. A theme which recurred throughout the discussion was the demise of adult literacy teaching as a profession. Conversely, the theme of teacher professionalism emerged as a discourse of resistance.

Interpretation of discourses

Everyone in the group denounced the new policies and the managers who were implementing new forms of control over teaching staff. The teachers were hurt, angry and bemused at the developments. A high level of consensus emerged from the intensity of their shared experiences. A collective adversarial subject position had been formed in opposition to the worldview and values associated with intimidatory management styles, marketisation, casualisation and the commodification of curriculum. They spoke as members of the teaching department, as members of a wider collectivity of teachers of ALBE and ESL and on behalf of the teaching profession in general. Almost all of the discussion was couched in the use of the 'we' ('we are at the cross roads', the 'we' being inter-changeable with terms such as 'teachers', 'the teaching profession', 'people'). The 'we' sometimes constructed teachers passively, as victims of the current policies and college management, but at other times as active subjects who were ready to take action (if they only knew what action to take) in defence of students and teachers and in defence of good peda-gogical practice.

In denouncing the new managerial and policy arrangements, partici-pants positioned themselves firmly within a discourse of teacher professionalism. 'Teacher professionalism' was in opposition to and in implicit dialogue with an 'enemy' discourse, which was referred to as the 'the new Zeitgeist', 'materialism' or 'economic rationalism'. I named the implied enemy discourse as a discourse of 'performativity', following Lyotard, Yeatman and Lankshear. 'Performativity' in my analysis was a meta-discourse that was implied by the teachers throughout their discus-sions, the meta-discourse which was associated with and which underlay the many unpopular changes which they described.

Teacher professionalism, as a discursive field, was constituted by a complex mélange of discursive elements. First, there was a discourse about the specialist skills and knowledges of the professional teacher: both the formal knowledge and the practical, intuitive knowledge, which are central to 'good practice'. There was a discourse about teaching as a profession in the wider sense. The discourse of professionalism constituted teachers as having rights and responsibilities, a level of individual and collective autonomy, a sphere of proper authority, intellectual and educational skills and resources and socially committed values expressed as professional ethics – a commitment to students and to the wider community of practice (Preston 1996). The discourse about teaching as a profession was also implied in the frustrated expectation of being involved in collegial decision-making structures within the college. There was also an element of 'boundary-keeping' in the expressions of concern about how aspects of what they saw as educational work – decisions about the placing of learners in courses and class groups – were now being taken over by bureaucrats from the Commonwealth Employment Service. Teacher professionalism also drew on a discourse of industrial rights and unionism that rested on traditions and histories of struggle for better teaching conditions as well as equity and access for students. Here, subject positions of solidarity, defiance against the oppressor, courage and collective action were being constructed.

The analysis shows the teachers shifting among and drawing upon all of these discourses of teacher professionalism as they talked about the many changes taking place. Preston (1996) claims that there is an inherent contradiction between the industrial and the professional discourses of the teaching profession; that is, that there is a contradiction between the 'elitist' and self-serving claims to special knowledge and privilege and the ethical and social commitments associated with teaching. In these texts, however, this dual positioning was not so much a 'contradiction' as a dimension of complexity in the way teachers saw themselves as professional workers.

The discourse of teacher professionalism was being used rhetorically, as a discourse of resistance, in response to the undermining of professional status and industrial conditions locally, especially the trend towards casualisation. Teacher professionalism was being invoked against the meta-discourse of performativity and its material and discursive effects. In asserting a (complex) discourse of teacher professionalism, the teachers were positioning themselves as ethical, professional subjects, *and* as workers who were being oppressed and exploited by the new wave of managerialism.

At the same time, a certain sense of powerlessness was evident in the anger and bitterness with which people denounced the new arrangements and those in managerial positions who made use of them to further their own agendas of power, institutional control, competitiveness and corporate advantage. The subject positions associated with the discourse of teacher professionalism seemed, in this case, to be insufficiently powerful to support positive visions of adaptation, survival or resistance.

Responses to discourse mapping

Most of the seven meetings were dominated by reports of the latest developments and expressions of distress about new happenings and industrial arrangements at the college. Each time we got together to consider (as I hoped) my latest analysis of discursive configuration, there had been a new series of distressing events which had to be talked about. The theoretical focus of my analysis was overwhelmed by the practical concern of all present to defend jobs, their professional standing and their notions of 'good practice'. While reading the transcript and considering my mapping of discourses within it, some were more interested in building and embellishing their story with new examples and more strident denunciations, than in reflecting on their own textual representations and the implications of these.

In an atmosphere of reduced of job security, worsening industrial situation and threats of non-renewal of contracts, it was not a priority to reflect on the transcripts of previous meetings and what might be learned from these about our discursive constitution as professionals. They were tired, anxious and in no state to engage in any depth with my post-structural analysis of their earlier discussion. Despite my best facilitatory efforts, the impact of their immediate problems meant they had little space to take up my invitation to use the analysis as a basis for reflection about their own discursive positioning and practice.

I had hoped that they would reflect upon the complex elements of the 'professional teacher' discourse they were using, and see the analysis as a resource for thinking about how they were positioning themselves as teaching professionals and how they might position themselves the light of an uncertain future.

I also had hoped they would follow up my observation, based on mapping the discourses in the text, of the disjunction between the (historically powerful) discourse of teacher professionalism they were drawing on and the sense of powerlessness they projected. Was this sense of powerlessness a reflection of their actual institutional and industrial situation at this time? Or was it more a question of how they were constructing and positioning themselves at a time of policy turmoil and institutional restructure? Were they being immobilised by the inherent contradiction in the discourse of teacher professionalism, as suggested by Preston (1996)? Or had the discourse of performativity colonised notions of teacher professionalism, and therefore undermined the ability to resist and oppose it? What were the sources of discursive and organisational power we could now draw on? Would it be possible to 'reconstruct' teacher professionalism in the new context, in such a way as to include some elements of performativity while still holding on to our basic beliefs about education and the teaching profession? This deeper level of questioning did not take place. Were the teachers resisting being drawn into and colonised by my theoretical interpretations of their struggles? Were they in fact resisting the 'discourse of discourse' as presented by me?

One obvious conclusion is that the immediate stress associated with being 'in the thick of battle' goes against the kind of meditational reflexivity which my discourse mapping exercise suggested. However, there was some evidence that my introducing the notion of discourse through feeding back a discursive analysis of their discussions may have contributed to more reflexive thinking about the broader issues.

Throughout many of the discussions, we kept returning to the question of 'why?' and how the local situation was reflective of the broader political context. We were practising the 'discourse of discourse' through using it in the light of our own texts and contexts. Increasingly, the teachers were using post-structural terms in their representations of what was going on and how they should best act in those circumstances. However, they (we) were not using it so much to interrogate their (our) own discursive positionings in those struggles.

I have also found a positive response in sharing my work among teachers more widely. That response suggests that the tools of post-structuralism are potentially useful to teachers and other practitioners addressing difficult issues of change. The 'discourse of discourse' is valuable precisely because it is an epistemology, a language and set of ideas which constantly directs attention to connections between text, subjectivity, and social structures and thus provides new and more complex insights into old problems.

Some methodological reflections

This was an informal, loosely structured version of action research based around a series of discussion and feedback sessions. Re-framing 'action research' in a post-structuralist framework, the 'action' was theorised as 'action in discourse'.

I had begun with three main aims: to support a group of teachers in a time of crisis, to produce data reflecting practices of discursive engagement and to explore the possibilities of combining post-structural discourse theory with action research. The aim of supporting a group of teachers by helping them to theorise their immediate struggles may have been achieved to some extent. The project provided opportunities for collective discussion and reflection away from the college, and there was support on the level of my personal friendship and solidarity. Without permanent tenure, however, this small group of teachers was powerless in an environment of contracting funds, marketisation and increasing managerial control. It is not clear how new insights and new ways of talking could have empowered them (in that particular situation) to negotiate these issues more effectively or more strategically.

The aim of testing out the usefulness to that group of ideas about discursive engagement was only partially achieved. The stress and 'chaos' experienced by the teachers during the course of the project, the many cancellations and the constant domination of the meetings by more urgent, practical issues made it impossible to facilitate processes which would enable them to study and reflect in depth on the theory I was offering. The feedback that I did get was mixed and inconclusive. The initial enthusiasm for the ideas waned during the period of crisis and then seemed to return in the final meetings.

Were the three research aims incompatible from the start? Was I attempting the impossible by combining research for academic purposes with a project which, if it were 'pure' action research, would have been owned by all the participants and shaped by their needs for knowledge and empowerment? In this case, the motivation and the momentum for the project came mainly from my research commitment. Although this in turn was part of a broader (shared) political project, the contradictions lingered. The teachers' participation was born of a mixture of genuine interest, their expressed need to make meaning of the current unsatisfactory situation, and loyalty to me as a colleague and friend. On one level, the meetings were about helping me; but they were also enjoyable social occasions at which they could let off steam and talk through the issues in a safe place. Some, but not all, of the group engaged critically with my re-framing of their issues.

At some stages, it seemed that my theoretical project would be overwhelmed by the teachers' imperative of self-defence and survival. The teachers' immediate issues kept bubbling up and crowding out the theoretical focus and I was never quite able to bring the theory together with the immediate practical concerns. It was not until much later, when the immediate period of crisis had been passed and after some teachers had left or had been relocated, that the two seemed to come closer together.

Throughout the project, I had been working with a divergent and in some ways contradictory set of aims. At the same time I was mediating complex currents of power (my theoretical 'power/knowledge' and my dependence on their willing collaboration), desire (strong personal relationships, the desire on all our parts to support each other) and emotion (anguish caused by difficult times and loss of jobs; my anxiety to produce appropriate data).

The contradiction I was experiencing at that time can be seen as a methodological problem common to many attempts at combining academic research with participatory action research. I was positioning the group on the one hand as co-researchers, and on the other hand as objects of *my* study and reporting, continuously iterating between *insider* and *outsider* positions (Cochrane-Smith and Lytle 1990). At the same time, I was trying to use each of those positions to interrogate the other, using the tensions to think critically and reflexively about what it means to do research (Schratz and Walker 1995) and to interrogate the ethical and professional basis of my own practice. In Fine's terms, I was attempting to 'work the self-Other hyphens' (Fine 1994: 72) to build a method which would be reflexively honest and rigorous within the terms of postmodern or post-structural enquiry.

Conclusion

In this 'postmodern' participatory action research project I used discourse mapping to analyse transcriptions of teachers' discussions about their work and progressively fed back my discursive interpretations to the participant teachers. Judged by the response within the meetings themselves, the project was only partially successful. The feedback I have received more broadly, however, leads me to maintain that the 'discourse of discourse' is a powerful tool in developing more reflexive and perhaps more strategic approaches to change, especially in the context of the profound changes now taking place in institutional, professional and industrial aspects of work.

This project aimed to produce useful knowledge about how teachers are resisting, surviving and engaging discursively during a period of radical institutional change and deteriorating industrial conditions. At the same time, it was an attempt to take up some of the methodological challenges posed to action researchers by postmodern and post-structural theory. Overall, this has meant thinking in more complex ways about the problem, the method, the texts produced and the outcomes. It has meant constantly interrogating my own purposes and investments, recognising 'the non-innocence of any practice of knowledge production … doing it and troubling it simultaneously' (Lather 1997: 67).

I am hopeful that the small research adventure recounted here will be of assistance to other ('postmodern') action researchers who are working with groups of people in coming to terms with unwanted change and struggling over how they might influence the direction of change.

Notes

1 In this text I use the term 'participatory' to mean that all participants have an active role in planning and doing the research and shaping the outcomes. In this project, as in many others, there was a high (but certainly unequal) degree of participation among those directly involved.

References

Cochrane-Smith, M. and Lytle, S.L. (1990) *Inside/Outside: Teacher Research and Knowledge*, New York: Teachers College Press.

Davies, B. (1994) *Poststructuralist Theory and Classroom Practice*, Geelong: Deakin University Press.

Ellsworth, E. (1989) 'Why doesn't this feel empowering? Working through the repressive myths of critical pedagogy', *Harvard Education Review* 59, 3: 297–324.

Fairclough, N. (1992) *Discourse and Social Change*, Cambridge: Polity Press.

Fine, M. (1994) 'Working the hyphens: re-inventing self and Other in qualitative research' in N.K. Denzin and Y.S. Lincoln (eds) *Handbook of Qualitative Research*, Thousand Oaks: Sage.

Fine, M. (1995) 'Dis-stance and other stances: negotiations of power inside feminist research' in A. Gitlin (ed.) *Power and Method: Political Activism and Educational Research*, New York: Routledge.

Foucault, M. (1980) *Power/Knowledge: Selected Interviews and Other Writings 1972–1977*, New York: Pantheon Books.

Foucault, M. (1981) *The History of Sexuality*, vol. 1, London: Penguin.

Fraser, N. (1989) *Unruly Practices: Power, Discourse and Gender in Contemporary Social Theory*, Cambridge: Polity Press.

Gore, J. (1991) 'On silent regulation: emancipatory action research in preservice teacher education', *Curriculum Perspectives* 11, 2: 47–51.

Hall, S. (1996) ' Reflexivity in emancipatory action research: illustrating the researcher's constitutiveness' in O. Zuber-Skerritt (ed.) *New Directions in Action Research*, London: Falmer Press.

Hargreaves, A. (1994) *Changing Teachers, Changing Times: Teachers' Work and culture in the Postmodern Age*, London: Cassell.

Hattam, R. (1995) 'Auditing Democracy in the Arena of Teachers' Work', *Newsletter of Flinders Institute for the Study of Teaching, The Flinders University of South Australia* 1 (June): 1.

Jennings, L.E. and Graham, A.P. (1996) 'Exposing discourses through action research' in O. Zuber-Skerritt (ed.) *New Directions in Action Research*, London: Falmer Press.

Kemmis, S. (1996) 'Emancipatory aspirations in a postmodern era' in O. Zuber-Skerritt (ed.) *New Directions in Action Research*, London: Falmer Press.

Kemmis, S. and McTaggart, R. (1988) *The Action Research Planner*, Geelong: Deakin University Press.

Lankshear, C. (forthcoming) *Literacy Policy and Postmodern Conditions*.

Lather, P. (1991) *Feminist Research in Education: Within/Against*, Geelong: Deakin University Press.

Lather, P. (1997) 'Methodology as subversive repetition: practices towards a feminist double science' in E. McWilliam, P. Lather and W. Morgan (eds) *Head Work, Field Work, Text Work: A Textshop in New Feminist Research*, Kelvin Grove: Queensland University of Technology.

Legge, D.G. (1999) *Rethinking Public Health*, NCEPH Tenth Anniversary Conference Papers, National Centre for Epidemiology and Population Health, Australian National University.

Lemke, J. (1995) *Textual Politics: Discourse and Social Dynamics*, London: Taylor & Francis.

Lyotard, J.-F. (1984) *The Postmodern Condition: A Report on Knowledge*, Manchester: Manchester University Press.

McTaggart, R. (1991) *Action Research A Short Modern History*, Geelong: Deakin University Press.

McTaggart, R. (1994) 'Participatory action research: issues in theory and practice', *Educational Action Research* 2: 313–37.

Preston, B. (1996) 'Professional practice in school teaching', *Australian Journal of Education* 40, 3: 248–64.

Sanger, J. (1996) 'Managing change through action research: a postmodern perspective on appraisal' in O. Zuber-Skerritt (ed.) *New Directions in Action Research*, London: Falmer Press.

Sanguinetti, J. (1995) *Negotiating Competence: The Impact of the CGEA on Teaching Practice*, Melbourne: National Languages and Literacy Institute of Australia.

Sanguinetti, J. (1998) 'The CGEA action research evaluation project: some methodological reflections' in *The Essence of Action Research (Proceedings from the ALRNNV Seminar)*, Geelong: Deakin Centre for Education and Change, Deakin University.

Sanguinetti, J. (1999) 'Within and against performativity: discursive engagement in adult literacy and basic education', unpublished PhD thesis, Deakin University.

Schratz, M. and Walker, R. (1995) *Research as Social Change*, London: Routledge.

Seddon, T. (1994). 'Changing contexts – new debates: ALBE in the 1990s', *Open Letter* 5, 1: 3–16.

Seddon, T. (1998) 'Remaking public education: after a nation-building state changes its mind' in A. Reid and E. Cox (eds) *Going Public: Education Policy and Public Education in Australia*, Canberra: Australian Curriculum Studies Association.

Stanley, L. and Wise, S. (1983) *Breaking Out Again*, London: Routledge.

Usher, R., Bryant, I. and Johnston, R. (1997) *Adult Education and the Postmodern Challenge: Learning Beyond the Limits*, London: Routledge.

Wadsworth, Y. (1991) *Everyday Evaluation on the Run*, Melbourne: Action Research Issues Association.

Weedon, C. (1987) *Feminist Practice and Poststructuralist Theory*, Oxford, UK, and Cambridge, Mass.: Basil Blackwell.

Weiner, G. (1994) *Feminisms in Education: An Introduction*, Buckingham: Open University Press.

Winter, R. (1996) 'Some principles and procedures for the conduct of action research' in O. Zuber-Skerritt (ed.) *New Directions in Action Research*, London: Falmer Press.

Yeatman, A. (1990) *Bureaucrats, Technocrats, Femocrats*, Sydney: Allen and Unwin.

Yeatman, A. (1994) *Postmodern Revisionings of the Political*, London: Routledge.

Zuber-Skerritt, O. (1996) 'Introduction: new directions in action research' in O. Zuber-Skerritt (ed.) *New Directions in Action Research*, London: Falmer Press.

14 Virtual research in performative times

Robin Usher and Richard Edwards

In this chapter we will look at the impact of new information/communication technologies (ICTs) on new forms of knowledge and changes in research or modes of knowledge production. A significant aspect of the contemporary moment is the proliferation of different forms of knowledge and of new modes and sites of knowledge production. The production of knowledge is now something that is not only done by academic researchers but engages many more – in different ways and forms – as learners and 'knowledge workers'. The proliferation of knowledge, knowledge production and knowledge producers has resulted in greater uncertainty as to the status of 'knowledge' – in effect, a deconstruction and 'decentring' of knowledge in its traditional forms, production and legitimation.

This chapter focuses on how the issues surrounding this 'decentring' of knowledge are played out and the significance of what have been called 'new modes of knowledge production' (Gibbons *et al.* 1994). In particular, we will look at the role and impact of ICTs and computer-mediated communication (CMC). We will argue that knowledge production is being reconfigured in the folds of globalisation and the cultural practices within which new technologies and modes of communication are implicated. In globalised conditions, ICTs have clearly enabled an increase in the sheer amount of information or data available. But this is not the end of the story for, at the same time, there has been a blurring of the hitherto tightly defined boundaries between knowledge and information, and a consequent breakdown of the hierarchies which have defined 'worthwhile' knowledge.

The contemporary situation is one where 'learning' rather than 'education' is foregrounded and where, consequently, notions of 'flexible learning' and the 'virtual university' now have some prominence, not only in the discourses favoured by those promoting learning in organisations, but in the policy-making domain generally. These notions can be seen as a reflection of the challenges to institutionalised education and face-to-face pedagogy and, as Kenway *et al.* (1993) point out, to the rise of alternative expectations about what constitutes worthwhile knowledge. These developments, linked to the so-called 'information society' and 'information age' (Webster 1995) are central in understanding the possibilities now being opened.

The dissemination and use of ICTs has challenged long-standing traditions of knowledge production in complex and contradictory ways, helping to facilitate, on the one hand, an emphasis on performativity – as the maximising of productivity and systemic efficiency (both within the academy and in the broader economic world) – and, on the other hand, an emphasis on outputs in a plurality of forms, in multiple sites, from diverse sources and related to a variety of aims.

As has been emphasised throughout this book, it has now become almost commonplace to argue that changes in conceptions of what constitutes 'worthwhile' knowledge and 'proper' research can be attributed to the radical epistemological and methodological questioning, the generalised doubt about universalistic truth-claims manifested in postmodern perspectives. Here, performativity is attributed a central place. We will examine performativity in relation to new modes of knowledge production and look at how this is played out ('performed') through the academy's increased engagement in collaborative research arrangements with commercial organisations. This engagement has helped to foreground (and is itself a manifestation of) the increased significance of the workplace as a source of knowledge, a site of research and an illustration of the postmodern condition.

First, however, we will look at the way knowledge is being reconfigured in the context of globalisation and the relationship particularly of this reconfiguration with the development and spread of ICTs. We will argue that knowledge production becomes not simply an issue of disciplines-based 'truth' but also subject to other criteria. We will explore what this implies for knowledge production and by doing so foreground the main theme of this chapter: that knowledge production can be seen as 'virtual' in two senses. One sense relates to the changing nature of *knowledge production* brought about by CMC. In this sense, we argue that the nature of the mediation is such that research has become 'virtual' and therefore radically different to traditional forms. Given this trend, the second sense relates to the question of whether certain kinds of research are 'virtual' to the extent that they are no longer 'really' research – as traditionally understood. It is in this 'doubt' about what constitutes 'real' research that questions about new modes and sites of research, new means of disseminating research findings, and new legitimations are raised in their most acute ways. And we argue these ways are most acute in relation to the research being conducted by the academy of the contemporary work-place.

Knowledge production and its legitimation

Lyotard (1984) posed the question of how the means for the production and transmission of a certain kind of knowledge is affected by the contemporary demands of performativity. He argues that these demands have progressively reconstructed the modernist educational project in terms related to the best efficiency and effectiveness of the contemporary socio-economic system, with its task being that of producing the knowledge needed by, and those with the skills indispensable to, that system. As we noted in Chapter 3, these have now become the knowledge and skills seen as necessary for staying ahead in the competitive world market conditions of globalised capital. With performativity, the question asked of knowledge is no longer is it true, or does it contribute to human progress, but what use is it and how will it enhance the performance of people and organisations? (Lyotard 1984: 4). Lyotard argued that ICTs have transformed knowledge production: 'Knowledge is and will be produced in order to be sold, it is and will be consumed in order to be valorised in a new production: in both cases the goal is exchange' (ibid.).

Knowledge is no longer valorised for its use value in terms of adding to the existing stock of knowledge or of contributing to human progress, but for its use in a system of exchange – in other words, for its exchange value. In this situation, knowledge becomes commodified, packaged and traded in the market-place of knowledge. Hence, the questions asked of it change, and therefore it is hardly surprising that the nature of what constitutes knowledge, and how and where it is legitimately produced, have now become subject to change and contestation.

At the same time, and indeed as a manifestation of commodification, knowledge – in its traditional, canonical, discipline-based sense – is superseded. Perhaps more accurately, it is 'reconfigured' by the demand for, and the configurations imposed by, computer-stored and -communicated information. Lyotard's argument was that anything not translatable into 'information' or 'data' would no longer be considered worthwhile. This draws attention to the significance and constitutive possibilities of the CMC medium itself, in particular the condition of virtuality to which it gives rise. This condition itself stimulates the demand for new skills and new kinds of knowledge. Poster (1997: 214) argues that 'canons and authorities are seriously undermined by the electronic nature of texts … as texts become "hypertexts" … the reader becomes an author, disrupting the stability of experts or "authorities"'. Through the internet, e-mail, CD-

ROMs and hypertext, possibilities are presented for individuals to access information, interact with it and other learners, and thus learn more flexibly and without the need to attend institutional centres or designated spaces of learning. New practices of reading and writing are made possible (Peters 1996). Equally, subjects (in the sense of bodies of disciplinary and canonical knowledge) and their transmission seem less significant in relation to, on the one hand, curriculum developments such as work-based learning, and, on the other, new skills and capacities such as multi-disciplinarity, multi-literacies and 'transcoding'. Even while the need for new knowledge and skills is stimulated, the conditions are created whereby knowledge and skills are more readily commodified – valued for their market and exchange value rather than for their social, cultural and epistemological significance.

We are witnessing, therefore, a process of 'dedifferentiation' at work, with a breakdown in the hierarchy of, and the distinction between, knowledge and information – with a consequent (dis)location or decentring of knowledge. Here, it is difficult to distinguish 'knowledge' from 'information'. What has hitherto been regarded simply as 'information' attains the status of 'knowledge', even if only because both are now located in an environment where epistemological boundary marking and policing is not so potent. Thus, changing conceptions of what is 'worthwhile' knowledge are constructed. Yet we would argue, *contra* Lyotard, that this is not simply a matter of knowledge being assimilated to computer-stored data. While it is undoubtedly the case that the mode of storage and dissemination has an impact on the way 'knowledge' is reconfigured and redefined, it is overly simplistic to ascribe all new forms of knowledge, and changes in the conception of what is knowledge, to the proliferation and ease of dissemination of computer-stored data. What we are witnessing is more complex. New modes of knowledge production, and changes in conceptions of what constitutes 'worthwhile' knowledge, can be understood as the enactments of decentring. Here there is a relationship between decentring and performativity, although the relationship is a complex one. For instance, Lyotard argued that there is a strong link between performativity and contemporary research to the extent that the latter has been transformed by the former. Research is expected to enhance the performativity of the education system in ensuring national economic competitiveness and external funding. Such enhancement can be enacted through collaborative arrangements between the academy, public and private organisations, and is now considered the hallmark of 'good' research.

A consequence of this linkage of 'good' research to external funding, argue Stronach and MacLure (1997), is that the spaces of social research have been 'compressed'. Furthermore, and perhaps more obviously as

McIntyre and Wickert assert in Chapter 9, research becomes politically influenced in the sense that it is now less autonomous or less answerable to its own knowledge-producing communities. Meanings are more 'negotiated'.

One way of understanding this is that social research largely gives up on any pretence it may have had of being 'disinterested'. There are now demands for 'relevance'. On the one hand, immediate policy pay-offs and direct instrumental contributions to funders are required. On the other hand, concessions have to be made to those measures that 'count' in research assessment exercises and evaluations of research quality. One argument is that, in effect, there is now more research with 'commitment'. Notwithstanding this argument, what emerges from this negotiation of meanings 'on the ground' is an intensification of research work through shorter contracts, job insecurity for researchers and greater control over the content and direction of research by state and quasi-state bodies and commercial organisations. Stronach and MacLure refer to this as 'Game 3 research' where mainstream research paradigms and cultures (Game 1 research) are now being played out in different milieu, with their key methodologies still deployed but at the same time transformed. They no longer signify what they once did – where research can now be seen as 'virtual', a simulacrum of what it once was.

Knowledge production is no longer, if indeed it ever was, a leisurely 'curiosity-driven' conversation confined exclusively to academic communities of practice; the need for results (or outcomes that 'perform') is greater and more urgent, and without it there is often limited opportunity for any kind of conversation at all! While it could be argued that the increased incidence, and changing nature, of research assessment still emphasises scholarship and research in a traditional sense, the amount and source of external funding has become a significant factor in assessing research 'performance'. The categories and criteria by which research performance is assessed lead still to a valorising of, for example, the single-authored book, the article in an academic journal and the refereed conference paper. These are traditional, scholarly criteria and categories. Conversely, the increased incidence and changing nature of research assessment has been accompanied by an increase in the number of universities and researchers who previously did not engage in scholarship and research in its traditional sense.

The new factor in the equation is the proliferation and diversification of research texts that has been enabled by ICTs. Examples of this are the expansion of traditional paper-based academic and professional journals, whose costs of production and distribution have been cut because of globalising technologies. Research is also made available through terrestrial and satellite television, videos, CD-ROMs and the like. There is also a proliferation and globalisation of research conferences made possible by cheaper television and enabled by the ease of communication afforded by e-mail and mobile phones. Even physical presence at a single conference location is no longer required with the growth and sophistication of video-conferencing. With the World Wide Web, there has been an explosion in developments that have made research available in a range of formats: for instance, through restricted bulletin boards, conferences or in formats following along the lines of traditional academic journals. Academics and researchers have themselves started to develop their own home pages on the web from which interested 'surfers' can download copies of articles and papers. Such developments can be seen as constitutive features of what Green (1998) termed the 'global academic' and manifestations of the contemporary virtuality of research.

While the place of research in the contemporary moment is ambiguous and the space it occupies unclear, it is possible to discern two trends pulling in opposite directions. The demands of performativity not only valorise outputs (as against inputs and process) but also outputs of a particular kind. This valorisation means that research in the academy is pulled towards closure and pushed towards a locking-in to an economy of the same. Research becomes more and more geared towards 'pay-offs' and the furtherance of systemic efficiency, valued in terms of how much funding it attracts and how happy the clients are with its immediate outcomes – and these are usually commercial in nature. Equally, this situation means that there are also more possibilities for a (dis)located research – a research that is aware of its own multi-locationality in both the closed and the open, the bounded and the unbounded, the traditional and the emerging. At the back of this (dis)location is what Stronach and MacLure (1997) refer to as a contemporary 'un-ruliness' of knowledge – a formulation with a deliberate ambiguity of meaning – referring to research which disrupts and subverts traditional assumptions, canons and modes, and, simultaneously, goes beyond the discipline (rules) of disciplinary communities. This 'un-ruliness' is partly attributable to the multiple sources of funding now available for research. As the state becomes more unable and unwilling to finance research out of block grants, funding from non-state sources becomes more significant, a tendency reinforced as research becomes more a matter of collaboration.

As Gibbons *et al.* (1994: 79) point out, while the targeting of research through the use of market mechanisms leads to more 'mission-oriented research', the 'greater pluralism of research funds [contributes] to intellectual diversity, counteracting perhaps other prevailing trends'. This is not the whole story, since the impact of ICTs has undoubtedly played a significant part in these developments. At one level, there is the greater possibility for the communication of research in diverse formats to diverse audiences. Traditional conceptions of the dissemination of research to a pre-constituted waiting audience at the end of a fixed research process are now increasingly questioned as to their adequacy and efficacy. There is, however, more to the matter than this. Peters (1996: 172) refers to the features such as dematerialisation, manipulability and the emergence of new discourse forms such as hypertext and hypermedia to argue that:

> Networked text distribution upsets the gatekeeping hierarchies of written texts surrounding the printing and publishing industries in ways that disturb both the market and traditional modes of regulation of the text … the computer is restructuring our economy of writing, changing the cultural status of writing and publishing, and altering both the relationship of the author to the text and of the author and text to the reader.

The 'unruliness' that Stronach and MacLure talk about can be understood as another way of referring to the decentredness of knowledge and dedifferentiation mentioned earlier, the breakdown of fixed and bounded rules, the dissensus about what constitutes knowledge and knowledge-production manifested in the epistemological and methodological questioning or doubting which is a feature of globalisation and postmodernity. With the impact of ICTs and their associated computer-mediated communication, we can begin to think of research as not only located in a hyper-real or virtual world (Baudrillard 1996), but as itself characterised by features that could be called hyper-real or virtual. It is here that we can begin to discern the connection between performativity, virtuality and decentredness. In this connection, performativity plays a significant although complex and ambiguous role since, in subverting the very notion of knowledge as something that has to be validated by a 'scientific' epistemology, and in undermining traditional ways of doing research, it requires both close and open possibilities. As Gibbons *et al.* (1994: 81) point out:

> Knowledge can no longer be regarded as discrete and coherent, its production defined by clear rules and governed by settled routines. Instead it has become a mixture of theory and practice, abstraction and aggregation, ideas and data. The boundaries between the intellectual world and its environment have become blurred.

Performativity contributes simultaneously to both the strengthening and loosening of boundaries, to both an economy of the same and to an economy of difference. It is paradoxical and has multiple significations. As Lyotard (1984) did point out, once knowledge is no longer an end in itself, its production and transmission ceases to be the exclusive responsibility of researchers and teachers in the academy and becomes, as it were, 'up for grabs' epistemologically and within diverse contexts of practice. Perhaps, therefore, it is apt to read Lyotard's perspective on technology as a metaphor for the knowledge transformative potential of computers, its opening up of new spaces where knowledge could be reconfigured in a more flexible, open and pragmatic way. Poster (1997: 214) puts it this way:

> The Internet seems to encourage the proliferation of stories, local narratives without any totalising gestures and it places senders and addressees in symmetrical relations ... moreover these stories and their performance consolidate the 'social bond' of the Internet 'community'.

In any event, Lyotard recognised that performativity accompanies (although he failed to recognise that performativity is a feature of) a world of decentred knowledge in which de-differentiation, hierarchies and absolute valorisations of particular forms of (instrumental) knowledge occur. Here, in a condition of endless production and dissemination that ICT and media technology enables, there is an accessibility for many more to much more than has ever been the case. Performativity, then, is a feature rather than simply an accompaniment of decentredness in that it is precisely in these conditions that performativity works best – each being the condition of the other!

According to Stronach and MacLure (1997), it is performativity that provides the conditions for new forms of Game 3 research. Despite its problematic nature, this can also be seen as another manifestation of the challenge to methodological realism: the hope for certainty through method, and 'pretensions to naked unadorned truth' (Green 1998: 1) which has conventionally structured knowledge production. Paradoxically, it is performativity itself which provides the possibility of (dis)located research as it simultaneously closes and opens the spaces of knowledge production. As we have argued, it is a (dis)located research located in the contemporary 'un-ruliness' about what constitutes knowledge and knowledge production.

New modes, new sites

The loss by universities of their dominant status as producers of a particular kind of knowledge and correspondingly of their monopoly as certifiers of competence in knowledge production has significant implications for how research is conceived. The developments surrounding this loss are both cause and consequence of changes in modes of knowledge production (and in their relative valorisation). These changes are intimately linked to the demands of performativity and to the impact of new technologies with their associated modes of communication. This has created an ambiguous situation where questions such as 'what is research?' and 'who is a researcher?' can be appropriately asked, but at the same time are largely unanswerable – or may have many possible answers. Again, ICTs have played a significant part in the way this situation has developed. For example, given the way that 'cyberspace' has developed through a logic that is both participatory and interactive, one of its effects has been to subvert the convention of 'authorship' and notions of 'authenticity', while at the same time foregrounding issues of textuality and intertextuality (Lankshear *et al.* 1996). As we noted earlier, what this has led to is a weakening of the distinction between informal communication and scholarly publication. In the process, this weakening gives rise to the interrelated issues of quality and, ultimately 'legitimacy', in the evaluation of that which is 'written' – the written itself now being *virtually embodied* and thus more than marks on paper. Academic conventions of peer review as a basis for establishing the validity and quality of research continue but are not necessarily any longer the only and final word. What's been made possible here is the repositioning of 'valid' knowledge production as no longer exclusively in the hands of university-based researchers. This repositioning is another aspect of the tendency for the commodification of knowledge and the individualising of learning that ICTs have helped bring about – although again, as we have been arguing, there is a countervailing trend for ICTs to enable collaborative approaches to learning by bringing together groups hitherto dispersed by physical (and emotional) distance.

Furthermore, in a move separate to but also interlinked with performativity and with the trend towards knowledge becoming increasingly commodified, knowledge production has begun to move – largely but not exclusively – out of the ivory tower and into the 'market-place'. For instance, ICTs enable the spread of knowledge, but as it becomes subject to commodification, its market value increases, thereby requiring more restricted access to it. It may thus be no accident that the issue of 'intellectual property rights' has surfaced as an attempt to police the spread and use of certain forms of knowledge, and perhaps also to bolster conventional notions of authorship which are increasingly under pressure. The potential commercial benefits of new knowledge to universities and their commercial funders and/or 'partners' cuts across the power of computer-mediated communication to spread participation. In turn, this commercial 'reality' has led to new forms of globalised hacking. As universities gradually lose their status as primary producers of a particular kind of knowledge (culturally concentrated knowledge), they become part of a wider and globalised 'knowledge market', forced to compete with R and D companies, consultants and highly paid think-tanks. Universities, both because of the demands of performativity and the sheer explosion and disseminability of knowledge which characterises globalised conditions, are now less able to control the production and exchange of knowledge and access to it. This is particularly so when 'knowledge' takes the form of 'information' – circulating promiscuously through the networks of CMC, even as attempts to police this promiscuity escalate.

As we shall see in a moment, different kinds of knowledge are now being produced through the academy's forging of collaborative research partnerships with government, industry and other organisations – collaborations which have forced academics to question conventional disciplines-sanctioned ways of doing research. As Gibbons *et al.* (1994: 13) put it:

> the parallel expansion in the number of potential knowledge producers on the supply side and the expansion of the requirement of specialised knowledge on the demand side are creating the conditions for the emergence of a new mode of knowledge production.

Not surprisingly, the requirements of performativity feature strongly in this situation with the emphasis in knowledge production switching from enquiry to application, from ideas to outcomes, and away from the traditional academic virtues of 'truth' and the 'disinterested' pursuit of knowledge. However, while knowledge production in performative times, with its tendency to conformity, can be understood as enfolded in an economy of the same, it is also simultaneously enfolded within an economy of difference. Our argument is that performativity creates a situation where anything becomes researchable and where knowledge is no longer limited or bounded by the epistemological police of disciplinary communities and their regimes of truth. The co-existence and intersection of these two dimensions allow for a performativity that is both closed and open, and, indeed, where the latter is enabled by the former.

Gibbons *et al.* (1994) distinguish between two modes of knowledge production which they refer to as Mode 1 and Mode 2. This distinction corresponds roughly to the distinction made by Luke (1996: 7–10) between 'culturally concentrated knowledge' (the outcome of Mode 1) and 'socially distributed knowledge' (the outcome of Mode 2). Mode 1 is defined as:

a form of knowledge production – a complex of ideas, methods, values, norms – that has grown up to control the diffusion of the Newtonian model to more and more fields of enquiry and to ensure its compliance with what is considered sound scientific practice.

(Gibbons *et al.* 1994: 2)

Mode 1 is what the academy would conventionally consider 'scientific' research to be – its cognitive and social norms determining 'what shall count as significant problems, who should be allowed to practise science and what constitutes good science' (ibid.: 3). Culturally concentrated knowledge is those intellectual products produced and consumed inside traditional research-monopolising universities. It is:

tradition-bound in practice as well as conventional in form ... produced on a campus by academic researchers in clearly demarcated scholarly disciplines to be transmitted first, to students in accredited degree programs or second, to clients in government, industry, or non-profit organisations through sponsored research contracts.

(Luke 1996: 7)

Mode 1 knowledge production is conducted by a disciplinary community oriented to knowledge accumulation – 'traditional "truths" accumulated over time ... universal, objective, disciplined, planned, tested and reliable findings' (ibid.: 8). Although Mode 2 is not exactly a new way of producing knowledge – and certainly socially distributed knowledge has been around for a while! – it is, according to Gibbons *et al.*, becoming increasingly prevalent and is taking its place in significance alongside the traditional and hitherto dominant Mode 1. In contrast then to Mode 1, Mode 2, the outcome of socially distributed knowledge, is:

an emergent gridwork of intellectual products increasingly produced and consumed outside of traditional university settings ... it arises from a material context of very short-run corporate outsourcings, task-specific government contracts or entrepreneurial venture capital start-ups.

(Luke 1996: 7)

Mode 2 knowledge production is characterised by being produced in the context of application – it has to be 'performative' in both senses in a contemporary situation where the sources of supply and demand for different forms of specialised knowledge are diverse and where the market process defines the contexts of application for that knowledge.

Furthermore, it is heterogeneous in terms of the skills deployed and trans-disciplinary in the sense that it cuts across and goes beyond conventional disciplinary structures.

Socially distributed knowledge has, as it were, found its moment within the folds of globalisation. Globalisation and flexible capital accumulation seem to depend upon the ability to reconfigure knowledge even while new modes of knowledge production can also be seen as a consequence of globalisation and the reconfiguration of capital. Lash and Urry (1994) have referred to contemporary socio-economic processes as a 'reflexive accumulation' where knowledge, flexibility and symbol processing skills are key. In this contemporary economic environment, technological innovation becomes the means of keeping ahead – and technological innovation requires the generation and deployment of new and specialised knowledge, and ICTs and the associated computer-mediated communication become the essential condition of this. As Luke (1996) points out, the capacity of labour to process information and generate knowledge is increasingly seen as the source of productivity and of economic growth, with notions of the knowledge economy gaining in popularity. Given this, therefore, it is perhaps hardly surprising that the place and status of socially distributed knowledge has become a key factor in researching the workplace – itself a site of Mode 2 knowledge production.

Since in-house knowledge production is now beyond the reach of most, we witness the growth of risk- and cost-sharing schemes. These take many forms, including R and D alliances, outsourcing and network firms, and the growth of firms whose business is itself specialised knowledge – the so-called 'knowledge industry', symbol processors, small value-adding firms and consultants who reconfigure knowledge and offer it for sale. These are the symbolic analysts identified by Reich (1993) as the key to the future of work. Now the kind of specialised knowledge needed to keep ahead is an applied, specific and commodifiable knowledge – one oriented to the identification and solution of problems generated in Mode 2 knowledge production. At the same time, as we have just noted, the demand for this knowledge also requires, and indeed depends upon, the sophisticated means of communication provided by ICTs. The new information technology with its global scope provides the means for the necessary access to knowledge production which itself is now global in its incidence.

As Gibbons *et al.* argue and as Lyotard foresaw, what is now needed is the bringing to bear of multi- and trans-disciplinary skills and perspectives to the solution of complex problems – a process 'being built around the clustering of innovations in information, computer and telecommunications technologies' (Gibbons *et al.* 1994: 125). Gibbons *et al.* (ibid.: 10) argue that the development of Mode 2 knowledge production is underpinned by an increase in the number of sites where research can be carried out, and ICTs have created a capability for these sites to interact leading to 'an explosion in the number of interconnections and possible configurations of knowledge and skill'. They go so far as to refer to a new information technology paradigm which they maintain is replacing one dominated by the technologies and organisations of mass production. This is a paradigm elaborated in debates about the existence, significance and causes of the shifts towards neo- and post-Fordism in the organisation of work to which ICTs are argued to be central.

The characteristics of Mode 2 knowledge production have certain implications and raise a number of important issues in thinking about the contemporary role and place of universities in globalised conditions. First, the global growth of higher education with consequent increases in the output of graduates has led to more and more people becoming familiar with and competent in research processes. Commitments to research-based professions and evidence-based practice and policy become a possibility if not always an actuality. Here, although there remain important hierarchies in the production, reading and evaluation of research, it is no longer an activity reserved for a select group of academics. With the parallel growth of 'knowledge' industries, many now work in ways which incorporate a research dimension but where the worksite is no longer the university. Thus research goes on, as we have already noted, outside disciplinary communities and in sites other than the university – although, as we shall see later, whether this research would be considered 'competent' in Mode 1 terms is a critically contested matter within the academy. Second, there has been an expansion in the demand for specialised knowledge. This is a critical factor in determining an organisation's comparative advantage. Organisations have now become involved in a complex array of collaborative arrangements – collaborations which very often, but not necessarily always, involve universities.

Mode 2 knowledge production, therefore, while not new, has assumed a large contemporary significance – certainly this is the argument that Gibbons *et al.* are putting forward. It is not answerable to 'truth' in the sense that the regimes of truth of disciplinary communities define truth (which does not mean that it produces knowledge that is untrue). It is not answerable to research paradigms and traditions in terms of the process by which it is produced and hence 'validated'. Most importantly for our purposes, Mode 2 knowledge production is output driven, not motivated simply by the spirit of curiosity and free enquiry and not seeking to discover the deep truths and underlying laws of the natural and social world. The focus is on application rather than contemplation. For all these reasons and because, as we have noted earlier, Mode 2 knowledge is specific and transient, the current situation can be understood as one where 'in Mode 1 terms much of the Mode 2 knowledge is automatically suspect; partisan, non-objective, undisciplined, ad hoc, unsupported or unreliable' (Luke 1996: 9).

It is, in effect, considered to be 'virtual' in the second sense of 'virtual' that we mentioned at the beginning of this chapter. Luke points out that there is now a strongly held view that the culturally concentrated knowledge structures are mostly ill adapted to producing the socially distributed knowledge needs of individuals as lifelong learners and organisations as learning organisations – although, as he also points out, universities should not necessarily be blamed for this, nor need they apologise for continuing Mode 1 forms of knowledge production.

It could be argued that Mode 2 knowledge production still needs Mode 1. And it is probably the case that Mode 2 researchers still need to be trained initially as Mode 1 researchers, hence the still important role universities have in research training and in building research capacity. Stronach and MacLure (1997), however, point out in their account of Game 3 research that the Mode 1 knowledge production process is not what it used to be – Game 3 having become a simulacrum of traditional Game 1 research! Furthermore, Mode 2 knowledge production poses particular problems for the traditional kind of university-based researcher. The authority of Mode 1 research in this environment means that the dominant mode of dissemination is the academic book, the scholarly refereed paper and the conference presentation. Mode 2 knowledge is disseminated much more informally, if at all, through such means as the summary report and, increasingly, through on-line postings and other forms of electronically mediated communication. Traditional research assessment puts an emphasis on certain kinds of output – which do not include the summary report and the on-line posting. What 'counts' as research, as we shall see in a moment, is being rendered increasingly problematic with the impact of ICTs. The important point to note, however, is that what is involved here is not a matter simply of the most efficient and effective means of disseminating knowledge. It is about the very *legitimacy* of different kinds of knowledge production. It is research assessment in contemporary conditions of globalisation which brings these questions of legitimacy to the fore. They are questions about what is to count as worthwhile research and how what is countable is to be demonstrated, performed and, as Rhodes puts it in Chapter 12, 'done'.

The performative and the virtual

As universities lose their position as the only site of a particular way of producing knowledge – with 'legitimate' knowledge now generated outside the university, sometimes in partnership with the university and sometimes not – the accountability of academics is accentuated. Research assessment exercises are now not only a means for rewarding outputs but also an instrument of state performativity – a technology to respond to the need 'to tell and show people what you do'. Research has to be demonstrated in terms of the relevance of its outcomes and its impact, whether this be in terms of research assessment exercises or in terms of collaborative projects with organisations in the 'real world'. In other words, performativity also implies and indeed requires performance for its realisation. Those working in the academy in contemporary globalised conditions are now involved in new ways of producing knowledge at a time when, as we have seen, definitions of what constitutes 'research' and 'knowledge' are changing.

To take ourselves as an example: as we write this chapter, as we inscribe ourselves (literally), we actively demonstrate the outcomes of our knowledge production and, at the same time, are inscribed and identified as particular kinds of knowledge workers. We are in the business of demonstrating (or not!) that we are producing 'relevant' and assessable knowledge. In this sense, our writing is a performance, an enactment.

Equally, our writing could be seen as in the service of performativity and in that sense located in an economy of the same. But since it is a critique of performativity and since also it is a discursive text foregrounding the constructive power of language and discourse, it is also located in an economy of difference. While we would not want to suggest that what we have written is not in some sense a 'truth' (it certainly is not false) nor that it is not about the 'real world', its 'truth' and its 'relevance' are not its main significance. This chapter, and indeed the book as a whole, is both performative and a performance – but within a practice that now relates not only, or even mainly, to an academic community but is heavily implicated in the folds of globalisation.

This argument is supported if we look again at the so-called new modes of knowledge production. Contrary to what Gibbons *et al.* are arguing, these are neither new nor dichotomously opposed to one another. Mode 2 has been around for a while, although, of course, there is an important set of new factors here – on the one hand, the post-Fordist organisation of work and, on the other, the impact of ICTs and computer-mediated communication – both of these contributing to transforming the impact and significance of Mode 2 knowledge production. At the same time, research has always (and not only in Mode 2) been shifting between the fundamental and the applied. In his review of Gibbons *et al.*, Benoit Godin (1998) argues very convincingly that neither Mode 1 nor Mode 2 has ever existed in 'pure form'. Mode 1 is what university researchers thought they were doing rather than what they were actually doing – what Gibbons *et al.* are pointing to in their notion of Mode 2 knowledge production is an artefact purely of discourse and contemporary forms of governmentality.

When it is put this way, this seems very convincing. In effect, Gibbons *et al.* are actually doing two things in one – they are both explaining what they take to be a new organisation of knowledge production and, at the same time, participating in its realisation. And maybe it is the latter that is most significant! In other words, the work of Gibbons *et al. is* performative – it is actually creating that of which it speaks. It is taking part in the creation of what Foucault calls a ' discursive domain' – a realm of thought and action. From this perspective, Mode 2 knowledge production assumes the place of a social technology.

Within the folds of globalising processes, the introduction of information technologies and CMC into research practices foregrounds, and radicalises perhaps as never before, both the textuality and virtuality of research practices, including their status as performative and mediated inscriptions. Here we are not referring simply to the computer as a handy tool for writing, significant though this is. We are speaking about the implications of the hyper-real for the very identity of the researcher and the research process.

At the heart of the hitherto dominant modernist way of understanding research are embedded deep epistemological and ontological assumptions about research as representation – as representing the search for truth, where the rational and humanistic researcher seeks to make original contributions to knowledge. This powerful narrative of how researchers should be governed and how they should govern themselves sees the identity of the researcher as forged by reason and the liberal values of the elite university. It is a narrative where knowledge production is enmeshed in the practices of academic communities which, even as they 'police' research texts, also establish boundaries for the identity of the researcher. These boundaries are grounded in the 'discipline', in both senses, of the particular community. But this identity formation is not explicit. Rather, the process is one where the external 'real world' is mirrored in a constructed internal 'real world' of the researcher. When research is understood as truthful representation of an external real world – independent of mediating influences – the researcher is represented as an autonomous authentic self, consciously governed by reason, liberal values and untouched by mediation. In other words, the 'real world out there' is posited upon and posits a 'real world in here' (Edwards 1997). Researcher identity is centred, unified and authentic, mirroring the nature of the world that it comes to know through research.

With globalisation rendering modernist notions of a centred world problematic, and with knowledge itself decentred, so too there is a reconfiguring of researcher identity and a reconceptualisation of the research process. In a hyper-real world of simulacra (copies without originals), a narrative of authenticity no longer has the same legitimating power as it once had. Furthermore, the policing of boundaries is no longer so potent, since the copy no longer relies for its meaning on the original. The possibilities of simulation in the production of research texts enabled by ICTs means that there are many and diverse researchers producing a multiplicity of texts in a diversity of formats and in diverse sites. With this proliferation and diversity of research texts, their differential production schedules and, with the possibility for continual re-working, authenticity, origins and originality become deeply problematic.

Research texts, as we have noted, can now appear in a variety of forms and formats, and increasingly there is recognition of the need to foreground intertextuality and significatory effects in practices of writing. 'Copy', 'cut' and 'paste' are not simply procedures in the literal construction of research texts, but also functions as a metaphor for the identity of the researcher in a hyper-real world of hyper-real texts. As we have noted earlier, ICTs have brought in their train new kinds of reading and writing practices, new sites of research and new ways of doing it. Of course, the identity of researchers has always been shaped in one way or another. It is not a matter of modernist narratives of identity being overthrown for a situation where there is no regulation and no identity formation. Knowledge production and knowledge producers are always subject to some form of mediation and some form of regulation and shaping of identity. But electronically mediated communication, with its dematerialisation, manipulability and new discursive forms – what we have called 'virtuality' – adds another and new dimension. CMC is not just a convenient way of disseminating and discussing research findings. It is that, but it is also something more as CMC changes the nature of what constitutes findings, how those findings are arrived at and how they are communicated.

This brings us to a conclusion which takes us back to the thematic which motivates this chapter. First, however, a reflexive note. This chapter would not have been possible without the advent of ICTs and the mediated communication that it makes possible. Not only does it constitute the subject matter of this chapter but it was enabled, and indeed would have been quite different – possibly would never have happened – given that one of us is located in Australia and the other in the UK. We are truly enfolded in globalisation!

We have argued that with globalising trends and their manifold effects comes a contemporary 'un-ruliness' of knowledge, a dissensus about what constitutes worthwhile or legitimate knowledge, a questioning of epistemological and methodological paradigms, academic values and cultures, and a growth of new forms and sites of knowledge. The performative, which itself takes different forms with different significations, both reflects and contributes to this postmodern condition of knowledge. The production of knowledge outside the academy, the virtuality of research, and the conflicts over whether such research is really 'valid' make it necessary to think anew about what constitutes knowledge, knowledge production and the knowledge producer in the (dis)locations of intensifying globalisation.

References

Baudrillard, J. (1996) *Selected Writings*, Cambridge: Polity Press.
Edwards, R. (1997) ' "Plagiarising" the self? Research texts as simulacra' in T. Evans, V. Jakupec and D. Thompson (eds) *Research in Distance Education 4*, Geelong: Deakin University Press.
Gibbons, M., Limoges, C., Nowotny, H., Schwartzman, S., Scott, P. and Trow, M. (1994) *The New Production of Knowledge: The Dynamics of Science and Research in Contemporary Societies*, London: Sage.
Godin, B. (1998) 'Writing performative history: the new New Atlantis', *Social Studies of Science* 28, 3: 465–83.
Green, B. (1998) 'All over the world … speculative notes on the global academic', paper presented at the annual conference of the AARE, 'Making Research Count', Adelaide, Australia.
Kenway, J. with Bigum, C. and Fitzclarence, L. (1993) 'Marketing education in the postmodern age', *Journal of Education Policy* 8, 2: 105–22.
Lankshear, C., Peters, M. and Knobel, M. (1996) 'Critical pedagogy and cyberspace' in H.A. Giroux, C. Lankshear, P. McLaren and M. Peters (eds) *Counternarratives*, London: Routledge.
Lash, S. and Urry, J. (1994) *Economies of Signs and Space*, London: Sage.
Luke, T.W. (1996) 'The politics of cyberschooling at the virtual university', paper presented at the International Conference on the Virtual University, University of Melbourne, Australia.
Lyotard, J.-F. (1984) *The Postmodern Condition: A Report on Knowledge*, Manchester: Manchester University Press.
Peters, M. (1996) *Poststructuralism, Politics and Education*, Westport: Bergin and Garvey.
Poster, M. (1997) 'Cyberdemocracy: Internet and the public sphere' in D. Porter (ed.) *Internet Culture*, London: Routledge.
Reich, R. (1993) *The Work of Nations*, London: Simon and Schuster.

Stronach, I. and MacLure, M. (1997) *Educational Research Undone: The Postmodern Embrace*, Buckingham: Open University Press.

Webster, F. (1995) *Theories of the Information Society*, London: Routledge.

Part IV

Conclusions

15 Inside the knowledge works

Reviewing the terrain

Carl Rhodes and John Garrick

At the outset of this book, we suggested that workplaces have changed and are changing from sites of physical labour to sites of knowledge construction. Importantly, this claim is made in the context of 'post-industrialism', 'knowledge work' and growing numbers of 'knowledge workers'. This is a context of late capitalism where manufacturing-based economies have shifted to service-based societies in which information and knowledge are *the* currency (Winsor 1992). In this brief reviewing chapter, we elaborate on the notion of 'post-industrialism' which has developed largely since the early 1970s, as this is a condition in which many of those in paid work are now immersed (including, of course, ourselves).

The use of this term 'post-industrialism' is suggestive of 'a shift in the structure of industrial capitalism away from mass production and bureaucracy and indicating changing production technologies, a growth in the service sector and changes in the knowledge requirements of work' (White and Jacques 1995: 48). In post-industrial economies the management of work has also changed through the impact of information technology and the development of alternative organisational forms. What was important to organisations in the industrial past was the harnessing of people's bodies – the need to control the people who were physical parts of the machinery of production as epitomised in the automated production lines of the Model T Ford and subsequent 'Fordist' workplaces. For many contemporary workplaces, however, nothing of an 'object' nature is produced and people's capability and willingness to engage in physical activity appears to be less important. The 'information economy' that has emerged through post-industrialisation is one where people spend their time at work using computers, reading, writing, talking and listening. The predominant way that work is mediated is textual, not physical. In this milieu there is a reduced need to control the bodies of workers and an increased need to manage the way that people produce and consume texts.

Further to these changes in the nature and organisation of work are the ways that knowledge is produced and scrutinised in society. Workplaces are both the producers *and* consumers of knowledge, and the ways that this 'working knowledge' is legitimised is important to contemporary understandings of those workplaces. Working knowledge can be viewed as a new game as it has new rules and is played in new sites beyond the academy and the research centre and into places of work. Here, the capacity for knowing is distributed throughout organisations and their environs and is not reliant on 'experts' whose abstract models are no longer ontologically secure (Boje 1997). In such a game, the scientific discourse that has dominated academic and 'pure' conceptions of knowledge is no longer as powerful as it once was and knowledge is, increasingly, legitimated in and through the practice of work.

In questioning the authority through which knowledge is legitimated, Lyotard (1984) asked the question: 'Who decides what knowledge is, and who knows what needs to be decided?' (p. 9). In some ways, this book has been an attempt to examine these questions and conceptualise key aspects of working knowledge in terms of how it is understood by different stakeholders. This has led to a point where the nature of research and knowledge are no longer tied to the confines of what might be classified as 'science'. Instead, knowledge is increasingly classified in terms of its contri bution to organisational effectiveness – where the notion of science might only be used as a means to an end and where, if alternative (non-scientific) means can better achieve this end, 'hard' science is not necessary. Knowledge, in this sense, has worth in its use value – its ability to achieve something outside of itself. Lyotard argues that this value is no longer drawn from the 'grand narratives' of humanity, liberty and progress, but rather from 'performativity' – an improved 'input output equation' (ibid.: 46). Such performativity would then measure knowledge on the basis of efficiency and saleability where:

> the transmission of knowledge is no longer designed to train an elite capable of guiding the nation towards emancipation, but to supply a system with players capable of acceptably fulfilling their roles at the pragmatic posts required by its institutions ... [resulting in] the mercantilisation of knowledge.
>
> (Lyotard 1984: 51)

In this notion, saleability and efficiency become the criteria for establishing worthwhile knowledge. As such, it is useful knowledge, not science itself, that is being made legitimate. Lyotard's argument also proposes that 'a self-sustaining system must cultivate performance satisfying skill amongst its members. Learning is [therefore] increasingly reduced to the technical transmission of a stock of knowledge' (Power 1990: 115).

It is now more than two decades since Lyotard published the French edition of what became (in English) *The Postmodern Condition: A Report on Knowledge*, but his commentary on changes to knowledge in contemporary society is still relevant – perhaps even more so. In particular, his argument that contemporary, 'postmodern', society has disrupted the unifying view that social progress can be achieved through the growth and application of science. This disruption has been played out in ways that might not have been imaginable before. The collection of essays contained in this book have teased out some of the ways that this disruption has occurred by exploring how knowledge and research are, and can be, deployed and legitimised through work practices. Reviewing this terrain of work and knowledge has taken the book into discussions from a range of local perspectives and contexts in which changes to knowledge can be accounted for. What we have here are forms of research that neither require nor desire the sanctity or legitimation of 'science', or of the 'academy', in order to get their work done. Instead, the knowledge produced and the research done are means to other (often commercial) ends. There is a range of ethical questions about this state of affairs that warrant explication: 'Is working knowledge about performativity – simply for its own sake?' 'Is this a form of knowledge whereby efficiency becomes a "core value" that is less open to scrutiny?' 'Are work organisations, as today's dominant institutions, governed solely by instrumental and economic rationalities?' These questions are important to how we understand the changes that are happening to work organisation and the new production of meaning.

It has been suggested that these changes represent a movement away from an industrial past and bring into question the work-based knowledge practices that focus on the 'instrumentalisation' of both people and nature. In this transition to more information-based societies, scientific-technical knowledge can be used 'to accomplish predictable results measured by productivity and technical problem solving leading to the "good" economic and social life, primarily defined by accumulation of wealth by production investors and consumption by consumers' (Alvesson and Deetz 1996: 194).

The technologies of representation that allow such a conception of organisational pasts and presents (for instance, modernism/postmodernism, industrialism/post-industrialism), should not, however, be taken at face value. To suggest, using Boje's (1997) 'reflexive parody', that 'the evil modernists [have been] screwing up the environment and downsizing human potential in their worship of performativity and the scientific method' (ibid.: 3) is obviously a way of telling stories about organisations that is mounted on a simplistic rendering of the history of work and knowledge. Instead, knowledge and work are intertwined through the knowledge that informs our understanding of work, and also the knowledge that is generated through the practices of work. This, then, emphasises that knowing and doing are not separate phenomena. What remains important is the need to reflexively examine commonly held perceptions about historical changes to knowledge and work in ways that support making wise judgement.

Arguably, 'organization, in its most general sense, is the appropriation of order from disorder and the exercise of *power* to overcome the "essential undecidability" of organizational reality' (Power 1990: 121). Writing about organisations and about work is, similarly, an exercise of power – to write about changes to work and knowledge, as has been done in this book, is not to avoid that power, but rather to employ particular textual practices of overcoming the 'undecidability' of knowledge at work. What this achieves in terms of working knowledge practices is that they go beyond an interrogation of the relevance of different theories about work and knowledge – they question academic knowledge *tout court* (White and Jacques 1995). Working knowledge is thus connected inextricably with power. An effect of this use of power can be to disrupt narratives of work that propose performativity as *the* essential value. Contemporary working knowledge acknowledges that both performativity – as a criteria of judging knowledge – and its critique are narratively produced. Working knowledge, then, by definition, needs to be reflexive.

In some ways, the chapters in this book have suggested that the pressures of a performativity-based 'economic rationalist' discourse are increasingly important in determining knowledge practices. At the same time, these ineffable pressures lead to new forms of questioning, problematising and resisting such practices. Based on our reading of the contributions to this book, this questioning has not been nostalgic; it has not been done in longing for the recreation of a (mythical) past, where humanity, progress and the development of humankind were not yet incredulous. Instead, approaches to research that simultaneously construct, explore, resist and interrupt can be important practices that foreground the ethics of the contemporary states of working knowledge. Such research practices are concerned with 'what happens to ethics as knowledge frameworks are increasingly challenged and where no firm epistemological ground is to be found' (Garrick and Rhodes 1998: 182).

If any conclusion can be drawn from the chapters contained in this book, it is that knowledge and research are now 'at work'. They are at work in two senses: first, that they are *in situ* in workplaces, and second, that they are *at work* – employed, exploited and developed. Inside these knowledge works, although performativity, efficiency and economic rationalism are important, they only tell one (albeit powerful) story.

Understanding work as the context of research and knowledge plays an important part in the valuing of knowledge in society – its value being increasingly, but not necessarily, related to its pragmatic applicability to the working of organisations. To suggest that this value is, and can only be, derived in economic terms tells a dangerously reductive story that attempts to fix power/knowledge relations from a particularly one-dimensional perspective. It is our argument that by interrogating knowledge at work, from the perspective of the different discourses and localised practices through which it is produced and consumed, that some of the ethical questions related to working knowledge (that we have highlighted) can be accounted for. Examples of such perspectives have been included throughout the book, offering explorations of research and knowledge at work as it is produced in the nexus between theory (theoria), the doing, and the pursuit of 'practical wisdom' (phronesis). The term 'phronesis', for instance, has historically denoted the possibility that individual human actions should be guided towards *the good* through the exercise of a set of interrelated qualities – virtues – 'agreed upon and exercised within a moral community or *polis*, which can provide the standards against which the goodness of each of its citizen members can be judged' (Rose 1999: 169). Here, we use the idea of the *nexus* of different knowledge forms, not to urge a return to the kinds of specific virtues that Aristotle may have once espoused (such as prudence, temperance, courage, munificence and so on) as these were defined by a definite moral code and conducted under an epistemology whereby the individual was subordinate to an external truth-code. Rather, we draw on Alistair MacIntyre's view that 'what matters at this stage is the construction of local forms of community within which civility and the intellectual and moral life can be sustained through the new dark ages which are already upon us' (in Rose 1999: 170). For Rose (ibid.) this means a politics of virtue that takes the paradoxical form of 'an attempt to create, by political action, that which is to be the counterweight and antidote to political power itself'.

For us, the relationships between the various ways of knowing have the potential to create new understandings of knowledge practices – including informing a postmodern politics of virtue at work. In an increasingly global, technological, 'networked' society, such new understandings will invariably involve relationships between everyday working lives, managerialism, workplace practices, trade unionism, academic research, teaching and policy-making. Indeed, the very nature of capitalism itself has undergone a process of profound restructuring that has been characterised by:

> greater flexibility in management; decentralisation and networking of firms both internally and in their relationships to other firms;

considerable empowering of capital vis a vis labour with the concomitant decline of influence of the labour movement; increasing individualisation and diversification of working relationships, massive incorporation of women into the pre-paid labour force ... increasing geographic and cultural differentiation of settings for capital accumulation and management.

(Castells 1996: 1–2)

The knowledge that is produced by such contemporary relationships creates and is also created by different ways of 'doing knowledge'. It is our contention that at the heart of these transformations are complex transformations of value. As we have argued, working knowledge is increasingly turned into an organisationally explicit and measurable factor of organisational performance. For individuals in contemporary organisations, it is their know-how which is vital in the reproduction of capital and the search for a competitive edge. The vital insights that were once implicit in specific individuals now have to be made explicit (insofar as this is possible) to become part of the transformative capacity of the organization. Typically, the construction of these relations is embodied in managerial 'win/win' solutions and benevolent outcomes where everyone is represented as profiting. From the dark side of this dialectic, however, things can be seen differently – once the individual's intellectual capital is transfused, their vitality can become very vulnerable.

Notwithstanding some of the darker aspects of contemporary working knowledge raised in this volume, its more optimistic possibilities have also been examined. Interpretive research, dialogue, action research and virtual research are but a few of the possibilities which can be both exciting and, at the same time, disturbing. With the momentous changes continuing to occur in workplaces, such possibilities are in demand and, simultaneously, create new uses for knowledge and new practices of research. A result of this is the need to continually develop and scrutinise both the production and the effects of these practices. One message has been made clear throughout: that contemporary conditions of work are making possible the challenge to traditional modes of knowledge and are creating new modes of knowledge production and legitimation. There is a vitality that comes with such opportunity. However, as has been discussed in various ways throughout the book, such conditions can also lead to new forms of 'epistemological closure' unless ways are found to evaluate the new productions of working knowledge. For us, this does not mean judging it against supposed extra-discursive criteria of good and bad, but rather discerning its more subtle possibilities, limits and *in situ* ethics. In organisational life, these possibilities will invariably include, at times, 'taking sides' and opposing discourses of domination. At work this should not be expected to be too easy.

References

Alvesson, M. and Berg, P.O. (1992) *Corporate Culture and Organizational Symbolism*, Berlin: De Gruyter.

Alvesson, M. and Deetz, S. (1996) 'Critical theory and postmodernism approaches to organizational studies' in S.R. Clegg, C. Hardy and W.R. Nord (eds) *Handbook of Organization Studies*, London: Sage (pp. 191–217).

Boje, D. (1997) 'Getting off the runaway train', *Electronic Journal of Radical Organization Theory*, vol. 2, 1, http://www.mngt.waikato.ac.nz/depts/sml/journal/ejrot.htm

Castells, M. (1996) *The Rise of the Network Society*, vol. 1, Oxford: Blackwell.

Garrick, J. and Rhodes, C. (1998) 'Deconstructive organisational learning: the possibilities for a postmodern epistemology of practice', *Studies in the Education of Adults* 30, 2: 172–83.

Lyotard, J.-F. (1984) *The Postmodern Condition: A Report on Knowledge*, Manchester: Manchester University Press.

Power, M. (1990) 'Modernism, postmodernism and organization' in J. Hassard and D. Pym (eds) *The Theory and Philosophy of Organization*, London: Routledge (pp. 109–24).

Rose, N. (1999) *Powers of Freedom: Reframing Political Thought*, Cambridge: Cambridge University Press.

White, R.F. and Jacques, R. (1995) 'Operationalizing the postmodernity construct for efficient organizational change management', *Journal of Organizational Change Management* 8, 2: 45–71.

Winsor, R.D. (1992) 'Talking the post-Fordist talk, but walking the post-industrial walk', *Journal of Organizational Change Management* 5, 2: 61–9.

Index